THE ESSENTIAL
FINGER FOOD
COOKBOOK

THE ESSENTIAL
FinGer FOOD
COOKBOOK

THUNDER BAY
P·R·E·S·S
San Diego, California

Thunder Bay Press
An imprint of the Advantage Publishers Group
5880 Oberlin Drive, San Diego, CA 92121-4794
www.thunderbaybooks.com

ISBN 1-57145-961-8.
Library of Congress Cataloging-in-Publication Data available upon request.

Printed by Toppan Printing Hong Kong Co. Ltd. PRINTED IN CHINA
1 2 3 4 5   07 06 05 04 03

Series Editor: Wendy Stephen Managing Editor: Jane Price
Designer: Michèle Lichtenberger Design Concept: Marylouise Brammer
Food Editor: Kathy Knudsen Food Director: Jody Vassallo
Photographers (cover and special features): Chris Jones, Lindsay Ross
Stylist (cover and special features): Mary Harris
Stylist's Assistants (cover and special features): Kathy Knudsen, Michelle Lawton, Kerrie Mullins
Picture Librarian: Annette Irish

Chief Executive: Juliet Rogers
Publisher: Kay Scarlett
Production Manager: Kylie Kirkwood

OUR STAR RATING: When we test recipes, we rate them for ease of preparation.
The following cooking ratings are used in this book:
★ A single star indicates a recipe that is simple and generally quick to make—perfect for beginners.
★★ Two stars indicate the need for just a little more care, or perhaps a little more time.
★★★ Three stars indicate special dishes that need more investment in time, care, and patience—but the results are worth it. Even beginners can make these dishes as long as the recipe is followed carefully.

IMPORTANT: Those who might be at risk from the effects of salmonella food poisoning (the elderly, pregnant women, young children and those suffering from immune deficiency diseases) should consult their physician with any concerns about eating raw eggs.

FINGER FOOD

There is something about finger food that is remarkably attractive and indulgent. Maybe it's the wonderfully adult feeling of breaking all the rules we've grown up with: 'sit still while you're eating' and 'you can't leave the table until you've finished'. Finger food, reckless and hedonistic, means gliding around the room, usually with a drink in one hand and a tiny bite-sized treat in the other. The association is with parties—lots of people, new friends to be made and the freedom to flit, plateless, from one fabulous conversation to the next. Finger food should always look good, colourful and fresh, piled high, with everyone taking from the communal platter, a meeting place where the food can lighten the mood and provide a topic of conversation. Finger food can be exciting and sometimes a bit risky— even the most cautious will try a new taste sensation if it's only one bite. But, remember the golden rule: whether it's sophisticated miniature Peking duck, or party-sized potato rosti, there is one thing that all finger food should be—utterly irresistible.

CONTENTS

SPECIAL FEATURES

PLANNING & PARTYING

What is finger food? This is a question we've had to ponder quite carefully while devising the recipes for this book. We decided that ideally finger food should be one or two bites at most, removing any real need to hold cutlery and a plate while you're chatting and moving about the room. If you decide not to provide plates, your finger food shouldn't be messy and explosive, leaving your guests with food all over their hands and clothes, searching desperately for the nearest pot plant to hide the remains.

However, there are also some fabulous recipes that we didn't want to miss out on, for example for antipasto and marinated cheese or vegetables, where you might need to supply plates and cocktail sticks or small forks for your guests. And, obviously, some of our most popular finger foods are dips, where you'll need to provide bread or other 'dippers' to scoop up your delicious creation. So, as you can see, finger food can be a fairly wide variety of dishes. It is also not restricted to savouries. Sweet finger food has a place at many gatherings.

A NIBBLE OR A PARTY?

Finger food is ideal for many occasions. You might invite a small group of friends round for hors d'oeuvres before an evening out, or a late supper after going out, or perhaps you are having a special dinner party and want to hand round some canapés with the drinks beforehand. Alternatively, you might be hosting a wild party for 50 people, a marquee wedding for 250 or a simple picnic or brunch in your back garden. Finger food has its place at all these events.

HOW OUR CHAPTERS WORK

We have divided our finger food into chapters based on flavours, dishes and styles of food from around the world. This means that you can easily put together a whole themed menu using a few dishes from one chapter. If you are choosing to serve Tex-Mex nibbles, for example, you probably wouldn't want to mix them with dishes from other chapters because of the rather unique and strong flavours. Having said that, many of the chapters can easily be combined with

RIGHT: Marinated trout and cucumber tarts (page 80)

others... you might choose to serve a couple of large antipasto platters, accompanied by a few Tapas or Meze dishes and give your guests a Mediterranean evening. Some of the Indian dishes will complement a careful selection of Eastern food, perhaps Thai or Malaysian. And, of course, our chapters of purely party food and sweet things can be mixed and matched with just about anything else. The choice is yours.

PLANNING A MENU

Many factors will affect your choice of menu. What type of gathering are you intending to have? How long will it go on for? What time of day? What time of year? How many people will be attending? What are their tastes in food? What are their ages and interests? Are there many vegetarians, or seafood-haters? How much time will you have to prepare? How well-equipped is your kitchen?

With finger food it is best to keep it simple. Don't try to attempt too much. A few platters of well-chosen ideas will create more impact and give you more time and freedom than attempting 20 recipes with just small quantities of each. Simply double or treble the recipe quantities given, if necessary, and pile your platters high. If your guests are staying for the whole evening you might want to consider one or two sweet dishes to be brought out later on. The time of day and year will influence you in your choice of hot and cold dishes—in summer there is little need to serve hot dishes, so you'll immediately give yourself more time on the day if you don't need to be cooking and reheating right up until when your guests arrive.

Obviously your choice of guests will have a major bearing on your choice of menu. A gathering of the local football team is probably not going to be fully satisfied by a plate of party quiches and petits fours, while your Great Aunt Maud might be a little perplexed by a selection of Mexican corn dogs and stuffed chillies for her ninetieth birthday. You will have to make your own decisions here. However, a good rule of thumb with a mixed group is to serve a couple of conservative 'all-rounder' items such as quiches or tartlets, something more substantial and usually bread based (especially if you are serving alcohol) and perhaps one or two more innovative ideas. You will find with finger food that people are much more adventurous in their tastes when only a couple of mouthfuls are involved (so perhaps Aunt Maud might enjoy that chilli anyway).

Think about the variety of dishes that you're offering. Try not to repeat ingredients—so don't

serve prawn dumplings *and* prawn tempura (unless you're having an evening for local fishermen with a prawn theme). Think about the colours and textures and try to get a good, show-stopping variety of both. Think about complementary flavours—sour, salty, spicy, subtle, savoury, sweet, as well as hot and cold—and try to create an interesting balance.

HOW MUCH TO SERVE

One of the biggest quandaries people have when preparing finger food is how much to make. How do you know how many of those little pieces everyone will eat? How do you know which will be the most popular? And, horror of horrors, what happens if you run out of food?

You will find that most of our recipe serving quantities are given as 'makes 40' for single items such as tarts or pikelets, or 'makes about 20 pieces' to give you an idea of how generously something like a frittata or pizza should be cut.

ABOVE: Curried chicken pies (left); Lamb korma pies (page 104)

9

nibbles, not a full meal. If it's an all evening affair, let them know you'll be providing food equivalent to an evening meal. Obviously it's better to make too much food than have people leave feeling hungry.

BUFFET TABLE OR 'WAITER'?
Once you've decided what to serve, you need to decide how you are going to serve it. Once again you will be governed by how many people are attending and how much room and equipment you have available. If you are just having a few friends over, you will probably be quite happy to hand round the food yourself (or perhaps enlist a couple of friends to help). For a larger gathering you might decide to set up a buffet table, or even to hire waiting staff—either of these options obviously gives you much more freedom on the day.

If you are handing food round, whether you are providing plates or not, make sure to always have plenty of napkins handy. If you aren't providing plates, make sure there's somewhere for people to get rid of used cocktail sticks etc.

If you are using a buffet table, you will need to give its layout some thought. For a large gathering, if you have the space and tables, it is a good idea to set up two tables so that everyone isn't queuing together. If this isn't possible, set up your one table with duplicate dishes starting from each end so that people work from both sides. Have plates, forks, napkins etc. available at each end and, if you are serving sweet food, set it up on a separate table.

The whole idea is not to create a traffic jam. So don't set the buffet table right next to the drinks table or people will get under each other's feet. And, rather than making a general announcement that the food is served, you might want to gradually invite people over to the table in smaller groups. Once again, make sure there is somewhere for people to leave their dirty plates.

PRESENTATION
There is little point in creating wonderful food if you're then going to cram it messily on unsuitable plates or in baskets so that the whole impact is lost. Finger food should always look fabulously tantalizing, so presentation is important. Decorate the platter before arranging the food on top. A beautiful folded napkin, banana leaves or even grape leaves and sprigs of various fresh herbs all make good 'beds' for finger food. Linen napkins look better than paper doilies which can soak up grease and look off-putting when the plate is half empty.

However, some recipes (such as carpaccio or other antipasto dishes) are impossible to calculate in pieces and you will find the recipe states, say, 'serves 8'. By this we mean it will give 8 people one serving as part of a whole antipasto platter.

A rough idea for quantities for pre-dinner nibbles is to serve about 3–5 pieces per person, and for a short (say two to three hour) cocktail party you should allow about 4–6 pieces of food per hour for each person, for as long as the party is expected to continue. For a full-length party or occasion when finger food is being served in place of a sit-down meal (such as a wedding or birthday party), allow 8–12 pieces per person.

Chips and nuts and other stand-bys are not included in this calculation.

As far as variety goes, as we stated earlier, it's best to keep it simple and concentrate on a few fabulous dishes than have a vast quantity of mediocre ones. We advise for 10–20 people, preparing about six different dishes and, for any number higher than that, about eight dishes.

For a whole evening occasion, you would move through light canapés, to more substantial bites (this is when you would serve any hot dishes) and finish with sweet nibbles.

It is always sensible to give your guests a rough idea of what to expect, food-wise, when you issue the invite. So if you're planning to have a two-hour cocktail party, it's a good idea to put start and (assumed) finish times on the invitation: that way people will be expecting

ABOVE: Ham and olive empanadillas (page 193)

You could also experiment with flat baskets, bowls, steel or glass platters, tiles and wooden boards. The ideas are endless, as long as they are clean and hygienic. Think about the theme of your food when choosing your platters—Tapas and Meze can look stunning served on Mediterranean-style tiles.

Don't mix more than two items on a platter. If you pile your platter high with just one recipe you'll give it great impact, as well as making it much easier to top up when supplies run low. Garnishes should be fresh and small enough not to overshadow the main item.

BEING PREPARED

Choose some foods that can be prepared well ahead and frozen, some that can be made a couple of days in advance and refrigerated, and one or two that need to be finished on the day. At the end of many of our recipes you'll find an 'in advance' note that lets you know what can be done. Limit those to be made on the day to simply frying or baking or to simple garnishing. Last minute cooking should be avoided wherever possible. Cook earlier in the day and reheat just before serving.

Write a detailed list of what you need to buy, what can be prepared in advance and when you should do it. Non-perishable foods can be

DRINKS

★ There are 5 glasses of wine in a 750 ml bottle. For a two-hour wine and finger food party, allow 1 bottle between two people.

★ White wine is usually more popular than red so allow 1 bottle of red for every 2 white.

★ There are 6 glasses in a 750 ml bottle of Champagne. Allow 2½ glasses per person for a two-hour drinks party. Allow 1½ glasses per person as a drink before dinner.

★ Keep it simple. Serve drinks to fit your food 'theme', and not too many varieties.

★ ALWAYS supply soft drinks. For a two-hour drinks party, allow 1 glass per person. If only soft drinks are to be served and no alcohol, allow about 3 glasses per person.

★ If people are bringing their own drinks, provide 1 glass per person in addition.

★ Buy ice. Chill the drinks well in advance.

★ If making punch, freeze some in ice-cube trays to chill the punch without diluting it.

★ Freeze berries or tiny wedges of fruit in ice-cubes for decoration.

★ Provide twice as many glasses as there are guests—they are easily abandoned.

bought well ahead, while some foods such as fresh herbs and vegetables should be bought as close as possible to the day.

When freezing small items such as mini quiches, meatballs and pikelets, allow them to cool completely before placing on baking paper covered trays and freezing until firm. Then remove from the trays and transfer to freezer bags. Label and seal, pressing out as much air from the bag as possible. Alternatively, arrange in single layers between sheets of greaseproof paper in airtight containers, then seal and freeze. Marinated foods can be frozen in the marinade in plastic bags. Flatten the bag, excluding most of the air and freeze while flat—this will take less time to thaw out.

People often forget to to take a good look at the adequacy of their kitchen equipment. Check that your fridge and freezer are large enough to store all you have planned. Is your oven adequate to reheat large quantities of food? Do you have enough platters, plates, glasses and cutlery? If you don't, all is not lost. These can be easily hired or borrowed. Just don't forget to check beforehand and be prepared.

ABOVE: Lemon grass prawn satays (page 108)

ANTIPASTO

It is an understatement to say that food is important to the Italians. They love to eat and meals are prepared with great pride and affection as a daily highlight of family life. And what more delicious way to whet the appetite than with a colourful antipasto platter? The word translates literally as 'before the meal' and the tradition arose from the lengthy banquets of the Roman Empire. Today, antipasto doesn't have to mean 'before the meal', it can be the whole magnificent feast itself. So pour yourself (and your guests) a glass of vino and bring a little Italian passion into your kitchen. *Buon appetito.*

BLACK OLIVES
Olives are indispensable as a savoury nibble to accompany drinks and are an attractive addition to an antipasto platter. They also add a distinctive flavour to many Mediterranean dishes. Some varieties are larger, some rounder than others. When olives are unripe, they are green, hard and bitter. Black olives have been left on the tree to darken and mature. Olives can either be preserved in oil, sometimes flavoured with herbs, or in brine. Italian and Greek olives are considered the best.

ABOVE, FROM LEFT:
Carpaccio; Pasta frittata;
Stuffed cherry tomatoes

CARPACCIO

Preparation time: 15 minutes + freezing
Total cooking time: Nil
Serves 8

✮

400 g (13 oz) beef eye fillet
1 tablespoon extra virgin olive oil
rocket leaves, torn
60 g (2 oz) Parmesan, shaved
black olives, cut into slivers

1 Remove all the visible fat and sinew from the beef, then freeze for 1–2 hours, until firm but not solid. This makes the meat easier to slice thinly.
2 Cut paper-thin slices of beef with a large, sharp knife. Arrange on a serving platter and allow to return to room temperature.
3 Just before serving, drizzle with oil, then scatter with rocket, Parmesan and olives.
IN ADVANCE: The beef can be cut into slices a few hours in advance, covered and refrigerated. Drizzle with oil and garnish with the other ingredients just before serving.

PASTA FRITTATA

Preparation time: 15 minutes
Total cooking time: 25 minutes
Makes 8 wedges

✮

300 g (10 oz) spaghetti
4 eggs
50 g (1 3/4 oz) Parmesan, grated
2 tablespoons chopped fresh parsley
60 g (2 oz) butter

1 Cook the spaghetti in a large pan of boiling water for about 10 minutes, until just tender but still retaining a little bite, then drain well.
2 Whisk the eggs in a large bowl, then add the Parmesan, parsley and some salt and freshly ground black pepper. Toss with the spaghetti.
3 Melt half the butter in a 23 cm (9 inch) frying pan and add the spaghetti mixture. Cover and cook over low heat until the base is crisp and golden. Slide onto a plate, melt the remaining butter in the pan and flip the frittata back in to cook the other side (do not cover). Serve warm, cut into wedges.

STUFFED CHERRY TOMATOES

Preparation time: 15 minutes
Total cooking time: Nil
Makes 16

✯

16 cherry tomatoes
50 g (1 3/4 oz) goats cheese
50 g (1 3/4 oz) ricotta
2 slices prosciutto, finely chopped

1 Slice the tops from the tomatoes, hollow out and discard the seeds. Turn them upside-down on paper towel and drain for a few minutes.
2 Beat together the goats cheese and ricotta until smooth. Mix in the prosciutto, then season. Spoon into the tomatoes and refrigerate until required.

PROSCIUTTO WITH MELON

Preparation time: 20 minutes
Total cooking time: Nil
Makes 16

✯

1 rockmelon or honeydew melon
16 slices prosciutto
extra virgin olive oil

1 Remove the seeds from the melon, cut into thin wedges and wrap a slice of prosciutto around each. Drizzle with oil and grind black pepper over each. Refrigerate until required.

MARINATED EGGPLANT
(AUBERGINE)

Preparation time: 15 minutes + salting
 + marinating
Total cooking time: 15 minutes
Serves 6–8

✯

750 g (1 1/2 lb) slender eggplant (aubergine)
1/4 cup (60 ml/2 fl oz) olive oil
2 tablespoons balsamic vinegar
2 cloves garlic, crushed
1 anchovy fillet, finely chopped
2 tablespoons chopped fresh parsley

1 Cut the eggplant into thick diagonal slices, place in a colander and sprinkle well with salt. After 30 minutes, rinse and pat dry.
2 Whisk the oil, vinegar, garlic and anchovy until smooth. Season, to taste.
3 Heat a little oil in a frying pan and brown the eggplant in batches. Transfer to a bowl, toss with the dressing and parsley and marinate for 4 hours. Serve at room temperature.

CHERRY TOMATOES
There are many different types and sizes of cherry tomato, all low in acid and quite sweet. Most are an ideal size for stuffing with a filling, but some are as tiny as small grapes and are sold in clusters. Although these can't be stuffed, they can be used to add colour or to garnish a dish.

LEFT: Prosciutto with melon (left); Marinated eggplant

OREGANO AND PROSCIUTTO PINWHEELS

Preparation time: 30 minutes + chilling
Total cooking time: 10 minutes
Makes about 40

✷ ✷

1 red pepper (capsicum)
1 green pepper (capsicum)
1 yellow pepper (capsicum)
125 g (4 oz) cream cheese, softened
25 g (³⁄₄ oz) Parmesan, grated
2 spring onions, finely chopped
¹⁄₄ cup (7 g/¹⁄₄ oz) chopped fresh oregano
1 tablespoon bottled capers, drained and chopped
1 tablespoon pine nuts, chopped
12 thin slices prosciutto

1 Cut the peppers into quarters and remove the seeds and membrane. Cook, skin-side-up, under a hot grill until the skin blackens and blisters. Place in a plastic bag until cool, then peel.
2 Mix together the cream cheese, Parmesan, spring onion, oregano, capers and pine nuts.
3 Place the pepper pieces on the prosciutto slices and trim the prosciutto to the same size. Remove the pepper and spread some cheese mixture on the prosciutto. Top with the pepper and spread with a little more cheese mixture. Roll up tightly from the short end. Cover and refrigerate for 1 hour, or until firm. Slice into 1 cm (¹⁄₂ inch) rounds and serve on toothpicks.

PESTO-TOPPED CHERRY TOMATOES

Preparation time: 35 minutes
Total cooking time: Nil
Makes about 50

✷

60 g (2 oz) fresh parsley, chopped
2 cloves garlic, roughly chopped
2 tablespoons pine nuts, toasted
¹⁄₄ cup (60 ml/2 fl oz) olive oil
60 g (2 oz) Parmesan, grated
15 g (¹⁄₂ oz) fresh basil leaves
15 g (¹⁄₂ oz) butter, at room temperature
500 g (1 lb) cherry tomatoes

1 Finely chop the parsley, garlic, pine nuts and oil together in a food processor or blender.
2 Add the Parmesan, basil leaves, butter and freshly ground pepper, to taste, and process until well combined.
3 Slice the tops from the cherry tomatoes (a small amount of tomato flesh can be scooped out of each tomato first so you can use a generous amount of filling). Spoon a little mound of the pesto mixture into the top of each tomato.
NOTE: The pesto can be made several days ahead. Spoon into a container and cover the surface of the pesto with a thin layer of olive oil to exclude air, thus preventing discoloration. Alternatively, the pesto can be frozen. Spoon into a shallow container and press plastic wrap onto the surface, again to eliminate air.
IN ADVANCE: The tomatoes can be cut and scooped up to 2 hours ahead, then refrigerated.

HERBED GOATS CHEESE

Preparation time: 20 minutes
Total cooking time: 6 minutes
Serves 6–8

✷

200 g (6¹⁄₂ oz) vine leaves in brine
3 teaspoons bottled green or pink peppercorns, drained and chopped
1 tablespoon chopped fresh marjoram
3 x 100 g (3¹⁄₂ oz) rounds soft goats cheese
rye bread, for serving

1 Place the vine leaves in a heatproof bowl and cover with hot water to rinse away the brine. Drain well and pat dry with paper towels.
2 Combine the peppercorns and marjoram in a shallow bowl or on a plate. Toss the goats cheese in the mixture until the sides are well coated. Arrange a few vine leaves, shiny-side-down, on a work surface. Wrap each goats cheese round in a few layers of vine leaves. This will prevent the cheese from overcooking and losing its shape.
3 Cook the cheese on a barbecue hotplate or under a hot grill for 3 minutes each side, or until the outside leaves are charred. Transfer to a plate and cool to room temperature. (The cheese is too soft to serve when hot, but will firm as it cools.) Use scissors to cut away the vine leaves and serve the cheese with the sliced rye bread.
IN ADVANCE: The cheese can be wrapped in the vine leaves a few hours ahead.

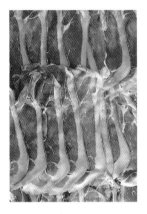

PROSCIUTTO
Prosciutto is an Italian ham that has been salted and dried in the air. It needs no cooking and is usually sold and served in wafer-thin slices. Its mellow flavour makes it ideal for eating as an antipasto with fruits such as sliced melons or fresh figs.

OPPOSITE PAGE: Oregano and prosciutto pinwheels (top); Herbed goats cheese

16

BASIL
Sweet basil is the most widely used of the many varieties of this aromatic, pungent herb. Although most well-known for its affinity with tomato, it is also the basis of pesto sauce and is used in many dishes and salads. Basil leaves bruise easily so they should be shredded rather than chopped. Fresh basil can be refrigerated for up to three days with the stems standing in a bottle of water.

PIZZETTA SQUARES

Preparation time: 20 minutes
Total cooking time: 40 minutes
Makes about 50

☆

2 tablespoons oil
4 onions, finely sliced
2 sheets frozen puff pastry, thawed
1/3 cup (90 g/3 oz) sun-dried tomato pesto
10 anchovies, finely chopped
15 g (1/2 oz) fresh basil leaves, finely shredded

1 Preheat the oven to moderately hot 200°C (400°F/Gas 6). Heat the oil in a large pan and cook the onion over medium heat for 20 minutes, or until soft and golden. Cool.
2 Lay each sheet of pastry on a lightly greased oven tray, then spread the tomato pesto evenly over the pastry. Scatter the onion over the top.
3 Sprinkle the anchovies and basil over the top and bake for 20 minutes, or until the squares are puffed and golden. Cool, then cut into squares. Serve warm or at room temperature.

ABOVE: Pizzetta squares

IN ADVANCE: Cook the onions 2 days ahead and refrigerate. Bake no earlier than 2 hours ahead.

PIZZA FRITTATA

Preparation time: 30 minutes
Total cooking time: 30 minutes
Makes 20 pieces

☆

20 g (3/4 oz) butter
60 g (2 oz) button mushrooms, finely chopped
1 small tomato, peeled, seeded, finely chopped
1 small red pepper (capsicum), seeded, finely chopped
1 small onion, finely chopped
1 stick cabanossi, finely chopped
1 teaspoon dried basil leaves
4 eggs
2/3 cup (170 ml/5 1/2 fl oz) cream
100 g (3 1/2 oz) Parmesan, grated

1 Preheat the oven to moderate 180°C (350°F/ Gas 4). Heat the butter in a pan, add the mushrooms, tomato, pepper, onion, cabanossi and basil and cook until soft.

2 Mix the eggs, cream and Parmesan. Add the mushroom mixture and pour into a greased 20 cm (8 inch) pie plate. Bake for 30 minutes. Cool to room temperature and cut into small wedges to serve.

NOTE: You can use chopped ham or salami instead of the cabanossi.

ASPARAGUS AND PROSCIUTTO ROLLS

Preparation time: 20 minutes
Total cooking time: 8 minutes
Makes 24

☆

12 slices prosciutto
24 asparagus spears
100 g (3¹/₂ oz) butter, melted
60 g (2 oz) Parmesan, grated
fresh nutmeg, grated
1 lemon

1 Preheat the oven to moderate 180°C (350°F/ Gas 4). Cut each slice of prosciutto in half. Cut off the base of each asparagus stem so that the spear is about 9 cm (3¹/₂ inches) long. Bring a pan of lightly salted water to the boil, add the asparagus and cook for 1 minute, or until just tender.

2 Drain the asparagus and pat dry. Brush with the melted butter, then roll the spears in the grated Parmesan. Wrap each asparagus spear in half a slice of prosciutto.

3 Brush an ovenproof dish, large enough to hold the asparagus in a single layer, with melted butter. Place the asparagus bundles in the dish. Sprinkle with any remaining Parmesan, grated nutmeg and cracked black pepper, to taste. Bake for 7 minutes. Squeeze a little fresh lemon juice over the top and serve.

NOTE: Thinly sliced bacon can be substituted for the prosciutto.

IN ADVANCE: The rolls can be assembled up to 6 hours ahead, covered and refrigerated. Cook just before serving.

NUTMEG
Nutmegs are available whole or ground. However, freshly grated nutmeg has a fresher and much more fragrant flavour than ready-ground, so buy whole nutmeg and a grater and grate your own when required. The spice is used in both sweet and savoury dishes.

LEFT: Asparagus and prosciutto rolls

MEDITERRANEAN PANTRY

Anchovy fillets: small fish fillets that are salt cured, canned or bottled in oil. The strong flavour and saltiness can be reduced by soaking in milk or water for a short time.

Arborio rice: Italian-grown, short-grain rice, used for making risotto because of the high starch content.

Artichoke hearts: the edible buds from a large plant of the thistle family. Available canned or bottled in brine or oil.

Pine nuts: high-fat nuts from a variety of pine tree. One of the more expensive nuts, due to the labour required to separate the nuts from the cones. Toasting brings out the flavour.

Parmesan: a hard cheese with a crumbly texture and distinctive flavour. Made from skimmed or partly skimmed cow's milk and aged for 2–3 years in large 'wheels'.

Mozzarella: a smooth, mild, white soft cheese. Originally made from buffalo milk, but now made from cow's milk or a mixture. Available sealed in plastic, or loose in whey or water. Bocconcini are small individual mozzarella balls.

Goats cheese: varies in texture from smooth and creamy to soft and crumbly, depending on the age of the cheese. Available plain or rolled in a variety of coatings from herbs to ash. Has a distinctive sharp taste.

Ricotta: a fresh, white, moist curd cheese, usually made from the whey drained off when making mozzarella. Slightly grainy, but smoother than cottage cheese.

Balsamic vinegar: gets its sweet and syrupy intense flavour and dark colour from being aged in a variety of wooden barrels. Use sparingly as a flavouring as well as a vinegar.

Olive oils: extra virgin olive oil is made from the first pressing of the olives and used mainly in uncooked dishes or dressings. Use a basic olive oil for cooking.

Olives: are black or green and varying sizes. Some are stuffed with anchovies, almonds or pimientos, others are cured in salt or marinated in oil.

Capers: flower buds of a bush native to the Mediterranean and parts of Asia. Sun-dried, then pickled in vinegar or brine. Available in several sizes. Also sold salted in jars.

Sun-dried tomatoes/peppers (capsicums): chewy, intensely flavoured and dark in colour. Available packed in oil or dry. The dry ones must be soaked in oil or other liquid to reconstitute before use.

Rocket: also known as arugula. A bitter, aromatic salad leaf with a peppery mustard tang. Available in bunches, sometimes with roots attached.

Feta: Firm white cheese with a crumbly texture and mild salty flavour. Originally made from goat and sheep's milk, now often made with cow's milk. Pressed into cakes and preserved in brine.

Haloumi: a firm, yet creamy, salty cheese. It is made from sheep's milk and matured in a whey and salt mixture. Smooth and creamy when melted.

Vine leaves: Available in jars or plastic packs in brine. Wash before use to remove saltiness. Fresh vine leaves need to be simmered before use to soften.

Pastrami: a well-seasoned dry-cured, smoked, cooked lean cut of beef, rubbed with a mix which can contain salt, pepper, cumin, paprika and garlic.

Prosciutto: salted and air-dried hind leg of pork. The salt removes some of the moisture. Pancetta is a good substitute.

Roma tomatoes: also known as egg or plum tomatoes. Egg-shaped with thick walls yielding a high flesh to seed ratio, making them great for cooking.

ARTICHOKES
When you are in a hurry, as you are quite likely to be when entertaining, marinated bottled or canned artichokes can be used instead of fresh artichokes which are quite fiddly and time consuming to prepare.

CANNELLINI BEAN SALAD

Preparation time: 20 minutes
Total cooking time: Nil
Serves 6–8

⭐

425 g (13¹/₂ oz) can cannellini beans
1 tomato
3 anchovy fillets
1 tablespoon finely chopped red onion
2 teaspoons finely chopped fresh basil
2 teaspoons extra virgin olive oil
1 teaspoon balsamic vinegar
bread, for serving

1 Rinse and drain the cannellini beans. Finely chop the tomato and slice the anchovies.
2 Mix the cannellini beans, tomato and anchovies with the red onion, basil, olive oil and balsamic vinegar. This can be spooned onto crusty sliced bread or slices of French bread stick lightly brushed with oil, then toasted and rubbed with garlic.
IN ADVANCE: The salad can be prepared up to a day ahead, covered and refrigerated.

ARTICHOKE FRITTATA

Preparation time: 20 minutes
Total cooking time: 25 minutes
Makes 8 wedges

⭐

30 g (1 oz) butter
2 small leeks, sliced
1 clove garlic, sliced
6 eggs
100 g (3¹/₂ oz) bottled marinated artichoke hearts, sliced
1 teaspoon chopped fresh tarragon
lemon juice, for drizzling

1 Heat the butter in a 20 cm (8 inch) non-stick frying pan, add the leek and garlic and cook until soft. Spread evenly over the bottom of the pan.
2 Lightly beat the eggs and season with salt and black pepper. Pour the eggs into the pan and arrange the artichoke slices on top. Sprinkle with the tarragon and cook over low heat until set (this will take about 10 minutes), shaking the pan occasionally to evenly distribute the egg.
3 Place under a hot grill to lightly brown. Cut into wedges and drizzle with a little lemon juice.

ABOVE: Cannellini bean salad (top left); Artichoke frittata

SCALLOP FRITTERS

Preparation time: 20 minutes
Total cooking time: 4–5 minutes per batch
Makes 40

⭐

250 g (8 oz) scallops
6 eggs
25 g (³/₄ oz) Parmesan, grated
3 cloves garlic, crushed
1 cup (125 g/4 oz) plain flour
2 tablespoons chopped fresh thyme
2 tablespoons chopped fresh oregano
oil, for shallow-frying
mayonnaise, for serving, optional

1 Clean and roughly chop the scallops. Lightly beat the eggs and combine with the Parmesan, garlic, flour and herbs. Stir in the scallops.
2 Heat 3 cm (1¼ inches) oil in a deep frying pan to 180°C (350°F). The oil is ready when a cube of bread browns in 15 seconds. Cook the fritters in batches. Using 1 tablespoon of batter for each fritter, pour into the oil and cook for 4–5 minutes, over moderate heat, until golden brown. Drain on crumpled paper towels and sprinkle lightly with salt. Can be served with mayonnaise for dipping.

SARDINES IN VINE LEAVES

Preparation time: 30 minutes + soaking
Total cooking time: 30 minutes
Makes 12

⭐

12 packaged or fresh vine leaves
3 tablespoons olive oil
1 clove garlic, crushed
1 spring onion, finely chopped
2 tablespoons pine nuts
3 tablespoons chopped fresh parsley
2 teaspoons finely grated lemon rind
3 tablespoons fresh white breadcrumbs
12 butterflied sardines

1 If using vine leaves in brine, soak in cold water for 30 minutes, drain and pat dry. For fresh leaves, place in a large heatproof bowl and cover with boiling water. Leave for 2–3 minutes,

rinse with cold water, drain and pat dry. Preheat the oven to moderate 180°C (350°F/Gas 4).
2 Heat 1 tablespoon of the oil in a frying pan and add the garlic, spring onion and pine nuts. Cook, stirring, over medium heat, until the pine nuts just begin to brown. Combine in a bowl with the parsley, lemon rind and breadcrumbs. Season with salt and freshly ground black pepper.
3 Fill the sardines with the breadcrumb mixture and wrap each in a vine leaf. Place in a single layer in a well greased baking dish. Drizzle with the remaining olive oil and bake for 30 minutes. Serve at room temperature.
IN ADVANCE: You can prepare and wrap the sardines the day before and store, covered, in the refrigerator. Remove, drizzle with the oil and bake a few hours ahead of time.

ABOVE: Scallop fritters (top); Sardines in vine leaves

SUPPLI

Preparation time: 40 minutes + chilling
Total cooking time: 1 hour
Makes about 30

✸ ✸

3 cups (750 ml/24 fl oz) chicken stock
60 g (2 oz) butter
1 small onion, finely chopped
1²/₃ cups (360 g/12 oz) arborio rice
¹/₂ cup (125 ml/4 fl oz) white wine
pinch of powdered saffron
50 g (1³/₄ oz) Parmesan, grated
2 eggs, lightly beaten
100 g (3¹/₂ oz) mozzarella cheese
1 cup (100 g/3¹/₂ oz) dry breadcrumbs
oil, for deep-frying

1 Put the stock in a pan, bring to the boil, reduce the heat and maintain at simmering point. Heat the butter in a large heavy-based pan. Add the onion and cook for 2–3 minutes, until softened but not brown. Add the rice and stir for another 2–3 minutes, until well coated with butter and onion.

2 Add the combined wine and saffron and stir until all the wine is absorbed. Add ¹/₂ cup (125 ml/4 fl oz) stock to the rice and stir continuously until absorbed, then continue adding the stock a little at a time, stirring, until ¹/₂ cup stock remains (about 15 minutes). Add the remaining stock and stir, then cover with a tight-fitting lid. Reduce the heat to very low and cook for 10–15 minutes, until the rice is tender. Allow to cool.

3 Gently stir through the Parmesan, eggs and salt and pepper, to taste. Cut the mozzarella cheese into 30 small cubes. With wet hands, form the rice mixture into 30 walnut-sized balls. Push a cube of mozzarella into the centre of each ball and mould the rice around it.

4 Coat each ball with breadcrumbs. Chill for at least 1 hour to firm. Fill a deep heavy-based pan one third full of oil and heat the oil to 180°C (350°F). The oil is ready when a cube of bread turns golden brown in 15 seconds. Fry 3–4 balls at a time for 4–5 minutes, or until golden brown. Drain on crumpled paper towels. Serve hot.
NOTE: The full name is Suppli al Telefono. Serve hot, so that when bitten into, the cheese filling pulls out into long thin strands like telephone wires.
IN ADVANCE: Cover and refrigerate for up to 3 days. Reheat in a warm oven for 15 minutes.

BELOW: Suppli

CHEESE FRITTERS

Preparation time: 15 minutes + chilling
Total cooking time: 10 minutes
Makes about 35–40

✸ ✸

175 g (6 oz) block firm feta cheese
125 g (4 oz) mozzarella cheese
¹/₃ cup (40 g/1¹/₄ oz) plain flour
1 egg, lightly beaten
¹/₂ cup (50 g/1³/₄ oz) dry breadcrumbs
oil, for deep-frying

1 Cut the feta and mozzarella into 2 cm (³/₄ inch) cubes. Combine the flour and ¹/₄ teaspoon black pepper on a sheet of greaseproof paper. Toss the cheese lightly in the seasoned flour and shake off the excess.

2 Dip the cheese into the egg a few pieces at a

Remove the head of the sardine, then cut through the gut to open the sardine out flat.

Carefully scrape the flesh away from the backbone, cut at either end and lift out the bone.

Spoon a little stuffing along the middle of each sardine and carefully lift onto a baking tray.

time. Coat with breadcrumbs and shake off the excess. Repeat the process with the remaining cheese and crumbs. Arrange on a foil-lined tray and refrigerate, covered, for 25 minutes.
3 Heat 3 cm (1¼ inches) oil in a deep frying pan to 180°C (350°F). The oil is ready when a cube of bread browns in 15 seconds. Cook a few pieces of cheese at a time over medium heat, for 2–3 minutes each batch, or until golden and crisp. Drain on crumpled paper towels. Serve.
NOTE: Serve cheese fritters with sweet chilli, plum or cranberry sauce or warmed mint jelly.

STUFFED SARDINES

Preparation time: 40 minutes
Total cooking time: 20 minutes
Makes 16

★ ★

16 large sardines
²/3 cup (65 g/2¼ oz) dry breadcrumbs
2 cloves garlic, crushed
2 tablespoons capers, drained and
   finely chopped
35 g (1¼ oz) Parmesan, grated
2 egg yolks, lightly beaten
juice of 2 lemons, to serve

1 Preheat the oven to moderately hot 200°C (400°F/Gas 6). Lightly grease a baking tray.
2 Remove the heads from the sardines, make a slit through the gut and open out flat. Remove the guts and carefully scrape the flesh away from the backbone; trim at the tail end, leaving the tail intact. Lift out the backbone; discard. Wash the sardines well and drain on paper towels.
3 Mix together the breadcrumbs, garlic, capers, Parmesan, freshly ground black pepper and enough egg yolk to bind the stuffing together. Spoon a little onto each open sardine, put on the baking tray and bake for 20 minutes, or until golden. Serve warm or cold, drizzled with lemon juice.
NOTE: You can buy sardines already filleted at some fishmongers. This makes the recipe quick and simple.
IN ADVANCE: The sardines and stuffing can be prepared a day ahead and refrigerated separately. Assemble several hours ahead.

ABOVE: Stuffed sardines

ITALIAN MEATBALLS

Preparation time: 25 minutes
Total cooking time: 20 minutes
Makes about 25

✵

250 g (8 oz) lean beef mince
1 small onion, grated
1 clove garlic, crushed
1/2 cup (40 g/1 1/4 oz) fresh white breadcrumbs
40 g (1 1/4 oz) pitted black olives, chopped
1 teaspoon dried oregano
1 tablespoon finely chopped fresh parsley
oil, for cooking

1 Combine the mince, onion, garlic, breadcrumbs, olives, oregano, parsley and salt and black pepper, to taste. Mix together thoroughly with your hands.
2 Form teaspoons of the mixture into balls. This is easier if you roll them with wet hands. Heat a little oil in a frying pan and cook the meatballs in batches until well browned and cooked through.
IN ADVANCE: You can prepare the meatballs, cover and refrigerate, then cook when you are ready, or cook them in advance and reheat them, lightly covered with foil, in a warm 160°C (315°F/Gas 2–3) oven. They can also be cooked and frozen, then reheated.

SMOKED COD FRITTATA

Preparation time: 20 minutes
Total cooking time: 20 minutes
Makes 12 slices

✵

500 g (1 lb) smoked cod
1 cup (250 ml/8 fl oz) milk
8 eggs
60 g (2 oz) Parmesan, grated
60 g (2 oz) Cheddar, grated
2 tablespoons chopped fresh thyme
30 g (1 oz) fresh basil leaves, torn
2 tablespoons olive oil

1 Place the smoked cod in a pan with the milk mixed with enough water to cover. Bring to the boil, then reduce the heat and simmer for 3–4 minutes. Remove with a slotted spoon and flake the flesh.

2 Whisk the eggs in a bowl and add the Parmesan and Cheddar, thyme, basil leaves and the fish. Mix together well.
3 Heat the oil in a large 23–25 cm (9–10 inch) heavy-based frying pan. Pour in the mixture and cook over medium heat for 10 minutes, or until nearly cooked. Place under a hot grill for 3–4 minutes, or until just set and lightly golden. Cut into wedges for serving.

MUSSELS WITH CRISPY PROSCIUTTO

Preparation time: 20 minutes
Total cooking time: 15–20 minutes
Makes about 20

✵

1 tablespoon oil
1 onion, finely chopped
6 thin slices prosciutto, chopped
4 cloves garlic, crushed
1.5 kg (3 lb) black mussels
60 g (2 oz) Parmesan, grated
60 g (2 oz) Cheddar, grated

1 Heat the oil in a small frying pan and add the onion, prosciutto, and garlic. Cook over medium heat for 5–8 minutes, until the prosciutto is crispy and the onion softened, then set aside.
2 Scrub the mussels with a stiff brush and pull out the hairy beards. Discard any broken mussels, or open ones that don't close when tapped on the bench. Add to a large pan of boiling water and cook for 5 minutes. Stir occasionally and discard any mussels that don't open. Remove the mussels from their shells, keeping half of each shell. Place 2 mussels on each half-shell and top each with a little of the prosciutto mixture.
3 Combine the Parmesan and Cheddar and sprinkle over the prosciutto. Cook under a preheated grill until the cheese has melted and the mussels are warmed through.
IN ADVANCE: The mussels can be scrubbed and beards removed several hours ahead of time.

OPPOSITE PAGE, FROM TOP: Italian meatballs; Smoked cod frittata; Mussels with crispy prosciutto

BRUSCHETTA

Crusty bread—whether it's an Italian loaf, French stick or sourdough—lightly toasted and topped with colourful fresh ingredients will satisfy the hungriest of guests.

SMOKED SALMON AND CAPERS

Cut 2 small French bread sticks into 1 cm (1/2 inch) slices and lightly grill until golden on both sides. Mix 250 g (8 oz) cream cheese with 2 tablespoons lemon juice and 15 g (1/2 oz) chopped chives. Spread over the toast and top with small slices of smoked salmon and a few baby capers. Garnish with sprigs of fresh dill before serving. Makes about 24.

GRILLED PEPPERS (CAPSICUMS)

Cut 2 yellow, 2 green and 2 red peppers (capsicums) in half lengthways. Remove the seeds and membrane, place skin-side-up under a hot grill and cook until the skins have blackened. Cool in a plastic bag, then peel off the skins. Thinly slice the peppers and place in a large bowl. Add 1 small red onion, sliced into thin wedges, 1 1/2 tablespoons olive oil, 1 1/2 tablespoons balsamic vinegar and

2 crushed cloves of garlic. Slice 2 small sourdough bread sticks into 1 cm (1/2 inch) slices. Lightly grill until golden on both sides. Top with the pepper mixture. Makes about 24.

ROCKET AND FETA

Cut a large French bread stick or an Italian loaf into 1 cm (1/2 inch) slices, brush with olive oil and grill until golden on both sides. Arrange rocket leaves over

each piece, using about 90 g (3 oz) altogether. Toss 200 g (6½ oz) crumbled feta with 2 teaspoons finely grated orange rind and 2 tablespoons olive oil. Spoon 2 teaspoons of the mixture over the rocket on each bruschetta. Grill 6 slices prosciutto until crispy, then crumble over the bruschetta. Makes about 30.

CAPRESSE

Mix 150 g (5 oz) finely diced bocconcini, with 3 tablespoons shredded fresh basil and 3 tablespoons warm extra virgin olive oil in a glass bowl. Season with salt and pepper, to taste. Cover and leave in a warm place for 1 hour to allow the flavours to develop. Cut a large French bread stick or an Italian loaf into 1 cm (½ inch) slices, brush with olive oil and grill until golden on both sides. Spread the bocconcini mixture over the toast. Makes about 30.

MUSHROOM AND PARSLEY

Cut a large French bread stick or Italian loaf into 1 cm (½ inch) slices, brush with olive oil and grill until golden on both sides. Heat 1 tablespoon of olive oil in a small frying pan, and fry 200 g (6½ oz) quartered small button mushrooms until just tender. Stir in 1 tablespoon lemon juice, 50 g (1¾ oz) crumbled goats cheese, a tablespoon of chopped fresh flat-leaf parsley and season, to taste. Spread over the toast. Makes about 30.

TOMATO AND BASIL

Cut a large French bread stick or Italian loaf into 1 cm (½ inch) slices, brush with olive oil and grill until golden on both sides. Finely chop 4 ripe tomatoes and mix with ½ cup (30 g/1 oz) finely shredded fresh basil and 2 tablespoons extra virgin olive oil. Spread over the toast. Makes about 30.

PASTRAMI AND HERBS

Cut a large French bread stick or Italian loaf into 1 cm (½ inch) slices, brush with olive oil and grill until golden on both sides. Combine 200 ml (6½ fl oz) of crème fraîche with 1 teaspoon each of chopped fresh parsley, chives and basil. Spread 1 teaspoon over each slice of toast. Halve 30 slices of pastrami, fold in half again and place 2 pieces over the crème fraîche. Mix 2 chopped tomatoes with ½ finely chopped red onion and 2 teaspoons each of balsamic vinegar and olive oil. Spoon over the top and garnish with small fresh basil leaves. Makes about 30.

FROM LEFT: Smoked salmon and capers; Grilled peppers; Rocket and feta; Capresse; Mushroom and parsley; Tomato and basil; Pastrami and herbs

CAPERS

Capers are the unopened flower buds of a small plant native to the Mediterranean. They are sold pickled and should be refrigerated after opening. The flavour is quite strong so they are used in small quantities. Smaller capers have a more subtle flavour and crunchier texture. Capers are also available coated and packed in salt. They should be rinsed before use.

FRITTO MISTO DI MARE

Preparation time: 30 minutes
Total cooking time: 12 minutes
Makes about 50 pieces

★ ★

Tartare sauce
1¹/2 cups (375 ml/12 fl oz) mayonnaise
1 bottled gherkin, chopped
1 teaspoon bottled capers, drained and finely chopped
1 tablespoon chopped fresh chives
1 tablespoon chopped fresh parsley
¹/4 teaspoon Dijon mustard
¹/4 small onion, finely grated

Batter
1 cup (125 g/4 oz) self-raising flour
¹/4 cup (30 g/1 oz) cornflour
1 tablespoon oil

500 g (1 lb) fish fillets, bones removed
12 sardines
8 raw medium king prawns, peeled

8 scallops, cleaned and deveined
1 calamari hood, cut into rings
flour, for coating
oil, for deep-frying
lemon wedges, for serving

1 For the tartare sauce, combine all the ingredients in a small bowl and mix well.
2 To make the batter, sift the flour and cornflour and a little salt and pepper into a large bowl. Make a well in the centre. Combine the oil and 1 cup (250 ml/8 fl oz) water and gradually whisk into the flour until a smooth batter is formed.
3 Cut the fish fillets into 5 cm (2 inch) strips. To prepare the fresh sardines, remove the heads and split them open down the belly, then clean with salted water. Ease the backbone out with your fingers and cut the backbone at the tail end with sharp scissors.
4 Dry the prepared seafood on paper towels, then coat in the flour and shake off the excess.
5 Heat the oil in a large deep pan to 180°C (350°F). The oil is ready when a cube of bread dropped into the oil turns golden brown in 15 seconds. Coat a few pieces of seafood at a time with batter and gently lower into the hot

ABOVE: Fritto misto di mare

oil with tongs or a slotted spoon. Cook for 2–3 minutes, or until crisp and golden brown. Drain on crumpled paper towels. Keep warm while cooking the remaining seafood. Serve with a bowl of tartare sauce and lemon wedges.

IN ADVANCE: The seafood for this dish can be prepared several hours ahead and kept covered in the refrigerator.

ROASTED BALSAMIC ONIONS

Preparation time: 15 minutes + overnight chilling
Total cooking time: 1 hour 30 minutes
Makes about 30

☆

1 kg (2 lb) pickling onions, unpeeled (see Note)
¾ cup (185 ml/6 fl oz) balsamic vinegar
2 tablespoons soft brown sugar
¾ cup (185 ml/6 fl oz) olive oil

1 Preheat the oven to warm 160°C (315°F/ Gas 2–3). Bake the onions in a baking dish for 1½ hours. Leave until cool enough to handle.

Trim off the stems and peel away the skin (the outer part of the root should come away but the onions will remain intact). Rinse a 1-litre wide-necked jar with boiling water and dry in a warm oven (do not dry with a tea towel). Put the onions in the jar.

2 Combine the vinegar and sugar in a small screw-top jar and stir to dissolve the sugar. Add the oil, seal the jar and shake vigorously until combined—the mixture will be paler and may separate on standing.

3 Pour the vinegar mixture over the onions, seal, and turn upside down to coat. Marinate overnight in the refrigerator, turning occasionally. Return to room temperature and shake the jar to thoroughly combine the dressing before serving.

NOTE: Pickling onions are very small, usually packed in 1 kg (2 lb) bags. The ideal size is around 35 g (1¼ oz) each. The sizes in the bag will probably range from 20 g (¾ oz) up to 45 g (1½ oz). The cooking time given is suitable for this range and there is no need to cook the larger ones for any longer. The marinating time given is a minimum time and the onions may be marinated for up to 3 days in the refrigerator. The marinade may separate after a few hours, which is fine—simply stir occasionally.

ABOVE: Roasted balsamic onions

HAM AND PINEAPPLE PIZZA WHEELS

Rub the chopped butter into the flour with your fingertips until the mixture resembles breadcrumbs.

Roll the dough into a rectangle and use a flat-bladed knife to spread all over with tomato paste.

Use the baking paper as a guide as you roll up the dough from the long side.

HAM AND PINEAPPLE PIZZA WHEELS

Preparation time: 25 minutes
Total cooking time: 20 minutes
Makes 16

✫ ✫

2 cups (250 g/8 oz) self-raising flour
40 g (1¼ oz) butter, chopped
½ cup (125 ml/4 fl oz) milk
4 tablespoons tomato paste
  (tomato purée)
2 small onions, finely chopped
4 pineapple slices, finely chopped
200 g (6½ oz) sliced ham, shredded
80 g (2¾ oz) Cheddar, grated
2 tablespoons finely chopped fresh parsley

1 Preheat the oven to moderate 180°C (350°F/ Gas 4). Brush 2 baking trays with oil. Sift the flour into a bowl, add the butter and rub into the flour with your fingertips until the mixture resembles fine breadcrumbs. Make a well and add almost all the milk. With a flat-bladed knife, mix with a cutting action until the mixture comes together in beads. Gather into a ball and turn onto a lightly floured surface. Divide the

dough in half. Roll out each half on baking paper to a 20 x 30 cm (8 x 12 inch) rectangle, about 5 mm (¼ inch) thick. Spread the tomato paste over each rectangle, leaving a 1 cm (½ inch) border.
2 Mix the onion, pineapple, ham, Cheddar and parsley. Spread evenly over the tomato paste, leaving a 2 cm (¾ inch) border. Using the paper as a guide, roll up the dough from the long side.
3 Cut each roll into 8 even slices. Place on the tray and bake for 20 minutes, or until golden. Serve warm.
IN ADVANCE: The wheels can be made in advance and gently reheated.

CAVIAR POTATOES

Cook some unpeeled baby potatoes (enough for your gathering) in a large pan of boiling water until tender. Allow to cool slightly. While still warm, carefully cut off the top and scoop out a little of the centre. Fill the hole with sour cream and top with caviar. You can mix finely chopped herbs or spring onion into the sour cream if you wish. Garnish with tiny sprigs of fresh dill. Serve warm.

ABOVE: Ham and pineapple pizza wheels

PESTO AND TOMATO TOASTS

Preparation time: 15 minutes
Total cooking time: 5 minutes
Makes about 30

☆

Pesto
1 cup (50 g/1¾ oz) fresh basil leaves
½ cup (50 g/1¾ oz) pecan nuts
¼ cup (60 ml/2 fl oz) olive oil
3 cloves garlic

1 French bread stick, thinly sliced
10 large sun-dried tomatoes, cut into thin strips
150 g (5 oz) Parmesan, thinly shaved

1 To make the pesto, mix the basil leaves, pecans, oil and garlic in a food processor until the mixture is smooth.
2 Toast the bread slices under a grill until brown on both sides.
3 Spread the pesto evenly over the pieces of toast. Top each slice with sun-dried tomatoes and some of the Parmesan.
IN ADVANCE: The pesto can be made several days ahead and stored in a jar. Pour a thin layer of olive oil over the top of the pesto to just cover. Pesto can also be frozen in ice cube trays and thawed when required.

MINI VEAL SALTIMBOCCA

Preparation time: 20 minutes + soaking
Total cooking time: 15 minutes
Makes about 40

☆ ☆

40 small wooden skewers (about 10 cm/
   4 inches) long
500 g (1 lb) piece veal fillet
8–10 slices prosciutto
60 g (2 oz) fresh sage leaves
30 g (1 oz) butter
2 teaspoons oil
2 tablespoons dry sherry

1 Soak the wooden skewers in warm water for about 20 minutes to prevent them burning while the meat is cooking. Cut the veal fillet into 40 thin slices, each measuring roughly 3 x 6 cm (1¼ x 2½ inches). Cut the prosciutto slices slightly smaller than the veal. Top each piece of veal with a piece of prosciutto, then a fresh sage leaf. Weave a skewer through all the layers to secure.
2 Heat half the butter and oil in a large frying pan, add half the skewers and cook over high heat until the veal is brown, then turn and brown other side.
3 Drizzle half the dry sherry over the cooked meat and gently shake the pan. Remove the skewers from the pan, pouring any juices over the skewers. Keep warm while you repeat with the remaining skewers. Serve soon after cooking, drizzled with any juices.
IN ADVANCE: The skewers can be prepared a day ahead. Keep covered in the refrigerator.

ABOVE: Pesto and tomato toasts

1 Pat the feta cheese dry with paper towels and cut into 2 cm (³/4 inch) cubes. Transfer to a bowl and sprinkle the oregano, coriander seeds and 1 tablespoon cracked black pepper all over the feta cheese.

2 Drain the sun-dried tomatoes over a bowl so that you retain all of the oil. Arrange the feta, chillies, rosemary and sun-dried tomatoes in a sterilized 3-cup (750 ml/24 fl oz) wide-necked jar with a clip-top lid. Cover with the reserved sun-dried tomato oil (you should have about 3 tablespoons) and top up with olive oil. Seal and refrigerate for 1 week before using. Serve at room temperature.

NOTES: To sterilize a storage jar, rinse with boiling water, then place in a very slow oven until completely dry.

The oil in the bottle will partly solidify when refrigerated, but will liquify when returned to room temperature.

IN ADVANCE: The marinated feta will keep in the refrigerator for 1–2 months. Use the oil to make salad dressings or to flavour pasta.

BLACK OLIVE AND PEPPER (CAPSICUM) TAPENADE

Preparation time: 15 minutes
Total cooking time: Nil
Makes about 1 cup (250 ml/8 fl oz)

⭐

75 g (2¹/2 oz) pitted black olives, sliced
75 g (2¹/2 oz) sun-dried peppers (capsicums)
  in oil, drained
1 tablespoon capers
1 large clove garlic
30 g (1 oz) flat-leaf parsley
1 tablespoon lime juice
90 ml (3 fl oz) extra virgin olive oil

1 Blend the olives, sun-dried peppers, capers, garlic and parsley together in a food processor or blender until finely minced. With the motor running, slowly add the lime juice and olive oil and process until just combined.

2 Transfer to a sterilized jar, seal and refrigerate for up to 2 weeks. Return to room temperature before serving.

3 Serve on bread or crackers, either as a spread by itself or spooned on top of ricotta cheese. It can also be served with pork and lamb skewers.

MARINATED FETA

Preparation time: 10 minutes
  + 1 week chilling
Total cooking time: Nil
Serves 6–8

⭐

350 g (11 oz) feta
1 tablespoon dried oregano
1 teaspoon coriander seeds
125 g (4 oz) sun-dried tomatoes
  in oil
4 small fresh red chillies
3–4 sprigs fresh rosemary
olive oil

ABOVE: Marinated feta

GARLIC AND HERB MARINATED ARTICHOKES

Preparation time: 20 minutes + overnight chilling
Total cooking time: Nil
Serves 8

★

2 cloves garlic, chopped
¹/₂ cup (125 ml/4 fl oz) olive oil
2 tablespoons finely chopped fresh dill
15 g (¹/₂ oz) finely chopped fresh parsley
2 tablespoons finely chopped fresh basil
2 tablespoons lemon juice
2 x 400 g (13 oz) cans artichoke hearts
3 tablespoons finely diced red pepper
   (capsicum)

1 To make the marinade, combine the garlic, oil, herbs and lemon juice in a bowl and whisk until well combined. Season with salt and cracked black pepper.
2 Drain the artichoke hearts and add to the marinade with the red pepper. Mix well to coat. Cover and marinate in the refrigerator

overnight. Serve as part of an antipasto platter or use in salads. Return the artichokes to room temperature before serving.
IN ADVANCE: The artichokes will keep in an airtight container in the refrigerator for up to a week.

SMOKED TROUT PUFFS

Cut 36 small squares from a sheet of ready-rolled puff pastry. Brush the tops lightly with beaten egg and sprinkle with sesame seeds. Place on greased baking trays and bake in a hot 220°C (425°F/Gas 7) oven for about 8 minutes, until puffed and well browned. Allow to cool, then gently split in half. Soften 250 g (8 oz) light cream cheese and blend with some finely chopped capers, finely chopped spring onion and chopped fresh dill. Spread on the bases of the squares, top with a small roll of smoked trout, then replace the pastry tops at a slight angle. Makes 36.

ABOVE: Garlic and herb marinated artichokes

FLAT-LEAF PARSLEY
Also known as continental parsley, flat-leaf parsley has a slightly stronger flavour than curly-leafed parsley and is available all year round. Both the stems and leaves are used in French cooking, whereas in Italy they normally just use the leaves. Buy parsley with firm stems and bright leaves, not yellowing. To store, stand the stalks in a jar of water in the refrigerator or wrap in paper towels and keep in the vegetable crisper.

ABOVE: Whitebait fritters

WHITEBAIT FRITTERS

Preparation time: 20 minutes + resting
Total cooking time: 15 minutes
Makes 12–15

★★

1/4 cup (30 g/1 oz) self-raising flour
1/4 cup (30 g/1 oz) plain flour
1/2 teaspoon bicarbonate of soda
1 egg, lightly beaten
3 tablespoons dry white wine
2 teaspoons chopped fresh flat-leaf parsley
1 clove garlic, crushed
1/2 small onion, grated
200 g (6 1/2 oz) Chinese or New Zealand
   whitebait
olive oil, for shallow-frying
lemon wedges, for serving

1 Sift the flours, bicarbonate of soda, 1/2 teaspoon salt and some freshly ground black pepper into a bowl. Stir in the egg and wine, whisk until smooth, then add the parsley, garlic, onion and whitebait. Cover and refrigerate for 20 minutes.

2 Heat about 2 cm (3/4 inch) of the oil in a deep frying pan to 180°C (350°F). The oil is ready when a cube of bread dropped into the oil turns golden brown in 15 seconds. Drop in level tablespoons of batter and, when the batter is puffed and bubbles appear on the surface, carefully turn to cook the other side.
3 Drain on paper towels and serve immediately with lemon wedges.
NOTE: The whitebait is very small and fine and is available fresh or frozen. There is no need to gut or scale them as they are so small.

WRAPPED PRAWNS WITH MANGO DIP

Blanch some snow peas (mangetout) and wrap around peeled cooked prawns. Secure each with a toothpick. Make a dip by mixing 1/2 cup (125 ml/4 fl oz) mayonnaise with 2 tablespoons mango chutney, 1 teaspoon curry paste and 1 tablespoon lime juice. Vary the amount of snow peas and prawns according to your needs and double the dip if you need more.

CHARGRILLED OCTOPUS

Preparation time: 15 minutes + marinating
Total cooking time: 10 minutes
Serves 6

★ ★

2/3 cup (170 ml/5 1/2 fl oz) olive oil
1/3 cup (10 g/1/4 oz) chopped fresh oregano
1/3 cup (10 g/1/4 oz) chopped fresh parsley
1 tablespoon lemon juice
3 small red chillies, seeded, finely chopped
3 cloves garlic, crushed
1 kg (2 lb) baby octopus

1 Combine the oil, herbs, lemon juice, chilli and garlic in a large bowl and mix well.
2 Use a small sharp knife to remove the octopus heads. Grasp the bodies and push the beaks out from the centre with your index finger; remove and discard. Slit the heads and remove the gut. If the octopus are too large, cut them into smaller portions.
3 Mix the octopus with the herb marinade. Cover and refrigerate for 3–4 hours, or overnight. Drain, reserving the marinade. Cook on a very hot lightly oiled barbecue or in a very hot pan for 3–5 minutes, or until the flesh turns white. Turn frequently and brush generously with the marinade during cooking.

MARINATED SEAFOOD

Preparation time: 40 minutes + chilling
Total cooking time: 10 minutes
Serves 8

★

500 g (1 lb) mussels, scrubbed, beards removed
1/2 cup (125 ml/4 fl oz) white wine vinegar
3 bay leaves
500 g (1 lb) small squid hoods, sliced
500 g (1 lb) scallops
500 g (1 lb) raw prawns, peeled and deveined
2 cloves garlic, crushed
1/2 cup (125 ml/4 fl oz) extra virgin olive oil
3 tablespoons lemon juice
1 tablespoon white wine vinegar
1 teaspoon Dijon mustard
1 tablespoon chopped fresh parsley

1 Discard any mussels that are already open. Put the vinegar, bay leaves, 3 cups (750 ml/24 fl oz) water and 1/2 teaspoon of salt in a large pan and bring to the boil. Add the squid and scallops, then reduce the heat to low and simmer for 2–3 minutes, or until the seafood has turned white. Remove the squid and scallops with a slotted spoon and place in a bowl.
2 Repeat the process with the prawns, cooking until just pink, then removing with a slotted spoon. Return the liquid to the boil and add the mussels. Cover, reduce the heat and simmer for 3 minutes, or until all the shells are open. Stir occasionally and discard any unopened mussels. Cool, remove the meat and add to the bowl.
3 Whisk the garlic and oil together with the lemon juice, vinegar, mustard and parsley. Pour over the seafood and toss well. Refrigerate for 1–2 hours before serving.
NOTE: Seafood should never be overcooked or it will become tough.

ABOVE: Chargrilled octopus (top); Marinated seafood

MINI PIZZAS

Is there anyone who doesn't love pizza? Make the basic pizza bases as instructed, then top them off with one, or several, of the following ideas. Then watch them walk off the plate.

PIZZA BASES

Mix 7 g (1/4 oz) dried yeast, 1/2 teaspoon sugar and 3/4 cup (185 ml/6 fl oz) warm water, cover and set aside for 10 minutes, or until frothy. Sift 2 cups (250 g/8 oz) plain flour and 1/2 teaspoon salt into a large bowl and make a well. Pour in the yeast mixture and add 1 tablespoon olive oil. Mix with a flat-bladed knife using a cutting action until the mixture forms a dough. Turn onto a lightly floured surface and knead for 10 minutes, or until smooth. Place in a lightly oiled bowl, cover with plastic wrap and leave for 45 minutes, or until the dough has doubled. Punch down the dough (give it one firm punch with your fist to remove the air) and knead for 8 minutes. Roll to 1 cm (1/2 inch) thick. Cut out 7 cm (2 3/4 inch) rounds with a cutter. Place the rounds on a lightly greased baking tray, top with one of the following fillings and bake in a moderately hot 200°C (400°F/ Gas 6) oven for 15 minutes. Makes 25.

BEEF AND ROAST PEPPER (CAPSICUM)

Press 1 1/2 tablespoons cracked black pepper onto a 250 g (8 oz) piece of rump steak. Heat a large frying pan, cook the steak for 5 minutes each side, then slice into thin strips. Cut a red pepper in half lengthways and remove the membrane and seeds. Grill skin-side-up until the skin is black and blistered. Place in a plastic bag until cool, then peel away the skin. Slice the flesh into thin strips.

Mix 1/3 cup (90 g/3 oz) tomato paste (tomato purée) with 2 teaspoons dried mixed herbs and spread the mixture over the pizza bases, leaving a small border. Sprinkle with 1/2 cup (75 g/2 1/2 oz) grated mozzarella cheese, then top each one with a few beef and pepper strips and bake for 15 minutes, or until the bases are crisp and golden. Mix 1/3 cup (90 g/3 oz) sour cream with 2 1/2 tablespoons seeded mustard, spoon over the pizzas and garnish with trimmed snow pea (mangetout) sprouts.

SPINACH AND BOCCONCINI

Spread 1 teaspoon tomato relish over each base (you will need 1/2 cup/125 ml/ 4 fl oz relish). Divide 60 g (2 oz) shredded English spinach leaves, 25 slices Roma (egg) tomato and 180 g (6 oz) sliced bocconcini among the pizza bases, then bake for 15 minutes, or until the bases are crisp.

PRAWN AND MANGO

Spread 1 teaspoon mango chutney over each base—you will need 1/2 cup (140 g/ 5 oz) chutney. Sprinkle with fresh coriander leaves and top each pizza with a peeled cooked prawn. Bake for 15 minutes, then top with thin slices of pepper brie cheese and allow to melt.

BRIE AND PEAR

Put 50 g (1 3/4 oz) brie, 1 tablespoon each of chopped fresh coriander, basil and parsley and 1 tablespoon each of cream, water and olive oil in a food processor and mix until smooth. Season, to taste, with a little salt. Core 2 small pears and cut each one into 14 thin slices. Spread half the brie mixture over the pizza bases, top each with a slice of pear and cover with the remaining cheese mixture. Bake for 15 minutes, or until the bases are golden and crisp. Serve immediately.

SUN-DRIED TOMATO PESTO AND CHICKEN

Fry 2 chicken breast fillets for 5–8 minutes on each side, or until golden. Cool slightly and slice into thin strips. Using 100 g (3 1/2 oz) sun-dried tomato pesto, spread 1 teaspoon pesto over each base, leaving a small border. Mix together 35 g (1 1/4 oz) grated mozzarella cheese and 25 g (3/4 oz) grated Parmesan, sprinkle over the bases and top with a few chicken strips. Bake for 15 minutes, or until the bases are golden and crisp. Garnish with small fresh basil leaves.

FROM LEFT: Beef and roast pepper; Spinach and bocconcini; Prawn and mango; Brie and pear; Sun-dried tomato pesto and chicken

BOCCONCINI

These small balls of fresh mozzarella cheese, found in some delicatessens and supermarkets, are often used in antipasto. Their creamy mild flavour combines well with tomato and basil. Smaller bocconcini are called ovolini, or sometimes cherry bocconcini. Store them in the refrigerator, fully covered in the whey in which they are sold, for up to three weeks. If you see any sign of yellowing, discard them.

BOCCONCINI TOMATO SKEWERS

Preparation time: 20 minutes + chilling
Total cooking time: Nil
Makes 20

☆

20 cherry bocconcini or ovolini, or 5 regular
   bocconcini, sliced into quarters
2 tablespoons olive oil
2 tablespoons chopped fresh parsley
1 tablespoon chopped fresh chives
20 small cherry tomatoes
40 small fresh basil leaves

1 Put the bocconcini in a bowl with the oil, parsley, chives, 1/4 teaspoon salt and 1/2 teaspoon ground black pepper. Cover and refrigerate for at least 1 hour, or preferably overnight.
2 Cut each cherry tomato in half and thread one half on a skewer or toothpick, followed by a basil leaf, then bocconcini, another basil leaf and then another tomato half. Repeat with more skewers and the remaining ingredients and serve.
IN ADVANCE: These can be served immediately, or covered and chilled for up to 8 hours.

MUSHROOM RISOTTO FRITTERS

Preparation time: 20 minutes + chilling
Total cooking time: 35 minutes
Makes 28

☆ ☆

3 1/4 cups (810 ml/26 fl oz) vegetable stock
1 tablespoon olive oil
20 g (3/4 oz) butter
1 small onion, finely chopped
1 cup (220 g/7 oz) arborio or short-grain rice
150 g (5 oz) button mushrooms, thinly sliced
35 g (1 1/4 oz) Parmesan, grated
oil, for shallow-frying

1 Put the stock in a pan, bring to the boil, reduce the heat and keep at simmering point.
2 Heat the oil and butter in a heavy-based pan, add the onion and stir over medium heat for 3 minutes, or until softened. Add the rice and stir for 2 minutes. Add the mushrooms and cook for 3 minutes, or until soft.
3 Add 1/2 cup (125 ml/4 fl oz) stock to the rice and stir continuously until absorbed. Add more stock, stirring constantly, until all the stock is

RIGHT: Bocconcini tomato skewers

absorbed and the rice is just tender and creamy. (This will take 15–20 minutes.) Stir in the Parmesan and remove from the heat. Transfer to a bowl. Cool, then refrigerate for at least 1 hour.
4 With wet hands, shape tablespoons of the mixture into flat rounds. Chill for 15 minutes.
5 Heat about 2 cm (³/4 inch) oil in a deep pan to 180°C (350°F). The oil is ready when a cube of bread dropped in the oil turns golden brown in 15 seconds. Cook the fritters in batches for 3 minutes each side, or until golden. Drain on crumpled paper towels. Can be served with relish.

HERB BAKED RICOTTA

Preparation time: 25 minutes + overnight marinating
Total cooking time: 30 minutes
Serves 4

★

1 kg (2 lb) wedge of ricotta (see Note)
2 tablespoons fresh thyme leaves
2 tablespoons chopped fresh rosemary
2 tablespoons chopped fresh oregano
3 tablespoons chopped fresh parsley
3 tablespoons chopped fresh chives
2 cloves garlic, crushed
¹/2 cup (125 ml/4 fl oz) olive oil
2 teaspoons cracked pepper

1 Pat the ricotta wedge dry with paper towels and place in a baking dish.
2 Mix the herbs, garlic, oil and cracked pepper in a bowl. Spoon onto the ricotta and press on with the back of a spoon. Cover and refrigerate overnight.
3 Preheat the oven to hot 220°C (425°F/Gas 7). Bake for 30 minutes, or until the ricotta is set. Delicious served with crusty bread.
NOTE: If you can only buy ricotta pieces, drain overnight in a colander over a bowl, in the refrigerator. Spread half the herb mixture in a 1.25 litre loaf tin. Spoon the ricotta in and spread with the remaining herbs before baking.

ABOVE: Herb baked ricotta

SEMI-DRIED TOMATOES

Preparation time: 10 minutes + overnight chilling
Total cooking time: 2 hours 30 minutes
Makes 64

★

16 Roma (egg) tomatoes
3 tablespoons fresh thyme, chopped
2 tablespoons olive oil

1 Preheat the oven to warm 160°C (315°F/
Gas 2–3). Quarter the tomatoes lengthways and
lay skin-side-down on a rack in a baking tray.
2 Sprinkle with 1 teaspoon each of salt and
cracked black pepper and the thyme and bake
for 2½ hours. Check occasionally to make sure
the tomatoes don't burn. Toss in the oil and cool
before packing into sterilized jars and sealing.
Refrigerate for 24 hours before using. Return to
room temperature before serving. Suitable for an
antipasto plate.
NOTE: To sterilize storage jars, rinse them
thoroughly with boiling water, invert and drain,
then place in a very slow oven to dry
thoroughly. Don't dry with a tea towel.
IN ADVANCE: Can be kept in an airtight
container in the fridge for up to 7 days.

*ABOVE: Semi-dried
tomatoes*

ARTICHOKE PANZAROTTI

Preparation time: 35 minutes + resting
  + chilling
Total cooking time: 20 minutes
Makes 24

★ ★

Oil and wine dough

2 cups (250 g/8 oz) plain flour
½ teaspoon baking powder
½ tablespoon caster sugar
1 egg, lightly beaten
⅓ cup (80 ml/2¾ fl oz) olive oil
¼ cup (60 ml/2 fl oz) dry white wine
beaten egg, to glaze

2 tablespoons olive oil
20 g (¾ oz) butter
100 g (3½ oz) lean bacon, diced
1 small red onion, sliced
2 cloves garlic, crushed
3 artichoke hearts, finely chopped
2 tablespoons finely chopped fresh parsley
150 g (5 oz) smoked mozzarella, diced
oil, for shallow-frying

1 Combine the flour, baking powder, sugar and ½ teaspoon salt in a bowl. Make a well in the centre of the dry ingredients, pour in the combined egg, oil and wine and mix with a flat-bladed knife to form a dough. Transfer to a floured surface and gather together into a ball.
2 Knead for 3–4 minutes, until smooth and elastic. Cover and set aside to rest at room temperature for at least 30 minutes.
3 Roll the dough out on a floured surface to 3 mm (⅛ inch) thickness. Rest for 10 minutes, then cut out twenty-four 8 cm (3 inch) circles. Brush around the edge with beaten egg.
4 While the dough is resting, heat the oil and butter in a frying pan, then add the bacon, onion, garlic and artichoke. Cook gently for 10 minutes, adding the parsley for the last 1–2 minutes. Remove from the heat, then drain.
5 Place 1 teaspoon bacon mixture in the centre of each circle of dough. Add some cheese, and salt and pepper, to taste. Fold one side of the dough over to meet the other, encasing the filling. Press firmly to seal, then press the edges with a fork. Place on a large plate or baking tray and refrigerate for 30 minutes.
6 Heat 2 cm (¾ inch) oil in a frying pan to 180°C (350°F). The oil is ready when a cube of bread dropped into the oil turns golden brown in 15 seconds. Fry the panzarotti, two or three at a time, until puffed and golden on both sides. Remove with a slotted spoon and drain on crumpled paper towels before serving.

MARINATED CHILLI MUSHROOMS

Preparation time: 20 minutes + marinating
Total cooking time: Nil
Makes 20–25

★

750 g (1½ lb) button mushrooms
2 cups (500 ml/16 fl oz) light olive oil
2 tablespoons lemon juice
1 clove garlic, finely chopped
¼ teaspoon caster sugar
1 red chilli, finely chopped
1 green chilli, finely chopped
1 tablespoon chopped fresh coriander
1 tablespoon chopped fresh parsley

1 Wipe the mushrooms with a damp paper towel to remove any dirt and place in a bowl.
2 Mix together the oil, lemon juice, garlic, sugar and chilli. Pour over the mushrooms and mix well so that the mushrooms are evenly coated. Cover with plastic wrap and marinate for at least 30 minutes. Just before serving, add the herbs, season and mix well.
NOTE: If you prefer a stronger flavour, add the herbs before marinating.
IN ADVANCE: The mushrooms can be marinated up to 1 week ahead and stored in the fridge.

BUTTON MUSHROOMS
Button mushrooms are commonly used for party dishes because of their uniform size and mild flavour. When buying them, make sure they are dry and firm. Refrigerate in a paper bag, not plastic, so they don't sweat. They don't need to be peeled but can be wiped over with damp paper towels if they need cleaning.

LEFT: Marinated chilli mushrooms

CANAPES

Canapés were originally small pieces of bread or toast spread with a savoury paste and served before the meal. The word 'canapé' comes from the French, meaning, surprisingly enough, 'couch'—the idea being that the toppings sit on the pieces of bread as if sitting on little sofas. Canapés have come a long way since then and, as well as bread, we now serve blinis, pikelets, polenta wedges, pastries and tartlets with an almost infinite variety of savoury toppings. The perfect canapé should be one, or at most two, dainty mouthfuls, requiring neither a fork nor a plate, thus allowing your guests to mingle at will, discussing what a fabulous chef you are.

the bread, flatten the slices well with a rolling pin and brush both sides with melted butter.

2 Spread the pepper mixture on each slice, leaving a 1 cm (½ inch) border. Roll up and secure with toothpicks. Cover and refrigerate for at least 2 hours.

3 Preheat the oven to moderate 180°C (350°F/ Gas 4). Cut each roll in half and secure with a toothpick. Bake on a baking tray for about 10–12 minutes, or until the rolls are crisp and pale golden. Sprinkle with paprika. Serve warm.

NOTE: The rolls can be served like mini rolled pizzas with different fillings. Brush bread slices with oil, then spread with tomato paste. Sprinkle with sliced olives, sun-dried tomatoes, grated Parmesan and chopped anchovies, mushrooms or other favourite fillings.

IN ADVANCE: These can be prepared and refrigerated up to a day in advance and baked just before serving.

HERB PANCAKES WITH AVOCADO BUTTER

Preparation time: 30 minutes
Total cooking time: 30 minutes
Makes about 50

★

½ cup (60 g /2 oz) plain flour
½ cup (60 g/2 oz) self-raising flour
1 egg, lightly beaten
½ cup (125 ml/4 fl oz) milk
20 g (¾ oz) chopped fresh mixed herbs
1 teaspoon cracked black pepper

Avocado butter
½ ripe avocado
60 g (2 oz) butter
1 tablespoon lemon or lime juice
½ teaspoon cracked black pepper

1 Sift the flours into a large bowl and make a well in the centre. Gradually add the combined egg, milk, herbs and pepper, whisking until the batter is smooth and free of lumps.

2 Heat a frying pan and brush with melted butter. Drop teaspoons of batter into the pan and cook until bubbles appear on top. Turn and cook until golden underneath. Keep warm.

3 Mix the avocado, butter, juice and pepper in a small bowl until smooth. Spread on top of the pancakes and serve.

PEPPER (CAPSICUM) ROLLS

Preparation time: 30 minutes + chilling
Total cooking time: 12 minutes
Makes 20

★

1 large red pepper (capsicum)
60 g (2 oz) Cheddar, grated
30 g (1 oz) Parmesan, grated
2 tablespoons whole egg mayonnaise
2 tablespoons finely chopped fresh parsley
1 teaspoon chopped fresh thyme
1 teaspoon chopped fresh oregano
2 drops Tabasco sauce
10 slices fresh bread
45 g (1½ oz) butter, melted
paprika

1 Halve the red pepper and remove the seeds and membrane. Cook skin-side-up under a hot grill until the skin is black and blistered. Place in a plastic bag and leave to cool, then peel. Finely chop the flesh and combine in a bowl with the Cheddar, Parmesan, mayonnaise, herbs, Tabasco and salt and pepper, to taste. Cut the crusts from

ABOVE: Pepper rolls

SMOKED SALMON PIKELETS

Preparation time: 15 minutes + standing
Total cooking time: 10–15 minutes
Makes about 50

★

Pikelets

1 cup (125 g/4 oz) self-raising flour
2 eggs, lightly beaten
1/2 cup (125 ml/4 fl oz) milk
1 tablespoon sour cream

Topping

1/2 cup (125 g/4 oz) sour cream
2 tablespoons mayonnaise
2 teaspoons lemon juice
1 tablespoon finely chopped fresh chives
1 tablespoon finely chopped fresh mint
125 g (4 oz) sliced smoked salmon
strips of lemon peel, to decorate

1 Sift the flour into a bowl and make a well in the centre. Mix the beaten egg, milk and sour cream and pour into the well. Stir into the flour until the batter is smooth and free of lumps. Set aside for 10 minutes.

2 Heat a large frying pan, brush with oil or melted butter, then drop teaspoons of mixture into the pan. When bubbles appear on the surface, turn the pikelets over and cook the other side. Remove and set aside. Repeat until all the batter has been used.

3 For the topping, stir the sour cream, mayonnaise, lemon juice, chives and mint together until well combined. Spoon a small amount onto each pikelet. Top with a piece of smoked salmon and decorate with strips of lemon peel.

IN ADVANCE: The pikelets can be made a day ahead, or frozen in single layers for up to a month. The sour cream mixture for the topping can be prepared a day ahead. You can assemble the pikelets up to an hour before you are going to serve them.

CHIVES
Although part of the onion family, fresh chives are used more like a herb. They impart a mild onion flavour to dips, vegetables and cheeses. If you grow some in a pot, you can just cut a little off when required. The grass-like stems are easy to snip with scissors.

LEFT: Smoked salmon pikelets

BACON

Lightly fried bacon is a vital ingredient in traditional quiche Lorraine. When covered with a creamy custard mixture and baked, the flavour of the bacon is enhanced. Bacon is fat and lean meat from the side and back of pigs. It has been preserved by dry salting (curing) and is usually smoked.

MINI QUICHE LORRAINES

Preparation time: 20 minutes
Total cooking time: 25 minutes
Makes 24

☆

3 sheets ready-rolled shortcrust pastry, thawed
60 g (2 oz) Gruyère cheese, grated
30 g (1 oz) butter
2 rashers bacon, finely chopped
1 onion, finely chopped
2 eggs
3/4 cup (185 ml/6 fl oz) cream
1/2 teaspoon ground nutmeg
fresh chives, cut into short strips, to garnish

1 Lightly grease two 12-hole round-based patty tins. Preheat the oven to moderately hot 190°C (375°F/Gas 5). Using a plain 8 cm (3 inch) cutter, cut rounds of pastry and fit in the tins. Divide the cheese evenly among the pastry bases. Cover and refrigerate while making the filling.
2 Heat the butter in a small pan and cook the bacon and onion for 2–3 minutes, until tender. Drain on paper towels. When cool, divide the mixture evenly among the bases. Whisk the eggs in a bowl with the cream, nutmeg and freshly ground black pepper. Pour or spoon carefully over the bacon mixture.
3 Place 2–3 strips of chive on top of each quiche to decorate. Bake for 20 minutes, or until lightly browned and set. Serve hot or warm.
IN ADVANCE: These quiches can be cooked up to 2 days ahead and stored in an airtight container in the refrigerator. They can be frozen in single layers for up to 2 months. Reheat in a moderate 180°C (350°F/Gas 4) oven.

ABOVE: Mini quiche Lorraines

CUCUMBER AND SALMON BITES

Preparation time: 20 minutes
Total cooking time: Nil
Makes about 40

★

250 g (8 oz) cream cheese or neufchatel
210 g (7 oz) can red or pink salmon, drained
1 tablespoon sour cream
1 tablespoon mayonnaise
1–2 teaspoons lemon juice
1 tablespoon finely chopped fresh coriander
1 tablespoon finely chopped fresh chives
2 teaspoons finely chopped fresh lemon thyme
4 Lebanese cucumbers, thickly sliced
sprigs of fresh dill or thinly shredded chilli or
    red pepper (capsicum), to decorate

1 Beat the cream cheese in a small bowl with electric beaters until soft and creamy. Add the salmon, sour cream, mayonnaise, lemon juice, coriander, chives, lemon thyme, and salt and pepper. Beat for 1 minute, or until combined.
2 Place a teaspoon of the cheese mixture on each cucumber round and decorate.
IN ADVANCE: The salmon mixture can be prepared a day ahead and refrigerated in an airtight container. Slice the cucumber into rounds and assemble just before serving.

PORT AND PEPPER PATE WITH MOON TOASTS

Preparation time: 40 minutes + overnight chilling
Total cooking time: 10 minutes
Makes about 30

★

450 g (14 oz) chicken livers, chopped
100 g (3½ oz) butter
1 onion, chopped
2 cloves garlic, crushed
⅓ cup (80 ml/2¾ fl oz) port
⅓ cup (80 ml/2¾ fl oz) cream
1 tablespoon chopped fresh chives
60 g (2 oz) can green peppercorns, drained
    and lightly crushed
10 slices bread
lemon pepper seasoning

1 Discard any green or discoloured parts from the livers. Heat the butter in a large, heavy-based pan. Add the liver, onion, garlic and port and stir over medium heat until the liver is almost cooked and the onion is soft. Bring to the boil and simmer for 5 minutes.
2 Remove from the heat and cool slightly. Combine in a food processor in short bursts until smooth. Press through a fine sieve into a bowl, then stir in the cream, chives and peppercorns. Spoon into a large dish, cover and refrigerate overnight, or until firm.
3 Preheat the oven to moderate 180°C (350°F/Gas 4). Line a baking tray with foil. To make the moon toasts, using a moon-shaped cutter, cut shapes out of the bread. Place on the tray and sprinkle with pepper. Bake for 5 minutes, or until pale golden and crisp. Cool on a wire rack.
IN ADVANCE: The pâté can be made 2 days ahead, and refrigerated, covered. The toasts can be made a week ahead and stored in an airtight container.

ABOVE: Cucumber and salmon bites

SMOKED TROUT TARTLETS

Preparation time: 40 minutes
Total cooking time: 20 minutes
Makes 34

⭐

1 loaf sliced white bread, crusts removed
60 g (2 oz) butter, melted
1 smoked trout (about 300 g/10 oz), skinned
   and boned
1 tablespoon chopped fresh chives
1/4 cup (60 g/2 oz) mayonnaise
2 spring onions, finely chopped
1 teaspoon horseradish cream
1 teaspoon seeded mustard
black olives, pitted and cut into strips,
   to garnish

1 Preheat the oven to very slow 120°C (250°F/
Gas 1/2). Flatten the bread slices with a rolling pin,
cut 8 cm (3 inch) rounds with a cutter, then brush
both sides with butter. Press into two 12-hole
round-based patty tins. Bake for 10 minutes, or
until crisp. Cool. Repeat to use all the bread.
2 Place the trout in a bowl and break the flesh
into small pieces with a fork. Add the chives,
mayonnaise, spring onion, horseradish cream and
mustard. Season with salt and pepper; mix well.
3 Spoon the filling into the tartlet cases, garnish
with strips of olives and serve immediately.
IN ADVANCE: The bread cases can be made
2 days ahead and stored in an airtight container.

SMOKED SALMON ROLLS

Preparation time: 30 minutes + chilling
Total cooking time: 5 minutes
Makes 36

⭐

6 eggs
3 teaspoons cornflour
125 g (4 oz) spreadable cream cheese
2 tablespoons chopped pickled ginger
2 tablespoons chopped fresh chives
200 g (6 1/2 oz) sliced smoked salmon,
   chopped
sprigs of fresh parsley, to garnish

1 Beat 1 egg in a bowl with 1 teaspoon water
and half a teaspoon of cornflour. Season.

2 Heat a frying pan and brush it lightly with oil.
Add the egg and cook over medium heat,
drawing the outside edges of the mixture into
the centre with a spatula, until the mixture is
lightly set. Cool in the pan for 2 minutes, then
carefully slide out onto a clean, flat surface with
the uncooked side upwards. Set aside to cool.
Repeat with the remaining eggs, beaten with
water and cornflour, to make five more omelettes.
3 Place each omelette on a sheet of baking paper
on a flat surface. Divide the cream cheese among
the omelettes, spreading over each. Sprinkle with
pickled ginger, chives and salmon. Season with
black pepper. Roll each gently but firmly, using
the paper to help pull the roll towards you. Chill,
wrapped in plastic wrap, for at least 3 hours.
4 Using a sharp knife, cut the rolls into 2 cm
(1/2 inch) slices, discarding the uneven ends.
Garnish with parsley sprigs.
IN ADVANCE: Can be made a day ahead, covered
and refrigerated. Serve at room temperature.

CARAMELIZED APPLES
ON PUMPERNICKEL

Preparation time: 30 minutes
Total cooking time: 15 minutes
Makes about 24

⭐

2 golden delicious or pink lady apples
2 tablespoons lemon juice
1/2 cup (60 g/2 oz) icing sugar
30 g (1 oz) butter
175 g (6 oz) blue cheese, crumbled
30 g (1 oz) walnuts, finely chopped
1 stick celery, finely chopped
250 g (8 oz) pumpernickel rounds

1 Peel and core the apples and slice each into
twelve wedges. Brush with lemon juice and
sprinkle generously with icing sugar. Heat the
butter in a frying pan and, when foaming, add a
few wedges and cook until brown and beginning
to caramelize. Cool on a sheet of baking paper.
Repeat with the remaining apple wedges, adding
more butter to the pan as needed.
2 Combine the cheese, walnuts and celery in a
bowl and spoon a little onto each pumpernickel
round. Top with an apple wedge.
NOTE: Granny Smith apples are not suitable.
IN ADVANCE: Prepare a few hours ahead and
refrigerate, covered with plastic wrap.

SMOKED
SALMON ROLLS

Cook the egg over medium
heat until lightly set. Use a
spatula to draw the outside
edges into the centre
during cooking.

Sprinkle pickled ginger,
chives and salmon over the
cream cheese.

Roll each omelette gently
but firmly, using the paper
to help pull the roll towards
you as you roll.

*OPPOSITE PAGE: Smoked
salmon rolls (top);
Caramelized apples
on pumpernickel*

HERBED CHEESE TARTLETS

Preparation time: 30 minutes + chilling
Total cooking time: 8–10 minutes
Makes 48

★

Pastry
4 cups (500 g/1 lb) plain flour
1 teaspoon paprika
250 g (8 oz) butter, chopped
1/3 cup (80 ml/2³/4 fl oz) lemon juice
8–10 tablespoons iced water

Filling
500 g (1 lb) cottage cheese
2 tablespoons chopped fresh chervil, plus extra
   to garnish
2 tablespoons chopped fresh tarragon
2 teaspoons chopped fresh chives
1/2 cup (125 ml/4 fl oz) thick (double) cream
24 black olives, pitted and sliced

1 Sift the flour and paprika with a pinch of salt into a large bowl. Add the butter and rub into the flour with your fingertips, until the mixture resembles fine breadcrumbs. Make a well in the centre and stir in the lemon juice and up to 8–10 tablespoons iced water. Mix with a flat-bladed knife until the mixture comes together in beads. Gently gather together and lift out onto a lightly floured surface. Flatten into a disc, wrap in plastic wrap and refrigerate for 15 minutes.
2 Preheat the oven to moderately hot 200°C (400°F/Gas 6). Grease two 12-hole round-based patty tins. Roll the dough out on a lightly floured surface to 3 mm (1/8 inch) thick and, using an 8 cm (3 inch) cutter, cut 48 rounds from the pastry and line the patty tins. Bake for 8–10 minutes, until golden brown. Repeat with the remaining pastry and ingredients.
3 To make the filling, beat together the cottage cheese, herbs and cream until smooth. Stir in the olives with salt and black pepper. Spoon into the cases and garnish each tart with a small sprig of chervil. Grind black pepper over the top and serve immediately.

CRAB AND LIME QUICHES

Preparation time: 15 minutes
Total cooking time: 20 minutes
Makes 18

★

2 sheets frozen puff pastry, thawed
2 eggs
3/4 cup (185 ml/6 fl oz) coconut cream
finely grated rind of 1 small lime
2 teaspoons lime juice
200 g (6¹/2 oz) can crab meat, drained
1 tablespoon chopped fresh chives

1 Preheat the oven to hot 210°C (415°F/Gas 6–7). Using two 12-hole round-based patty tins, lightly grease 18 of the holes. Cut 18 rounds of pastry, using an 8 cm (3 inch) cutter.
2 Beat the eggs lightly in a small bowl and add the remaining ingredients. Season with salt and white pepper. Spoon about 1 tablespoon of filling into each pastry case.
3 Bake for 20 minutes, or until golden. The quiches will rise during cooking, then deflate slightly. Serve warm.

ABOVE: Crab and lime quiches

CROSTINI WITH PEPPER (CAPSICUM) ROULADE

Preparation time: 30 minutes + chilling
Total cooking time: 10 minutes
Makes about 20

★★

2 red peppers (capsicums)
2 yellow peppers (capsicums)
8 English spinach leaves
1 tablespoon chopped fresh flat-leaf parsley
1 small French bread stick
2 tablespoons olive oil
shaved Parmesan, to garnish

1 Cut each pepper in half and remove the seeds and membrane. Cook skin-side-up under a hot grill until the skin is black and blistered. Place in a plastic bag and leave to cool. Peel.
2 Remove the stalks from the spinach and put the leaves in a bowl. Cover with boiling water and set aside for a couple of minutes until the leaves have wilted. Drain and cool. Squeeze out the excess water and spread the leaves out. Pat dry with paper towels.
3 Place two sheets of overlapping plastic wrap on a flat surface. Flatten out the red pepper to form a rectangle, overlapping the ends. Lay the spinach leaves over the pepper to make a second layer. Place the flattened yellow pepper on top to make a third layer, making sure there are no gaps, and overlapping the ends. Sprinkle with the parsley. Using the plastic wrap to assist, roll up the pepper tightly lengthways, sealing the ends. Wrap tightly in foil, twist the ends firmly and chill for 3 hours.
4 Preheat the oven to moderately hot 200°C (400°F/Gas 6). Cut the bread stick into 1 cm (½ inch) slices. Place on a baking tray, lightly brush with olive oil, sprinkle with salt and bake for 5–10 minutes, until golden.
5 Remove the plastic wrap, cut the roulade into 1.5 cm (⅝ inch) thick slices and place on the crostini. Drizzle with oil. Garnish with Parmesan.
IN ADVANCE: The topping and the bread can be prepared separately up to 6 hours in advance. However, don't top the bread any earlier than 30 minutes before serving as it may go soft.

CROSTINI WITH PEPPER ROULADE

After grilling the peppers and allowing them to cool, peel away the skin.

Layer the pepper and the spinach leaves onto the plastic wrap.

Unwrap the chilled roulade and cut it into thin slices with a sharp knife.

LEFT: Crostini with pepper roulade

CHIVE CREPE CORNETS WITH SMOKED TROUT

Cover the base of the pan with batter, then sprinkle with chopped chives.

Place the smoked trout on a work surface and carefully peel away the skin.

Lift the flesh away from the bones, keeping the trout as intact as possible. Remove any stray bones.

ABOVE: Chive crepe cornets with smoked trout

CHIVE CREPE CORNETS WITH SMOKED TROUT

Preparation time: 45 minutes + standing
Total cooking time: 15–20 minutes
Makes 20

☆ ☆

3/4 cup (90 g/3 oz) plain flour
I egg, plus I egg yolk, lightly beaten
I cup (250 ml/8 fl oz) milk
20 g (3/4 oz) butter, melted
2 tablespoons chopped fresh chives

Filling
250 g (8 oz) smoked trout
125 g (4 oz) cream cheese, at room
   temperature
1/4 cup (60 g/2 oz) sour cream
1/4 cup (60 ml/2 fl oz) cream
Tabasco sauce
2 teaspoons lemon juice
I tablespoon chopped fresh chives
I tablespoon drained capers, chopped
2 small gherkins, finely chopped

I carrot, cut into julienne strips
I celery stalk, cut into julienne strips
strips of fresh chives

I Sift the flour into a bowl, make a well and gradually add the combined egg, yolk, milk and butter, mixing until smooth and free of lumps. Pour into a jug, cover and leave for 30 minutes.
2 Heat a crepe or frying pan measuring 20 cm (8 inch) across the base and brush lightly with melted butter. Pour enough batter into the pan to thinly cover the base, pouring the excess back into the jug. (Add more milk if the batter is too thick.) Sprinkle some chopped chives over the batter and cook for about 30 seconds. Turn the crepe over and cook the other side until lightly brown. Transfer to a plate while cooking the remaining batter and chives.
3 Remove the skin from the trout. Carefully lift the flesh from the bones, keeping it as intact as possible and removing any stray bones. Divide into twenty even-sized pieces. Mix together the cream cheese, sour cream, cream, a few drops of Tabasco, lemon juice, chopped chives, capers and gherkins.
4 Blanch the carrot and celery in boiling water for 1 minute, then refresh in cold water. Drain and dry on crumpled paper towels.

5 Place a crepe on the work surface, chive-side-down. Spread with some of the filling mixture, then cut in half. Fold each half-crepe in half, so that the chives show decoratively. Repeat with the remaining crepes.

6 Arrange a piece of trout, a few sticks of carrot and celery, and 2–3 lengths of chives on each folded crepe, then roll up firmly like a cornet. The julienned vegetables should poke decoratively from the top of the crepe. Fold the top edge of each cornet over (you could use a little remaining filling to make them stick). Cover and refrigerate until ready to serve.

IN ADVANCE: Crepes and fillings can be made separately a day ahead and refrigerated. Alternatively, the crepes can be frozen in layers with greaseproof paper between them.

COCKTAIL TARTLETS

Preparation time: 30 minutes + chilling
Total cooking time: 10 minutes
Makes about 30

★

1 1/2 cups (185 g/6 oz) plain flour
100 g (3 1/2 oz) chilled butter,
   chopped
30 g (1 oz) Parmesan, grated
1 egg, lightly beaten

Fillings
pesto, sun-dried tomato and black olives
olive tapenade, hard-boiled quail eggs and fresh
   flat-leaf parsley
cream cheese, shredded sliced smoked salmon,
   thinly sliced Lebanese cucumber, and
   chopped fresh chives

1 Sift the flour and 1/4 teaspoon salt into a large bowl, add the butter and rub into the flour with your fingertips until the mixture resembles fine breadcrumbs. Stir in the Parmesan, then make a well in the centre. Add the egg and a little water and mix with a flat-bladed knife, using a cutting action, until the mixture comes together in beads. Gently gather together and lift out onto a lightly floured surface. Press together into a ball. Wrap in plastic wrap and refrigerate for 30 minutes.

2 Preheat the oven to hot 210°C (415°F/Gas 6–7). Lightly grease two 12-hole round-based patty tins. Roll the pastry out very thinly and using an 8 cm (3 inch) cutter, cut 30 rounds from the pastry. Press the pastry into the tins and prick lightly all over. Bake for 8–9 minutes, or until golden. Allow to cool in the tins. Remove and repeat with the remaining pastry.

3 Fill the cooled shells with the different fillings.

IN ADVANCE: The tartlet shells can be made up to a few days ahead and stored in an airtight container. If necessary, re-crisp briefly in a moderate 180°C (350°F/Gas 4) oven before use.

LEFT: Tartlets, from left: Olive tapenade, quail eggs and parsley; Pesto, sun-dried tomato and olives; Cream cheese, salmon, cucumber and chives

the pastry evenly with a fork and bake for 15 minutes, or until golden brown. Reduce the oven to moderate 180°C (350°F/Gas 4).

3 Heat the oil in a heavy-based pan. Add the mushrooms and stir over medium heat for 5 minutes, or until well browned. Remove from the heat and stir in the bacon, spring onion and parsley. Season with salt and pepper, to taste, and allow to cool.

4 Using electric beaters, beat the cream cheese and eggs in a small bowl for 5 minutes. Add the cooled mushrooms and stir to combine. Pour the mixture onto the cooked pastry base. Bake for 25 minutes, or until firm and lightly browned. Cool in the tin. Cut into triangles when cool.

NOTE: These bites are best eaten on the day they are made.

ROSEMARY AND CHEESE BISCUITS

Preparation time: 10 minutes + chilling
Total cooking time: 20 minutes
Makes about 50

★

1 cup (125 g/4 oz) plain flour
100 g (3½ oz) butter, chopped
1 tablespoon sour cream
60 g (2 oz) Cheddar, grated
65 g (2 oz) Parmesan, grated
3 teaspoons chopped fresh rosemary
3 teaspoons chopped fresh chives

1 Preheat the oven to moderate 180°C (350°F/ Gas 4). Lightly grease 2 baking trays with melted butter or oil. Sift the flour and some salt and cracked black pepper into a large bowl and add the chopped butter. Rub the butter into the flour with your fingertips until the mixture resembles fine breadcrumbs.

2 Add the sour cream, cheeses and herbs and mix with a flat-bladed knife. Press the mixture together with your fingers until it forms a soft dough. Press into a ball, wrap in plastic wrap and refrigerate for 15 minutes.

3 Roll level teaspoons of the mixture into balls and place on the prepared trays, leaving a little room between the biscuits for spreading. Flatten slightly with a lightly floured fork.

4 Bake for 15–20 minutes, or until lightly golden. Transfer to a wire cake rack and leave until cool.

BACON AND MUSHROOM CREAM BITES

Preparation time: 15 minutes
Total cooking time: 45 minutes
Makes 18

★

1 egg yolk, lightly beaten
2 sheets ready-rolled shortcrust pastry
2 tablespoons oil
375 g (12 oz) mushrooms, finely chopped
4 bacon rashers, finely chopped
4 spring onions, finely chopped
15 g (½ oz) fresh parsley, finely chopped
250 g (8 oz) cream cheese, softened
4 eggs

1 Preheat the oven to hot 210°C (415°F/ Gas 6–7). Brush a shallow 23 cm (9 inch) square cake tin with melted butter or oil.

2 Brush egg yolk over one sheet of pastry. Place the other sheet over the top and gently press together. Trim the edges to fit the tin. Prick

ABOVE: Bacon and mushroom cream bites

HERBED MUSSEL TARTS

Preparation time: 30 minutes
Total cooking time: 15 minutes
Makes 24

★

Filling

2 kg (4 lb) black mussels
90 g (3 oz) butter, softened
2 cloves garlic, crushed
2 tablespoons chopped fresh chives
2 tablespoons chopped fresh flat-leaf
   parsley

24 slices white bread
60 g (2 oz) butter, melted

1 Scrub the mussels with a stiff brush and pull out the hairy beards. Discard any broken mussels, or open ones that don't close when tapped. Rinse well. Bring 2 cups (500 ml/16 fl oz) water to the boil in a large pan, then add half the mussels. Cover and cook for 3–5 minutes, until just opened. Discard any unopened mussels.

Repeat with the remaining mussels. Cover the mussels immediately with cold water and remove the flesh from the shells (if the mussels are very large, cut in half). Pat dry with paper towels. Beat the butter until smooth. Add the garlic, chives and parsley and season, to taste.
2 Preheat the oven to moderate 180°C (350°F/ Gas 4). Flatten the bread slices with a rolling pin and, using an 8 cm (3 inch) biscuit cutter, cut a circle from each slice. Brush both sides of each circle with the melted butter, then press into two 12-hole round-based patty tins. Bake for 8 minutes, or until crisp and lightly golden.
3 Divide the mussels among the hot bread cases and carefully spread herb butter over the top. Bake for 5 minutes, or until the mussels are heated through. Serve at once.
IN ADVANCE: Bake the bread cases up to 6 hours ahead and store in an airtight container. Cook the mussels up to 2 hours ahead, cover and refrigerate. Assemble and reheat to serve.

BLACK MUSSELS

Black mussels are bivalve molluscs found on rocks and wharf piles or grown commercially. When you buy them, they should be firmly closed. Discard any broken mussels, or open ones that don't close when tapped on the bench. To prepare them for cooking, scrub the mussels with a stiff brush to remove all the dirt, then pull off the hairy beards. Rinse well. If the mussels are particularly gritty, soak them in salted water for 1 or 2 hours so they will expel sand and grit. Rinse and cook as per the instructions in your recipe. When they are all opened, they are cooked. At this stage, discard any unopened mussels and any with dried flesh.

LEFT: Herbed mussel tarts

TWISTS

Quick and simple, using frozen ready-rolled puff pastry, twists can be made up to three days in advance and stored in an airtight container. Crisp in the oven if they soften. All recipes can be doubled or trebled.

THYME TWISTS

Lay 1 sheet of puff pastry on a work surface and, when thawed, brush lightly with beaten egg. Remove the hard stems from a bunch of fresh thyme and sprinkle the leaves over the pastry. Gently press onto the pastry and top with a second sheet of pastry. Cut the pastry into 2 cm (¾ inch) strips. Holding both ends, twist the strip in opposite directions twice. Place on a lightly greased baking tray and bake in a hot 210°C (415°F/Gas 6–7) oven for 10–15 minutes, or until puffed and golden. Makes 12.

CHEESE TWISTS

Lay 1 sheet of puff pastry on a work surface and, when thawed, brush lightly with beaten egg and cut into 1.5 cm (⅝ inch) strips. Holding both ends, twist the strip in opposite directions twice. Place on a lightly greased baking tray and sprinkle 3 tablespoons finely grated Parmesan over the flat part of the twists. Bake in a hot 210°C (415°F/Gas 6–7) oven for 10 minutes, or until puffed and golden. Makes 16.

SESAME AND POPPY SEED TWISTS

Lay 1 sheet of puff pastry on a work surface and, when thawed, brush lightly with beaten egg, then sprinkle with 1 tablespoon sesame or poppy seeds and gently press onto the pastry. Cut the pastry into 1.5 cm (5/8 inch) strips. Holding both ends, twist the strip in opposite directions twice. Bake on a lightly greased baking tray in a hot 210°C (415°F/Gas 6–7) oven for 10 minutes, or until puffed and golden. Makes 16.

PROSCIUTTO TWISTS

Lay 1 sheet of puff pastry on a work surface and, when thawed, brush lightly with beaten egg and cut into 1.5 cm (5/8 inch) strips. Holding both ends, twist the strips in opposite directions twice.

Bake on a lightly greased baking tray in a hot 210°C (415°F/Gas 6–7) oven for 10 minutes, or until puffed and golden. Cut 8 slices of prosciutto in half lengthways. Wrap a slice around and down each twist. Makes 16.

ASPARAGUS SPEARS

Lay 1 sheet of puff pastry on a work surface and, when thawed, brush lightly with beaten egg and cut into 1.5 cm (5/8 inch) strips. Secure to one end of a blanched fresh asparagus spear (you will need 16). Wrap around and down the asparagus, brush the end of the pastry with egg and secure to the other end of the asparagus. Place on a lightly greased baking tray and bake in a hot 210°C (415°F/Gas 6–7) oven for 10–15 minutes, or until puffed and golden. Makes 16.

SUN-DRIED TOMATO PLAITS

Lay 1 sheet of puff pastry on a work surface and, when thawed, brush lightly with beaten egg and cut into 1 cm (1/2 inch) strips. Join 3 strips together at the top, by pressing. Plait them together, inserting slices of semi-dried tomato at intervals in the plait (you will need 40 g/1 1/2 oz tomatoes for this). Place on a lightly greased baking tray and bake in a hot 210°C (415°F/Gas 6–7) oven for 10–15 minutes, or until puffed and golden. Makes 8.

FROM LEFT: Thyme twists; Cheese twists; Sesame and poppy seed twists; Prosciutto twists; Asparagus spears; Sun-dried tomato plaits

ABOVE: *Turkey and cranberry pikelets*

TURKEY AND CRANBERRY PIKELETS

Preparation time: 25 minutes + standing
Total cooking time: 15 minutes
Makes about 30

☆

1 cup (125 g/4 oz) self-raising flour

1 egg, plus 1 egg yolk

1¼ cups (315 ml/10 fl oz) milk

25 g (¾ oz) butter, melted

3 tablespoons mayonnaise

150 g (5 oz) cooked turkey, shredded

3 tablespoons cranberry sauce

60 g (2 oz) alfalfa sprouts

3 hard-boiled eggs, sliced

1 Sift the flour and a pinch of salt into a bowl and make a well in the centre. Lightly whisk together the egg, egg yolk, milk and melted butter in a jug and gradually add to the flour, whisking to make a smooth, lump-free batter. Cover and leave for 30 minutes.

2 Heat a frying pan and brush lightly with melted butter or oil. Drop tablespoons of the batter into the pan, allowing room for spreading. Cook over medium heat until small bubbles begin to appear on the surface and the undersides are golden. Turn the pikelets over and cook the other sides. Transfer to a plate, cover with a tea towel and leave to cool while cooking the remaining batter.

3 Spread mayonnaise over each pikelet and top with turkey, cranberry sauce, alfalfa sprouts and a slice of egg.

IN ADVANCE: Pikelets can be made a day ahead and stored, covered, in the refrigerator. They can be frozen if you prefer, in single layers, for up to 2 months.

MUSHROOMS EN CROUTE

Preparation time: 40 minutes
Total cooking time: 20 minutes
Makes 48

★

8 slices white bread, crust removed

80 g (2³/4 oz) butter, melted

1 tablespoon olive oil

1 clove garlic, crushed

¹/2 small onion, finely chopped

375 g (12 oz) small button mushrooms,
    finely sliced

1 tablespoon dry sherry

¹/3 cup (80 g/2³/4 oz) sour cream

2 teaspoons cornflour

1 tablespoon finely chopped fresh parsley

1 teaspoon finely chopped fresh thyme

30 g (1 oz) Parmesan, grated

1 Preheat the oven to moderate 180°C (350°F/ Gas 4). Brush both sides of the bread with the butter. Cut each slice in half vertically, then each half into three horizontally. Bake on a baking tray for 5–10 minutes, or until golden and crisp.
2 Heat the oil in a large frying pan, add the garlic and onion and cook, stirring, over low heat until the onion is soft. Add the mushrooms and cook over medium heat for 5 minutes, or until tender. Season with salt and pepper.
3 Pour the sherry into the pan. Blend the sour cream and cornflour, add to the mushrooms and stir until the mixture boils and thickens. Remove from the heat and stir in the herbs. Allow to cool.
4 Spread the mushroom mixture onto each croûte and sprinkle with the Parmesan. Place on a baking tray and bake for 5 minutes, or until heated through. Serve decorated with small sprigs of fresh herbs, if desired.
NOTE: To serve as a pâté, purée the mushroom mixture, spoon into small dishes, then chill.
IN ADVANCE: Bake the bread up to 4 days in advance and store in an airtight container. Make the topping and assemble just prior to serving.

ABOVE: Mushrooms en croûte

2 Melt the butter in a pan, add the onion and bacon and cook over medium heat for about 3 minutes, until softened but not browned. Stir in the flour and cook for 2 minutes. Remove from the heat and gradually stir in the reserved liquid. Return to the heat and stir until the sauce boils and thickens. Stir in the cream, juice and parsley, reserving a little parsley. Season.
3 Heat the vol-au-vent cases in the oven for 5 minutes. Reheat the sauce, stir in the seafood and warm through. Divide among the cases, garnish with parsley and serve.

GOATS CHEESE TARTLETS

Preparation time: 40 minutes + chilling
Total cooking time: 25 minutes
Makes 30

☆

2 cups (250 g/8 oz) plain flour
150 g (5 oz) chilled butter, chopped
2–4 tablespoons milk

Filling

12 sun-dried tomatoes, sliced
200 g (6½ oz) goats cheese, chopped
2 tablespoons chopped fresh basil
20–30 pitted black olives, sliced
2 tablespoons chopped spring onion tops
4 eggs, lightly beaten
1 cup (250 ml/8 fl oz) cream

1 Sift the flour and a pinch of salt into a bowl. Add the butter and rub in until the mixture resembles fine breadcrumbs. Make a well and add enough milk to mix to a soft dough, using a knife. Lift onto a floured surface and gather into a ball. Chill in plastic wrap for 30 minutes.
2 Preheat the oven to moderate 180°C (350°F/ Gas 4). Roll out the pastry to 2 mm (⅛ inch) and cut 30 rounds with an 8 cm (3 inch) cutter. Line two lightly greased 12-hole patty tins, prick the pastry lightly and bake for 7 minutes, or until cooked but not coloured. Bake all the rounds.
3 Arrange the sun-dried tomatoes in the bases and cover with the cheese, basil, olives and spring onion. Combine the eggs and cream in a small bowl and season with salt and pepper. Spoon the mixture over the filling and bake, for 15 minutes, or until the filling is just set. Repeat with the remaining pastry and filling. Serve warm or at room temperature.

PRAWN AND SCALLOP VOL-AU-VENTS

Preparation time: 25 minutes
Total cooking time: 20 minutes
Makes 36

☆

1 cup (250 ml/8 fl oz) fish stock
1 cup (250 ml/8 fl oz) white wine
250 g (8 oz) scallops
250 g (8 oz) raw prawns, peeled
60 g (2 oz) butter
4 spring onions, finely chopped
1 bacon rasher, finely chopped
¼ cup (30 g/1 oz) plain flour
½ cup (125 ml/4 fl oz) cream
1 teaspoon lemon juice
½ cup (30 g/1 oz) finely chopped fresh parsley
36 small ready-made vol-au-vent cases

1 Heat the stock and wine in a pan until simmering. Add the scallops and prawns and cook gently for 2–3 minutes. Remove with a slotted spoon, cool and chop. Reserve 1 cup (250 ml/8 fl oz) of the cooking liquid. Refrigerate the seafood while making the sauce. Preheat the oven to warm 160°C (315°F/Gas 2–3).

ABOVE: Prawn and scallop vol-au-vents

Turn the bread slices over after about 5 minutes of baking and continue to bake until lightly browned.

Squeeze out the excess liquid from the softened spinach leaves and put on paper towels to dry.

Spread the pimiento evenly over the cheese mixture before rolling up, using the plastic as a guide.

CHEESE AND SPINACH ROULADE BRUSCHETTA

Preparation time: 30 minutes
Total cooking time: 10 minutes
Makes about 24

☆☆

1 French bread stick

2 tablespoons oil

500 g (1 lb) English spinach

90 g (3 oz) spreadable cream cheese

90 g (3 oz) goats cheese

3 tablespoons canned pimiento, drained and
    finely chopped

1 Preheat the oven to moderately hot 200°C (400°F/Gas 6). Cut the bread into 24 thin slices and lightly brush both sides with oil. Bake in a single layer on a baking tray for 10 minutes, or until lightly browned, turning once. Remove and allow to cool.

2 Remove the stalks from the spinach and place the leaves in a bowl. Cover with boiling water and leave for a couple of minutes, or until the leaves have wilted. Drain and leave to cool. Squeeze out the excess liquid and drain on crumpled paper towels.

3 Lay the spinach leaves flat, overlapping, on a piece of plastic wrap, to form a 25 x 20 cm (10 x 8 inch) rectangle. Beat the cheeses together until soft and smooth. Spread the cheese mixture evenly and carefully over the spinach. Top the cheese evenly with pimiento. Using the plastic wrap as a guide, carefully roll up the spinach to enclose the cheese. Remove the plastic wrap and cut the log into thin slices using a sharp knife. Serve on the toast.

NOTE: Be sure to thoroughly drain the spinach and pimiento to avoid a watery result.

IN ADVANCE: The bread slices can be baked several days ahead and stored in an airtight container. The roulade can be made a day ahead and stored, wrapped in plastic wrap, in the refrigerator. Assemble them together just before serving time.

ABOVE: Cheese and spinach roulade bruschetta

PARMESAN
TUILE CONES

Place the cutter back over each circle and sprinkle with the Parmesan and paprika mix, spreading evenly to the edges.

Lift each round from the tray with a spatula and wrap around the end of a cream horn mould to form a cone.

OPPOSITE PAGE: Tuna tartlets with apple mousseline mayonnaise (left); Parmesan tuile cones

TUNA TARTLETS WITH APPLE MOUSSELINE MAYONNAISE

Preparation time: I hour + curing + freezing
Total cooking time: 10–15 minutes
Makes about 48

✷ ✷

375 g (12 oz) tuna, in one piece, skinned
24 hard-boiled quail eggs, halved lengthways, to garnish
45 g (1½ oz) fresh coriander leaves, to garnish

Cure
500 g (1 lb) rock salt
1½ cups (375 g/12 oz) sugar
½ teaspoon ground black peppercorns
1 teaspoon ground ginger

Filo tartlets
250 g (8 oz) filo pastry
250 g (8 oz) unsalted butter, melted

Apple mousseline mayonnaise
2 tablespoons smooth apple sauce
1 cup (250 ml/8 fl oz) whole egg mayonnaise
2 tablespoons cream, whipped

1 Choose a large flat glass dish for curing. Cut the tuna into 3 cm (1¼ inch) strips the length of the tuna, then cut the lengths to fit the dish.
2 Mix the cure ingredients and cover the base of the dish with a layer of the cure, then a layer of tuna. Continue layering, finishing with a layer of cure. Weigh down and refrigerate for 4 hours.
3 Remove the tuna from the cure. Wash the tuna under cold running water, then dry thoroughly. If not using right away, wrap in a lightly oiled cloth to prevent drying out. Refrigerate before slicing.
4 Preheat the oven to moderately hot 190°C (375°F/Gas 5). For the filo cups, layer 6 sheets of filo on top of one another, brushing each with butter. Keep the remainder under a damp cloth.
5 Cut 8 cm (3 inch) rounds of the layered filo with a cutter. Cut through with scissors if necessary. Line two 12-hole round-based patty tins with the rounds, butter-side-down. Press into the holes and prick with a fork. Arrange on baking trays and freeze for at least 10 minutes. (This can be done a day ahead.) While chilling, prepare the remaining filo rounds, but keep covered to prevent them drying out.

6 Bake the pastry cases for 4–5 minutes. Remove from the tins and cool on a wire rack. Repeat with the remaining filo rounds.
7 For the apple mousseline mayonnaise, fold the apple sauce into the mayonnaise, then fold in the cream. Taste and add salt and pepper if necessary.
8 Do not assemble until just before serving. Slice the tuna across the grain in paper-thin slices with a sharp knife. Spoon a teaspoonful of mayonnaise into each case. Top with a slice of tuna, half a quail egg and a coriander leaf. Serve at once.
NOTE: Cook quail eggs in boiling water for 5 minutes, then place in cold water to cool.

PARMESAN TUILE CONES

Preparation time: 40 minutes
Total cooking time: 30 minutes
Makes 36

✷ ✷

150 g (5 oz) Parmesan, finely grated
pinch of paprika
150 g (5 oz) ricotta cheese
2 teaspoons lemon juice
1½ tablespoons milk
2 teaspoons fresh chopped chives, plus extra, cut into short lengths, to garnish
3 slices prosciutto
2 fresh figs, cut into small pieces

1 Preheat the oven to hot 220°C (425°F/Gas 7). Line two baking trays with baking paper. Using a 7 cm (2¾ inch) cutter as a guide, draw circles on the paper. Invert the paper onto the trays. Place the cutter back over each round and sprinkle with 3 teaspoons of Parmesan combined with the paprika, spreading evenly to the edges.
2 Bake only 3–4 at a time for 3 minutes, or until melted and golden. Remove each round from the tray, using a spatula, and wrap around the end of a cream horn mould to form a cone shape. Cool. If they begin to harden too quickly, return to the oven for 10 seconds to soften again.
3 Beat the ricotta cheese, lemon juice and milk in a bowl until smooth. Stir in the chopped chives and salt and cracked black pepper, to taste.
4 Grill the prosciutto until crisp. Allow to cool, then break into pieces about 2 cm (¾ inch) long. Carefully spoon 2 teaspoons of the cheese mixture into each Parmesan tuile. Decorate the end of each tuile with a piece of fig, prosciutto and chives.

SESAME SHAPES

Preparation time: 35 minutes + standing
Total cooking time: 15–20 minutes
Makes about 30

☆

1¹/₂ cups (185 g/6 oz) self-raising flour
4 tablespoons sesame seeds, toasted
2 teaspoons finely grated orange rind
2 eggs
2 teaspoons sesame oil
1 cup (250 ml/8 fl oz) milk
4 tablespoons orange juice
125 g (4 oz) sun-dried tomatoes,
   finely chopped

Filling
200 g (6¹/₂ oz) soft cream cheese
2 tablespoons chopped fresh
   coriander

1 Sift the flour and a pinch of salt into a bowl, stir in the sesame seeds and orange rind and make a well in the centre. With a fork, gradually whisk in the combined egg, sesame oil, milk and orange juice to make a smooth lump-free batter. Set aside for 15 minutes.
2 Heat a frying pan and brush lightly with melted butter or oil. Pour ¹/₃ cup (80 ml/ 2³/₄ fl oz) batter into the pan and cook over medium heat for 3–4 minutes, or until bubbles appear on the surface. Turn over and cook the other side. Transfer to a plate and cover with a tea towel while cooking the remaining batter.
3 Use biscuit cutters to cut out various shapes (you will be sandwiching 3 of each shape together so make sure you have the right number of each).
4 To make the filling, mix the cream cheese and coriander and use to sandwich together three pikelet shapes. Decorate with sun-dried tomato.
IN ADVANCE: Pikelets can be joined and cut into shapes a day ahead. Store in an airtight container in the refrigerator.

SUN-DRIED TOMATOES
Sun-dried tomatoes are usually halved, sprinkled with salt and left to dry in the sun. Sometimes they are dried in the oven. The salt preserves them, but makes them too salty to eat so they are soaked in water for a few hours to swell and rid them of salt. Sometimes they are soaked in vinegar and water, drained, dried, then stored in a mix of olive oil and flavourings such as herbs and garlic. They are readily available and add flavour to many dishes.

RIGHT: Sesame shapes

RED PEPPER (CAPSICUM) PIKELETS WITH PROSCIUTTO

Preparation time: 30 minutes + resting
Total cooking time: 25 minutes
Makes about 20

☆

1 small red pepper (capsicum)

1 cup (125 g/4 oz) plain flour

1/2 teaspoon bicarbonate of soda

1 1/4 cups (315 ml/10 fl oz) buttermilk

1 egg

50 g (1 3/4 oz) butter, melted

130 g (4 1/4 oz) can corn kernels, drained

1 tablespoon finely chopped fresh chives,
    plus some for garnish

1 cup (250 ml/8 fl oz) crème fraîche
    or sour cream

5 slices prosciutto, cut into strips

1 Cut the red pepper into large flattish pieces and remove the seeds and membrane. Cook, skin-side-up, under a hot grill until black and blistered. Place in a plastic bag and leave to cool, then peel. Chop the flesh finely.
2 Sift the flour, bicarbonate of soda and a pinch of salt into a bowl and make a well in the centre. Gradually add the combined buttermilk, egg and melted butter and mix until just combined and lump-free. Stir in the pepper, corn and chives. Do not overmix.
3 Heat a frying pan and brush with melted butter or oil. Drop 2 teaspoons of batter into the pan for each pikelet, leaving a little room for spreading. Cook until bubbles begin to form on the surface. Turn over and cook the other side. Transfer to a plate and cover with a tea towel to keep warm while cooking the remaining batter.
4 Top each pikelet with a teaspoon of crème fraîche and a strip of prosciutto. Garnish with fresh chives.

ABOVE: Red pepper pikelets with prosciutto

MINI QUICHES

Make the pastry cases as directed, then fill with one of our quiche mixtures. Making two trays of quiches takes no extra time, as they can be baked side by side.

PASTRY CASES

Preheat the oven to moderately hot 200°C (400°F/Gas 6). Grease two round-based shallow 12-hole patty tins. Lay 2 sheets of ready-rolled shortcrust pastry on a work surface and cut 12 rounds from each with an 8 cm (3 inch) cutter. Line the tins with pastry, fill with one of the following suggestions and bake as instructed. Remove from the tins while warm and cool on wire racks. Makes 24.

CARAMELIZED ONION AND BACON

Heat 2 teaspoons oil in a large pan. Add 1 large, finely chopped onion, cover and cook over medium-low heat for 30 minutes, or until golden (caramelized onion is slow-cooked to bring out the sweetness, so don't rush this step). Transfer to a bowl to cool. Add 125 g (4 oz) finely chopped bacon to the pan and cook until crisp. Mix with the onion, add 3 teaspoons

wholegrain mustard and season with pepper. Place a small amount in each pastry case. Beat 2 eggs with ½ cup (125 ml/4 fl oz) milk and pour over the onion and bacon. Bake for 15–20 minutes, or until puffed and golden.

GOATS CHEESE AND SEMI-DRIED TOMATO

Mix together 60 g (2 oz) crumbled goats cheese and 60 g (2 oz) chopped semi-

dried tomatoes and place a small amount in the bottom of each pastry case. Beat 2 eggs with ½ cup (125 ml/4 fl oz) milk and 3 tablespoons chopped fresh basil. Season and pour into the cases. Bake for 15–20 minutes, or until puffed and golden.

CURRIED APPLE AND ONION

Heat a little oil in a pan. Lightly brown a small thinly sliced onion, then add a small peeled and grated green apple. Add ¼ teaspoon curry powder and stir for 1 minute. Cool slightly. Spoon heaped teaspoons into the pastry cases. Mix ½ cup (125 ml/4 fl oz) milk, 2 lightly beaten eggs and 2 tablespoons cream in a jug and pour enough into each pastry case to cover the onion. Sprinkle with a little grated Cheddar—you'll need about 20 g (¾ oz) altogether. Bake for 15–20 minutes, or until puffed and golden.

CREAMY HERB

Mix together 2 beaten eggs, 2 tablespoons milk, ½ cup (125 ml/ 4 fl oz) cream, 2 teaspoons chopped fresh chives and 1 teaspoon each of chopped fresh dill, thyme and parsley. Pour into the pastry cases and sprinkle with grated Parmesan, using only about 2 tablespoons altogether. Bake for 15–20 minutes, or until puffed and golden.

SMOKED SALMON

Put 100 g (3½ oz) cream cheese, ¼ cup (60 ml/2 fl oz) cream and 2 eggs in a food processor and mix together, then add some cracked black pepper, to taste. Sprinkle a little finely chopped smoked salmon into the pastry case—you will need about 100 g (3½ oz) smoked salmon. Pour the cream cheese mixture over the top and bake for 15–20 minutes, or until puffed and golden.

CORN AND RED PEPPER
(CAPSICUM)

Drain a 130 g (4 oz) can corn kernels and mix with ⅓ cup (40 g/1½ oz) grated Cheddar and half a finely chopped red pepper. Beat 2 eggs, ⅔ cup (170 ml/ 5½ fl oz) cream, 2 teaspoons Dijon mustard and a dash of Tabasco sauce in a jug and season with salt and pepper. Spoon the corn mixture into the pastry cases, dividing evenly among them, and top with the egg mixture until almost full. Bake for 15–20 minutes, or until puffed and golden.

QUICHES, FROM LEFT: Caramelized onion and bacon; Goats cheese and semi-dried tomato; Curried apple and onion; Creamy herb; Smoked salmon; Corn and red pepper

69

RED ONIONS
These onions are quite sweet and mild compared to other onions and are often finely chopped or sliced and used raw in salsas and salads. They are best kept in the vegetable crisper in the refrigerator.

CRAB CAKES WITH AVOCADO SALSA

Preparation time: 25 minutes + chilling
Total cooking time: about 15 minutes
Makes 20

★

2 eggs
340 g (11 oz) can crab meat, drained
2 spring onions, finely chopped
1 tablespoon mayonnaise
2 teaspoons sweet chilli sauce
1¼ cups (100 g/3 oz) fresh white breadcrumbs
oil, for shallow-frying

Avocado salsa
2 ripe Roma (egg) tomatoes, chopped
1 small red onion, finely chopped
1 large avocado, finely diced
3 tablespoons lime juice
2 tablespoons fresh chervil leaves
1 teaspoon caster sugar

1 Beat the eggs lightly in a bowl. Add the crab meat, spring onion, mayonnaise, sweet chilli sauce and breadcrumbs, and stir well. Season, then cover and refrigerate for 30 minutes.
2 To make the avocado salsa, combine all the ingredients in a bowl, season with salt and pepper, and toss gently to combine.
3 Using wet hands, form the crab mixture into 20 small flat cakes. Heat 3 cm (1¼ inches) oil in a large heavy-based pan and cook the crab cakes over medium heat for about 3 minutes each side, or until golden brown on both sides. Drain well on crumpled paper towels and serve immediately, with avocado salsa to spoon onto the top.
IN ADVANCE: The crab mixture can be made a day ahead, then covered and refrigerated. Prepare the salsa close to serving time.

ABOVE: Crab cakes with avocado salsa

PINE NUTS

Pine nuts have a sweet flavour and are an important ingredient in pesto. They are also used in salads, rice pilafs, pasta dishes and stuffings for vegetables and poultry. As pine nuts have a high fat content, they can go rancid quite quickly, so they are best stored in an airtight container in the freezer or the refrigerator.

MUSHROOMS IN BASIL PESTO ON SOURDOUGH

Preparation time: 20 minutes
Total cooking time: 20–25 minutes
Makes 24

☆

Basil pesto

25 g (³/4 oz) fresh basil leaves

30 g (1 oz) Parmesan, grated

2 tablespoons pine nuts, toasted

2 tablespoons olive oil

1 small clove garlic, crushed

2¹/2 tablespoons olive oil

1 sourdough bread stick, cut into 24 x 1 cm
 (¹/2 inch) thick slices

500 g (1 lb) small flat mushrooms, thinly sliced

3 teaspoons balsamic vinegar

80 g (2³/4 oz) thinly sliced prosciutto

1 For the basil pesto, finely chop the basil leaves, Parmesan and pine nuts in a food processor. Gradually add the olive oil in a thin stream, with the motor running, and process until smooth. Season with salt and pepper.

2 Combine the garlic with 2 tablespoons of the olive oil in a small bowl and brush it over both sides of the bread slices. Place on baking trays and cook both sides under a medium-hot grill until golden brown.

3 Heat the remaining ¹/2 tablespoon of olive oil in a large frying pan. Add the mushrooms and cook over medium heat for 3–4 minutes, or until the mushrooms are heated through. Drain away any liquid. Add the pesto and the vinegar to the mushrooms, stir to combine, then cook over low heat for 1–2 minutes, or until heated through.

4 Preheat the oven to moderately hot 200°C (400°F/Gas 6). To assemble, top the toasts with mushroom, then torn and folded prosciutto. Bake on baking trays for 6 minutes, or until the prosciutto is crisp. Serve immediately.

IN ADVANCE: The basil pesto can be made up to 3 days ahead. Cover and refrigerate. Alternatively, it can be made well ahead and frozen in ice cube trays or a small container. Any other type of bread stick can be used if sourdough is not available.

ABOVE: Mushrooms in basil pesto on sourdough

FLORENTINE SCONES WITH MORTADELLA AND ARTICHOKE

Preparation time: 30 minutes
Total cooking time: 15 minutes
Makes 60

★★

100 g (3½ oz) English spinach leaves
20 g (¾ oz) butter
3 spring onions, finely sliced
1¼ cups (155 g/5 oz) self-raising flour
50 g (1¾ oz) Parmesan, grated
⅓ cup (80 ml/2¾ fl oz) milk, approximately
2 teaspoons milk, extra
200 g (6½ oz) artichokes in olive oil, drained
¼ cup (60 ml/2 fl oz) thick (double) cream
100 g (3½ oz) thinly sliced mortadella
1½ tablespoons finely chopped pistachio nuts

1 Preheat the oven to hot 220°C (425°F/Gas 7). Wash the spinach and cook, covered, in a saucepan over medium heat for 2 minutes, or until wilted. Drain and cool. Squeeze the spinach with your hands to remove as much liquid as possible, then chop finely.
2 Heat the butter in a small pan, add the onion and cook over medium heat for 2 minutes, or until very soft.
3 Sift the flour into a bowl and stir in the spinach, onion mixture and Parmesan. Make a well and use a flat-bladed knife to stir in enough milk to mix to a soft, sticky dough. Turn onto a lightly floured surface and knead lightly until just smooth. Roll out to about 1.5 cm (⅝ inch) thickness, then cut 30 rounds with a 4 cm (1½ inch) cutter. Lightly grease a baking tray and place the rounds on it so they are almost touching. Brush the tops lightly with the extra milk and bake on the middle shelf for 10–12 minutes, or until cooked and golden brown.
4 Meanwhile, chop the artichokes in a food processor until smooth. Add the cream and process quickly until combined. Do not overprocess or the mixture may curdle. Season with salt and pepper, to taste.
5 To assemble, split the scones horizontally in half, top each half with artichoke cream, then torn and folded pieces of mortadella. Sprinkle with pistachio nuts.
IN ADVANCE: The scones are best made on the day of serving. The artichoke cream can be prepared a day ahead and refrigerated.

LAMB ON POLENTA

Preparation time: 15 minutes
Total cooking time: 15 minutes
Makes 24

★

3 cups (750 ml/24 fl oz) chicken stock
¾ cup (110 g/3½ oz) instant polenta
2 tablespoons grated Parmesan
2 lamb fillets (150 g/5 oz)
oil, for frying
¼ small cucumber, thinly sliced
3 tablespoons natural yoghurt

1 Lightly grease a 20 x 30 cm (8 x 12 inch) shallow tray. Pour the stock into a saucepan and bring to the boil. Add the polenta and stir over medium heat for 5 minutes, or until thick. Remove from the heat. Stir in the Parmesan and salt and pepper, to taste. Spread into the tray; cool.
2 When cool, cut the polenta into rounds with a 4 cm (1½ inch) cutter. Trim the lamb of any excess fat and sinew.
3 Heat a little oil in a frying pan, add the lamb and cook until brown all over and cooked as desired, about 3 minutes each side for medium. Remove the lamb fillets from the pan and wipe the pan clean. Add more oil to the pan and fry the polenta rounds until lightly browned on both sides. Remove from the pan.
4 Cut the cucumber slices into quarters. Thinly slice the lamb and place on top of the polenta. Top with yoghurt and a piece of cucumber.
NOTE: For extra flavour, the lamb can be rolled in cracked black peppercorns prior to cooking.

ASPARAGUS BOATS

Cut 3 sheets ready-rolled shortcrust pastry into 25 cm (10 inch) squares. Cut at 6 cm (2½ inch) intervals to make rectangles. Cut in half. Use to line twenty-four 8 cm (3 inch) lightly greased metal boat-shaped tins; chill. Fry 2 crushed cloves garlic and a finely chopped small onion in 30 g (1 oz) butter until soft. Cool, then stir in 2 beaten eggs, ¾ cup (185 g/6 oz) sour cream and 4 tablespoons grated Parmesan. Season. Spoon into the boats and place on baking trays. Bake in a moderately hot 200°C (400°F/Gas 6) oven for 15 minutes, or until golden. Top with blanched asparagus spear tips (cut in half if too thick). Makes 24.

SPRING ONIONS
Sometimes called scallions or green onions, spring onions are immature onions harvested before the bulb has formed. They are sold in bunches. Trim off the roots and tips and wash thoroughly before using. They do not need much cooking to soften them. Sometimes they are added to a dish just before serving and are often added raw to salads to give a mild onion flavour.

OPPOSITE PAGE:
Florentine scones with mortadella and artichoke (top left); Lamb on polenta

FIGS
There are hundreds of varieties of the fig, which has a history dating back to the leaves that are associated with Adam and Eve. It is thought figs originated in Syria, but they are now grown in many countries. A lot of today's varieties are cultivated in Italy. Some are round, others pear-shaped and the size varies considerably. When buying figs, avoid any with mould or broken skin. They should be plump and slightly soft. Dried figs are also available.

ABOVE: Mini scones with ham, leek and port figs

MINI SCONES WITH HAM, LEEK AND PORT FIGS

Preparation time: 40 minutes + chilling
Total cooking time: 45 minutes
Makes about 40

★ ★

2 cups (250 g/8 oz) plain flour
3 teaspoons baking powder
110 g (3½ oz) chilled butter
100 g (3½ oz) Stilton cheese
2 tablespoons chopped fresh chives
¾ cup (185 ml/6 fl oz) milk

Filling

1 cup (250 ml/8 fl oz) port
6 large dried figs, stems removed
1 teaspoon sugar
1 large leek
1 teaspoon Dijon mustard
2 teaspoons red wine vinegar
1 tablespoon olive oil
150 g (5 oz) shaved ham

1 Sift the flour, baking powder and ¾ teaspoon salt into a large bowl. Coarsely grate the butter and cheese into the flour and rub in with your fingertips until the pieces are the size of coarse breadcrumbs. Stir in the chives. Pour in the milk and combine with a fork until large clumps form. Turn onto a floured surface and press into a ball.
2 On a floured surface, roll the dough into a 15 x 25 cm (6 x 10 inch) rectangle. With the long edge of the dough facing you, fold in both ends so they meet in the centre, then fold the dough in half widthways. Roll again into a 15 x 25 cm (6 x 10 inch) rectangle, about 1 cm (½ inch) thick. Cut rounds close together with a 3 cm (1¼ inch) cutter. Push the scraps together and roll and cut as before. Place 2.5 cm (1 inch) apart on a baking tray and refrigerate for 20 minutes. Preheat the oven to hot 220°C (425°F/Gas 7) and bake for 10–12 minutes, or until lightly browned.
3 In a small pan, heat the port, figs and sugar. Bring to the boil, reduce the heat and simmer for 15 minutes. Remove the figs and, when cooled, roughly chop. Simmer the liquid for about 3 minutes, until reduced and syrupy. Put the figs back in and stir to combine. Set aside.
4 Discard any tough leaves from the leek, then rinse the leek. Trim off the dark green tops. Slit

the leek lengthways, almost to the bottom, roll a quarter turn and slit again. Wash well, drain and steam for about 10 minutes, or until very soft. Roughly chop, then combine with the mustard, vinegar and oil. Season with salt and pepper.

6 Cut the scones in half. Put a folded piece of ham on each bottom half, top with a teaspoon each of leek and fig mixture, then replace the tops.

GOATS CHEESE AND APPLE TARTS

Preparation time: 10 minutes
Total cooking time: 25 minutes
Makes 32

☆

2 sheets frozen puff pastry
300 g (10 oz) goats cheese, sliced
2 cooking apples
2 tablespoons extra virgin olive oil
1 tablespoon chopped fresh lemon thyme

1 Preheat the oven to hot 210°C (415°F/ Gas 6–7). While the pastry is still frozen, cut each sheet into four squares and then each square into quarters. Place slightly apart on a lightly greased baking tray. Set aside for a few minutes to thaw and then lay the cheese over the centre of each square of pastry, leaving a small border.

2 Core the unpeeled apples and slice them thinly. Interleave several slices over the pastry, making sure the cheese is covered completely. Lightly brush the apples with oil and sprinkle with lemon thyme and a little salt and pepper, to taste.

3 Bake the tarts for 20–25 minutes, or until the pastry is cooked through and golden brown at the edges. The tarts are best served immediately.

IN ADVANCE: The pastry can be topped with cheese, covered and refrigerated overnight. Top with the apple just before cooking.

ABOVE: Goats cheese and apple tarts

3 Place the croissants on a lightly greased baking tray and refrigerate for about 30 minutes. Preheat the oven to moderately hot 200°C (400°F/Gas 6). Brush each croissant with beaten egg, then bake for 20 minutes, or until puffed and golden. **IN ADVANCE:** Croissants can be prepared up to 6 hours ahead. Bake just before serving.

GARLIC TOAST WITH SALMON MAYONNAISE

Preparation time: 35 minutes
Total cooking time: 30 minutes
Makes 32

☆

1 pepper (capsicum)
1 tomato
8 slices of bread, crusts removed, cut into triangles, or French bread stick, sliced
1/3 cup (80 ml/2³/4 fl oz) olive oil
2 cloves garlic, crushed
2 tablespoons olive oil, extra
1 onion, finely chopped

Salmon mayonnaise
2 egg yolks
2 cloves garlic, crushed
2 teaspoons lemon juice
3/4 cup (185 ml/6 fl oz) olive oil
60 g (2 oz) sliced smoked salmon

1 Remove the seeds and membrane from the pepper and finely chop the flesh. Peel the tomato by scoring a cross in the base, soaking in hot water for 30 seconds, then plunging in cold water. Peel the skin away from the cross. Scoop out the seeds and finely chop the flesh.
2 Preheat the oven to moderate 180°C (350°F/Gas 4). Brush both sides of the bread with the combined oil and garlic and bake on a baking tray for 10–15 minutes. Turn halfway through cooking. Set aside.
3 Heat the extra oil in a frying pan, add the pepper, tomato and onion and fry until the onion is soft. Remove from the heat.
4 For the salmon mayonnaise, whisk the egg yolks, garlic and lemon juice together in a small bowl. Beat the oil into the mixture, about a teaspoon at a time, ensuring all the oil is combined before adding more. The mixture will have the consistency of thick cream.

MINI CROISSANTS

Preparation time: 30 minutes + chilling
Total cooking time: 40 minutes
Makes 30

☆

40 g (1¹/4 oz) butter
3 onions, finely chopped
12 pitted black olives, finely sliced
2 tablespoons chopped fresh parsley
3 sheets frozen puff pastry, thawed
1 egg, beaten

1 Melt the butter in a frying pan and cook the onions over medium-low heat for 20 minutes, or until golden and sweet tasting. Remove from the heat and stir in the olives, parsley, salt and cracked black pepper, to taste. Allow to cool.
2 Cut each sheet of pastry in half, then each half into 5 triangles with a base (shortest side) of 8 cm (3 inches). You will have a couple of odd shapes left at each end. Place a little onion mixture at the base of each triangle and roll up towards the point, enclosing the filling. Curl the ends around to form a croissant shape.

ABOVE: Mini croissants

5 Transfer the mayonnaise to a food processor, add the salmon and freshly ground pepper, to taste, then process until smooth.

6 Serve the garlic toasts topped with some pepper mixture, then salmon mayonnaise.

IN ADVANCE: The mayonnaise and garlic toast can both be made a day ahead. Cover, separately, and refrigerate. Assemble close to serving.

PUMPKIN AND HAZELNUT PESTO BITES

Preparation time: 20 minutes
Total cooking time: 35 minutes
Makes 48

★

750 g (1 1/2 lb) butternut pumpkin
3 tablespoons oil
35 g (1 1/4 oz) roasted hazelnuts
35 g (1 1/4 oz) rocket
3 tablespoons grated Parmesan

1 Preheat the oven to moderately hot 200°C (400°F/Gas 6). Peel the pumpkin and cut into 2 cm (3/4 inch) slices, then cut into rough triangular shapes about 3 cm (1 1/4 inches) along the base. Toss with half the oil and some salt and cracked black pepper, until coated. Spread on a baking tray and bake for 35 minutes, or until cooked.

2 For the hazelnut pesto, process the hazelnuts, rocket, 1 tablespoon of the Parmesan and the remaining oil, until they form a paste. Season with salt and cracked black pepper.

3 Spoon a small amount of the hazelnut pesto onto each piece of pumpkin and sprinkle with the remaining Parmesan and black pepper if desired. Serve warm or cold.

IN ADVANCE: Pesto can be made several days ahead. Pour a film of oil over the surface to prevent discoloration. Tip the oil off before using the pesto.

BELOW: Pumpkin and hazelnut pesto bites

BEEF EN CROUTE WITH BEARNAISE

Preparation time: 20 minutes
Total cooking time: 30–35 minutes
Makes 40

★★

500 g (1 lb) piece beef eye fillet, trimmed
2 teaspoons oil
60 g (2 oz) butter, melted
1 clove garlic, crushed
2 small bread sticks, cut into very thin slices
25 g (3/4 oz) mustard cress, cut in short lengths

Béarnaise
200 g (6 1/2 oz) butter, melted
1/3 cup (80 ml/2 3/4 fl oz) white wine vinegar
1 bay leaf
1 tablespoon chopped fresh tarragon
6 black peppercorns
3 parsley stalks
2 egg yolks
2 teaspoons chopped fresh tarragon, extra

1 Preheat the oven to moderate 180°C (350°F/ Gas 4). Tie the beef with string at even intervals; season. Heat the oil in a pan and fry the beef to brown all over. Transfer to a small baking dish and bake for 20–25 minutes for medium to medium-rare. Remove and set aside.
2 Combine the butter and garlic in a bowl and brush over both sides of the bread. Bake on baking trays for 10 minutes, or until just golden.
3 For the Béarnaise, melt the butter slowly over low heat, remove from the heat and leave for 2–3 minutes to allow the milky mixture to separate to the bottom. Pour off the butter, leaving the milky sediment behind; discard the sediment. Combine the vinegar, bay leaf, tarragon, peppercorns and parsley in a pan and simmer briefly until reduced to 1 tablespoon; strain. Beat the egg yolks and the reduced sauce in a heatproof bowl over a pan of simmering water until slightly thickened. Remove from the heat and drizzle in the butter a few drops at a time, beating continuously until thick. Stir in the extra tarragon and season, to taste. If the mixture becomes too thick (it should be the consistency of mayonnaise), stir in a little water. If the butter is added too quickly, the mixture will separate.
4 Cut the beef into very thin slices, drape on each crouton and top with Béarnaise. Place the mustard cress on the Béarnaise.

SWEET ONION TARTS

Preparation time: 25 minutes + chilling
Total cooking time: 40 minutes
Makes 20

★

1 cup (125 g/4 oz) plain flour
75 g (2 1/2 oz) butter, chopped
1 tablespoon bottled green peppercorns, drained
1 egg yolk
1 teaspoon Dijon mustard

Sweet onion filling
2 tablespoons olive oil
3 onions, sliced
1 clove garlic, sliced
2 teaspoons sugar
2 tablespoons balsamic vinegar
3 tablespoons raisins

1 tablespoon olive paste
75 g (2 1/2 oz) feta cheese

1 Lightly grease 20 holes in two 12-hole round-based patty tins. Sift the flour and 1/4 teaspoon salt into a bowl and add the butter. Rub in with your fingertips until the mixture resembles fine breadcrumbs. Make a well in the centre. Crush the peppercorns with the back of a knife and chop finely. Add to the flour with the egg yolk, mustard and up to 2 teaspoons water. Mix with a flat-bladed knife until the mixture comes together in beads. Turn onto a lightly floured surface and press together into a ball. Wrap in plastic wrap and refrigerate for 20 minutes.
2 Preheat the oven to moderately hot 200°C (400°F/Gas 6). Roll the dough out on a lightly floured surface to 2–3 mm (about 1/8 inch). Cut 20 rounds with an 8 cm (3 inch) cutter. Put in the patty tins and prick with a fork. Bake for 8–10 minutes, or until golden.
3 For the filling, heat the oil in a heavy-based pan. Add the onion and garlic and cook, covered, over low heat for 30 minutes, or until the onion is very soft and beginning to brown. Increase the heat to moderate, add the sugar and vinegar and cook, stirring, until most of the liquid has evaporated and the onion is glossy. Stir in the raisins.
4 Spread a little olive paste into the base of each pastry case. Spoon the onion mixture over it and crumble the feta cheese on top. Serve warm or at room temperature.

OPPOSITE PAGE: Beef en croute with Béarnaise (top); Sweet onion tarts

LEMONS

Lemons are probably the most versatile and useful citrus fruit to have in the kitchen. The juice and rind add flavour to a wide variety of dishes. A sprinkling with the juice preserves the colour and enhances the flavour in many fruits and vegetables such as bananas, avocados and apples. The juice is used in marinades to flavour and tenderise. And, of course, lemons are synonymous with fish. Lemons are available all year round. Choose fruit that is firm, brightly coloured and heavy for its size. Refrigerate if the weather is humid.

ABOVE: Marinated trout and cucumber tarts

MARINATED TROUT AND CUCUMBER TARTS

Preparation time: 30 minutes + standing + freezing
Total cooking time: 10 minutes
Makes 20

★ ★

Filling
300 g (10 oz) ocean trout fillet
1/4 cup (60 ml/2 fl oz) lemon juice
2 tablespoons extra virgin olive oil
1/2 small Lebanese cucumber, finely chopped
2 spring onions, finely sliced
1 tablespoon chopped fresh dill or chervil
20 baby English spinach leaves

1 cup (125 g/4 oz) plain flour
2 tablespoons grated Parmesan
75 g (2 1/2 oz) chilled butter, cubed
1 egg, lightly beaten

1 Remove the skin from the trout, then, using kitchen tweezers, remove the bones. Freeze the fish in plastic wrap for 1 hour. Whisk the lemon juice and oil in a bowl. Cut the fish into strips about 3 x 1 cm (1 1/4 x 1/2 inch) and add to the lemon juice marinade. Cover and set aside at room temperature for 20 minutes, or until the fish turns opaque (in summer, refrigerate—the process will take a little longer). Drain off most of the marinade, leaving just enough to moisten the fish. Add the cucumber, spring onion, dill or chervil, and season with salt and black pepper.
2 While the fish is marinating, sift the flour and a pinch of salt into a large bowl and add the Parmesan and butter. Rub in with your fingertips until the mixture resembles fine breadcrumbs. Make a well, add the egg and stir in with a flat-bladed knife until the mixture comes together in beads. Turn onto a lightly floured surface and gather into a ball. Wrap in plastic wrap and refrigerate for 30 minutes.
3 Preheat the oven to hot 210°C (415°F/Gas 6–7). Lightly grease two 12-hole round-based patty tins. Roll out the pastry to about 2 mm (1/8 inch) thick and cut 8 cm (3 inch) rounds to line 20 holes. Prick the pastry lightly with a fork and

bake for 8–10 minutes, or until golden. Remove from the tins and set aside to cool. Place a spinach leaf in each tart case and top with 1 level tablespoon of filling. Serve at once.

IN ADVANCE: Prepare the tart cases up to 2 days ahead and store in an airtight container.

STILTON, PEAR AND WATERCRESS SHORTBREADS

Preparation time: 20 minutes
Total cooking time: 20–25 minutes
Makes 20

☆☆

125 g (4 oz) Stilton cheese
100 g (3 ¹/₂ oz) butter
2 cups (250 g/8 oz) plain flour
250 g (4 oz) walnuts, finely chopped
2 small ripe pears
¹/₂ cup (125 ml/4 fl oz) crème fraîche or light
    sour cream
watercress leaves, to garnish

1 Preheat the oven to moderate 180°C (350°F/ Gas 4). In a small bowl, beat the cheese and butter with electric beaters for 2–3 minutes, until pale and creamy. Add the flour and walnuts and season with black pepper. Stir until the mixture forms a stiff paste, then turn out onto a lightly floured surface and gather together.

2 Press the mixture into a 30 x 20 cm (12 x 8 inch) shallow tin and score with a knife into 20 even pieces. Bake for 20–25 minutes, or until the shortbread begins to brown. While hot, cut into individual biscuits following the score lines. Cool in the tin.

3 Quarter, core and thinly slice the pears close to serving. To assemble, dot a small amount of crème fraîche in the centre of each biscuit to hold the pear in place. Top the biscuit with slices of pear. Spoon the remaining crème fraîche on top of the pear and garnish with watercress leaves.

IN ADVANCE: The shortbread biscuits can be made up to 3 days ahead and stored in an airtight container when cold. If you need to assemble the whole dish a while before serving, lightly brush all over the sliced pear with a little lemon juice to prevent the pear browning.

ABOVE: Stilton, pear and watercress shortbreads

FLAVOURS OF INDIA

If your friends enjoy the spice of life, why not give your finger food an Indian theme? Some of the dishes—samosas, pakoras, chicken tikka—are well-known and loved favourites. But spicy doesn't have to mean fiery and Indian food can also be delicate and amusing—lamb korma pies and bread bowls filled with dhal combine the flavours of the hot country but are hardly the robust fare we have come to expect. For a large and hungry gathering offer a selection of our miniature flatbreads to scoop up colourful side dishes and chutneys.

TANDOORI COOKING

In India and Pakistan, special charcoal-fired clay tandoor ovens are used for tandoori cooking. Traditionally, the food is marinated in a mixture of crushed garlic, grated fresh ginger, natural yoghurt, lemon juice and spices. It is then threaded onto a spit and lowered over the hot coals into the ovens. A variety of foods, including chicken, fish and meat can be cooked this way.

ABOVE: Chicken tikka

CHICKEN TIKKA

Preparation time: 30 minutes + overnight
　marinating
Total cooking time: 15 minutes
Makes 25–30 skewers

☆

750 g (1 1/2 lb) chicken thigh fillets
1/4 onion, chopped
2 cloves garlic, crushed
1 tablespoon grated fresh ginger
2 tablespoons lemon juice
3 teaspoons ground coriander
3 teaspoons ground cumin
3 teaspoons garam masala
1/3 cup (90 g/3 oz) natural yoghurt

1 Cut the chicken into 3 cm (1 1/4 inch) cubes. Soak 30 wooden skewers in cold water for several hours.
2 Finely chop the onion, garlic, ginger, juice and spices together in a food processor. Transfer to a bowl and stir in the yoghurt and 1/2 teaspoon salt.

3 Thread 4 pieces of chicken onto each skewer and place in a large baking dish. Coat the chicken with the spice mixture. Cover and refrigerate for several hours, or overnight.
4 Barbecue, fry or grill the chicken skewers, turning frequently, until cooked through.
IN ADVANCE: Skewered chicken can be left to marinate in the refrigerator for 1–2 days.

TANDOORI CHICKEN

Preparation time: 40 minutes + overnight
　marinating
Total cooking time: 10 minutes
Makes about 60

☆

1.5 kg (3 lb) chicken thigh fillets
2 cups (500 g/1 lb) natural yoghurt
1/3 cup (80 ml/2 3/4 fl oz) white wine vinegar
1 tablespoon lemon juice
1 tablespoon ground sweet paprika
1 tablespoon cayenne pepper

1 tablespoon ground coriander

1 tablespoon ground cumin

6 cloves garlic, crushed

1 tablespoon grated fresh ginger

2 bay leaves

3 green peppers (capsicum), seeded and cut
   into small squares

1 Cut the chicken into bite-sized pieces and put
in a large glass or ceramic bowl. Add the
yoghurt, vinegar, juice, spices, garlic, ginger and
bay leaves and mix well. Cover and refrigerate
overnight. At the same time, soak 60 small
wooden skewers in cold water overnight.
2 Thread the chicken onto the skewers,
alternating with the pepper squares. Grill for
5–10 minutes, or until the chicken is tender and
cooked through, turning often. Serve hot.

BEEF SAMOSAS WITH MINT CHUTNEY DIP

Preparation time: 50 minutes
Total cooking time: 15 minutes
Makes about 20

★

2 tablespoons oil

1 onion, finely chopped

2 teaspoons finely chopped fresh ginger

400 g (13 oz) beef mince

1 tablespoon curry powder

1 tomato, peeled and chopped

1 potato, cubed

1 tablespoon finely chopped fresh mint

6 sheets ready-rolled puff pastry

1 egg yolk, lightly beaten

1 tablespoon cream

Mint chutney dip

20 g (3/4 oz) fresh mint leaves

4 spring onions

1 red chilli, seeded

1/4 teaspoon salt

1 tablespoon lemon juice

2 teaspoons caster sugar

1/4 teaspoon garam masala

1 Heat the oil in a pan, add the onion and
ginger and cook over medium heat for

3–5 minutes, or until the onion is soft.
2 Add the mince and curry powder and stir
over high heat until the beef has browned.
Add 1 teaspoon salt and the tomato and cook,
covered, for 5 minutes. Add the potato and
3 tablespoons water and cook, stirring, for
5 minutes. Remove from the heat, then cool.
Stir in the mint.
3 Preheat the oven to hot 210°C (415°F/
Gas 6–7). Cut the pastry into 13 cm (5 1/4 inch)
circles using a cutter or small plate as a guide,
then cut in half. Form cones by folding each
in half and pinching the sides together.
4 Spoon 2 teaspoons of the mince into each
cone. Pinch the top edges together to seal. Place
on a lightly greased baking tray. Beat the egg
yolk with the cream and brush over the pastry.
Bake for 10–15 minutes, or until puffed and
golden brown. Serve with mint chutney dip.
5 To make the dip, roughly chop the mint
leaves, spring onion and chilli and place in a food
processor or blender with 3 tablespoons water
and the remaining ingredients. Mix thoroughly
and serve with the hot samosas.
IN ADVANCE: Prepare the samosas up to a day
ahead and refrigerate. Cook just before serving.

*ABOVE: Beef samosas
with mint chutney dip*

ONION BHAJIS WITH TOMATO AND CHILLI SAUCE

Preparation time: 30 minutes
Total cooking time: 40 minutes
Makes about 25

★ ☆

Tomato and chilli sauce
2–3 red chillies, chopped
1 red pepper (capsicum), seeded, cut into
   small dice
425 g (14 oz) can chopped tomatoes
2 cloves garlic, finely chopped
2 tablespoons soft brown sugar
1 1/2 tablespoons cider vinegar

Bhajis
1 cup (125 g/4 oz) plain flour
2 teaspoons baking powder
1/2 teaspoon chilli powder
1/2 teaspoon ground turmeric
1 teaspoon ground cumin
2 eggs, beaten
4 onions, very thinly sliced
50 g (1 3/4 oz) fresh coriander leaves, chopped
oil, for deep-frying

1 To make the sauce, combine all the sauce
ingredients with 3 tablespoons water in a
saucepan. Bring to the boil, lower the heat and
simmer for about 20 minutes, until it thickens.
Remove from the heat. Season, to taste, with salt
and freshly ground pepper.
2 For the bhajis, sift the flour, baking powder,
chilli powder, turmeric, cumin and 1 teaspoon
salt into a bowl and make a well in the centre.
Gradually add the combined egg and 3 tablespoons
water, whisking to make a smooth lump-free
batter. Stir in the onion and chopped coriander.
3 Fill a deep, heavy-based pan one third full of
oil and heat the oil to 180°C (350°F). The oil is
ready when a cube of bread dropped into the
oil turns golden brown in 15 seconds. Drop
small rough balls of batter, about the size of a
golf ball, into the oil and fry in batches for about
1 1/2 minutes each side, or until crisp and golden.
Drain on crumpled paper towels. Serve hot with
the tomato and chilli sauce.
IN ADVANCE: These are best served freshly fried,
but can be made ahead of time and reheated in a
moderately hot 200°C (400°F/Gas 6) oven for
about 5 minutes.

BREAD BOWLS FILLED WITH DHAL

Preparation time: 25 minutes
Total cooking time: 35 minutes
Makes 24

★ ☆

1/2 cup (125 g/4 oz) red lentils, rinsed and
   drained
1 cup (250 ml/8 fl oz) vegetable stock
24 slices white bread
60 g (2 oz) ghee or butter
1/2 teaspoon cumin seeds
1/2 teaspoon ground coriander
1/4 teaspoon yellow mustard seeds
2 cloves garlic, crushed
1/2 teaspoon chopped red chilli
2 tablespoons chopped fresh coriander leaves

1 Preheat the oven to moderately hot 200°C
(400°F/Gas 6). Combine the red lentils and
stock in a heavy-based pan. Bring to the boil,
reduce the heat and simmer, covered, for
10 minutes, or until tender. Stir occasionally
and check that the mixture is not catching on
the bottom of the pan. Remove from the heat.
2 Meanwhile, using an 8 cm (3 inch) cutter,
cut 24 rounds of bread. Roll each to 1 mm
(1/16 inch) thick with a rolling pin. Melt half
the ghee or butter, brush on both sides of the
bread, then push into two 12-hole mini muffin
tins to form little bowls. Bake for 12–15 minutes,
or until firm and golden.
3 Heat the remaining ghee or butter in a small
frying pan and add the cumin, ground coriander
and mustard seeds. Cook until the mustard seeds
begin to pop, then add the garlic and chilli.
Cook stirring, for 1 minute, or until fragrant. Stir
the spice mixture into the cooked lentils, return
to the heat and simmer over very low heat,
stirring frequently until the dhal is thick and
creamy. Season, to taste, with salt and set aside
to cool a little before serving
4 Fill each bread bowl with 2–3 teaspoons of
warm dhal, scatter with the chopped coriander
and serve immediately.
IN ADVANCE: Bread bowls and dhal can be
made 2 days ahead and stored separately. Store
the bread bowls in an airtight container and the
dhal, covered, in the refrigerator. Gently reheat
the dhal and fill the bread bowls with warm dhal
close to serving time.

CORIANDER
Fresh coriander is an
ancient plant. The leaves
look like parsley but they
are a lighter green and,
when chopped, the aroma
is quite distinctive. All
parts of the plant, including
the roots, leaves, stems
and seeds (dried), are used
in some cuisines, especially
Thai. Sometimes coriander
is called cilantro or
Chinese parsley. Stand the
roots, which are still
attached when you buy a
bunch, in a jar of water in
the refrigerator and
coriander will keep for
several days.

*OPPOSITE PAGE: Onion
bhajis with tomato and
chilli sauce (top left);
Bread bowls filled
with dhal*

AROMATIC PANTRY

Besan flour: pale yellow, finely milled flour made from dried chickpeas (garbanzo beans). High in protein, it is used in many dishes, including doughs and sauces. Also known as gram flour.

Chilli powder: made by finely grinding whole dried red chillies. Flavour varies from mild to fiery hot, so add sparingly to dishes until the heat of the particular chilli powder has been ascertained. Sometimes available as a blend containing chilli, oregano, cumin and garlic.

Curry leaves: small shiny, bright green pointed leaves from a tree native to India. Fresh leaves are used in many Indian dishes. Much of the flavour is lost from dried leaves.

Fennel seeds: greenish brown seeds from the fennel plant. Have a light licorice taste, not overpowering if used sparingly. Also available ground. Used in both sweet and savoury dishes and to flavour some liqueurs.

Garam masala: a mixture of dry-roasted ground spices, usually including cinnamon, pepper, coriander, cumin, cardamom, cloves and either mace or nutmeg. Some variations contain up to 12 spices.

Kaffir lime leaves: dark, shiny, double leaves with a distinctive citrus flavour and strong perfume rich in aromatic oils. Remove the central thick vein and slice thinly. Dried leaves may need soaking before use.

Coriander seeds: small pale yellow/brown, slightly ridged round seeds with a mild fragrance. Also available ground. Often used in conjunction with fresh coriander. The flavours are completely different.

Lemon grass: The tough exterior leaves are removed and the white interior is used in cooking, sliced or pounded into a paste. The bruised stem can be used in soups or curries and removed before serving.

Red lentils: tiny round flat pulses. Can also be deep orange or yellow. Not necessary to soak before cooking. Widely available.

Fresh coriander: a pungent herb, also known as cilantro and Chinese parsley. All parts of the plant are edible. Whole dried seeds or ground coriander also available.

Curry powder: blend of up to 20 spices. Varies depending on the region, but ranges from mild to hot. Will lose flavour after two months and should be bought in small quantities.

Cumin seeds: small, pale brown aromatic seeds which have a warm pungent earthy flavour. Also available ground.

Brown mustard seeds: small golden brown seeds. Hotter and more aromatic than the yellow mustard seeds.

Kalonji/nigella seeds: small black seeds with a slight peppery onion flavour. Available in speciality stores.

Ghee: pure clarified butter with no milk solids, so it can be heated to a high temperature without burning. Available in tins or the refrigerated section of the supermarket.

Palm sugar: made from the boiled sap of palm trees. Sold in blocks or jars, it is thick and crumbly and is generally grated before use. Soft brown sugar makes a good substitute.

Ground turmeric: dried ground root of fresh turmeric, a member of the ginger family. Has a mild musky flavour and imparts a distinctive yellow colour to food.

SESAME PRAWNS WITH TANGY MINT CHUTNEY

Preparation time: 20 minutes
Total cooking time: 20 minutes
Makes 24

★ ★

1 kg (2 lb) raw king prawns (about 24)
1/4 cup (30 g/1 oz) plain flour
1 egg, lightly beaten
2/3 cup (65 g/2 1/4 oz) dried breadcrumbs
1/2 cup (80 g/2 3/4 oz) sesame seeds
oil, for deep-frying

Tangy mint chutney
50 g (1 3/4 oz) fresh mint leaves
1/2 cup (140 g/4 1/2 oz) fruit chutney
2 tablespoons lemon juice

1 Peel the prawns, leaving the tails intact. Carefully cut the prawns down the back, devein and flatten slightly.
2 Toss the prawns in the flour and shake off the excess. Dip the floured prawns in the beaten egg and coat with the combined breadcrumbs and sesame seeds.
3 Fill a deep, heavy-based pan one third full of oil and heat the oil to 180°C (350°F). The oil is ready when a cube of bread dropped into the oil turns golden brown in 15 seconds. Deep-fry the prawns, in batches, for about 2 minutes each batch, until golden brown. Remove from the oil with tongs or a slotted spoon. Drain on crumpled paper towel.
4 To make the tangy mint chutney, combine the mint, chutney and lemon juice in a blender or food processor for 15 seconds, or until smooth. Serve as a dip.
IN ADVANCE: The prawns can be crumbed a day ahead. Place in a single layer on a tray, cover and refrigerate. Alternatively, freeze in a single layer and when frozen, place in a plastic bag and seal. Thaw in a single layer on a baking tray in the refrigerator. Prepare the mint chutney close to serving time.

ABOVE: Sesame prawns with tangy mint chutney

SPICY PUMPKIN PUFFS

Preparation time: 20 minutes
Total cooking time: 50 minutes
Makes 20

★ ★

1 tablespoon vegetable oil

1 onion, finely chopped

3 fresh or dried curry leaves

1 tablespoon brown mustard seeds

2 teaspoons mild Madras curry powder

1/2 teaspoon chilli powder

1/2 teaspoon ground turmeric

350 g (11 oz) pumpkin, diced

1/2 cup (80 g/2 3/4 oz) frozen peas

3/4 cup (185 ml/6 fl oz) chicken stock

5 sheets ready-rolled puff pastry

1 egg, lightly beaten

1 Heat the oil in a frying pan and cook the onion for 2–3 minutes over moderate heat. Add the curry leaves and mustard seeds and fry for 1–2 minutes, or until the mustard seeds pop. Add the curry powder, chilli powder and turmeric to the pan and stir for about 30 seconds, or until combined.

2 Add the pumpkin to the pan and stir for 1–2 minutes, or until the pumpkin is well coated with spices. Add the peas and stock to the pan and simmer gently for 8–10 minutes, or until the pumpkin is tender and most of the liquid has evaporated. Remove from the heat and allow to cool completely.

3 Preheat the oven to hot 220°C (425°F/Gas 7). Lightly brush two baking trays lightly with oil. Cut four 10 cm (4 inch) circles from each of the pastry sheets and spoon 1 tablespoon of the mixture into the centre of each. Brush the edges with the beaten egg and fold over to enclose the filling. Seal the edges by rolling and folding, or pressing with a fork. Place the puffs on the trays and lightly brush with the remaining beaten egg. Bake for 25–30 minutes, or until puffed and golden.

IN ADVANCE: Can be made 2 days ahead or frozen for up to 2 months.

SPICY PUMPKIN PUFFS

Add the curry leaves and the mustard seeds to the onion in the pan and fry until the seeds pop.

To check whether the pumpkin is tender, gently insert the point of a knife into a piece.

Brush around the edges of each pastry circle with lightly beaten egg.

Seal the edges of the puffs by rolling and folding, or pressing lightly with a fork.

LEFT: Spicy pumpkin puffs

PALM SUGAR
Palm sugar is made by boiling the sap of either the sugar palm or the palmyra palm both of which grow wild in Malaysia and Indonesia. It is a thick, crumbly sugar with quite a rich flavour. The colour varies from pale caramel to dark brown. It is sold in Asian food speciality stores in block form, or in jars, and keeps for months in an airtight container.

ABOVE: Coconut-crusted lamb cutlets

COCONUT-CRUSTED LAMB CUTLETS

Preparation time: 10 minutes + marinating
Total cooking time: 10 minutes
Makes 24

★

24 thin, lean lamb cutlets
1 large onion, grated
2 cloves garlic, crushed
2 teaspoons ground turmeric
1 tablespoon soft dark brown or palm sugar
2/3 cup (60 g/2 oz) desiccated coconut
2 teaspoons soy sauce
2 tablespoons lemon juice

1 Trim the meat of excess fat and sinew. Combine all the remaining ingredients in a bowl with 1 teaspoon of salt and 1/2 teaspoon of freshly ground black pepper. Stir until the coconut is thoroughly moistened.
2 Add the lamb cutlets and press the coconut mixture onto the surface of each one. Cover with plastic wrap and marinate in the refrigerator for 2 hours.
3 Preheat and lightly oil the grill, then grill the cutlets for 3–5 minutes on each side, or until crisp and golden brown.

IN ADVANCE: This recipe can be prepared a day or two ahead and refrigerated, covered. Bring to room temperature before grilling.

CURRIED MINCE MEATBALLS

Preparation time: 40 minutes + chilling
Total cooking time: 40 minutes
Makes 25–30

★ ★

2 tablespoons olive oil
1 large onion, finely chopped
1 clove garlic, finely chopped
45 g (1 1/2 oz) butter
1 tablespoon curry powder
2 tablespoons plain flour

¾ cup (185 ml/6 fl oz) milk

1 tablespoon mango or tomato chutney

400 g (13 oz) minced, cooked, cold lamb, beef
  or chicken

¼ cup (30 g/1 oz) plain flour, extra, for coating

2 eggs

1¼ cups (125 g/4 oz) dry breadcrumbs

oil, for deep-frying

mango or tomato chutney, extra, for serving

1 Heat the oil in a medium saucepan, add the
onion and cook over medium heat for about
5 minutes, or until soft and golden. Add the
garlic and cook for 30 seconds. Add the butter to
the pan and, when melted, stir in the curry
powder until aromatic. Add the flour and cook
for 1 minute, or until foaming. Remove from
the heat and gradually stir in the milk. Return to
the heat and stir constantly over medium heat
until the sauce boils and thickens. Reduce the
heat and simmer for 2 minutes. Add the chutney
and ¼ teaspoon each of salt and black pepper.
Remove from the heat and add the meat, stirring
until the mixture is well combined. Cool, cover

with plastic wrap and refrigerate for at least 1 hour.
2 Using wet hands, form tablespoons of the
mixture into balls and place on greaseproof paper
covered trays.
3 Place the extra flour on a plate. Beat the eggs
in a shallow bowl. Put the breadcrumbs on a
sheet of greaseproof paper. Lightly coat the balls
in flour, shake off any excess, dip in egg and
then coat with breadcrumbs. Cover and
refrigerate on paper-covered trays for 1 hour,
or overnight.
4 Fill a deep heavy-based pan one third full of
oil and heat the oil to 180°C (350°F). The oil is
ready when a cube of bread dropped into the oil
turns golden brown in 15 seconds. Deep-fry the
meatballs in batches for about 2 minutes each
batch, or until golden brown all over. Remove
from the oil with a slotted spoon and drain on
crumpled paper towels. Serve with chutney.
NOTE: You can use any leftover roast meat.
Mince it in a food processor or cut finely with
a sharp knife.

IN ADVANCE: The meat mixture can be made
up to 2 days ahead. The crumbed balls can be
frozen for up to 2 months. Allow to thaw
thoroughly before frying.

*ABOVE: Curried mince
meatballs*

BREADS
Traditionally used in India to accompany curries and mop up the sauces, these wafer-thin or sometimes puffy flatbreads can also be broken up and served with creamy vegetable- or yoghurt-based dips, or sambals.

GHEE
Ghee, or clarified butter, used in India, keeps longer than butter and can be heated to a higher temperature without burning. To make your own, melt unsalted butter over very low heat, without stirring, until frothy. Remove from the heat, scoop off the foam, then gently pour the liquid into a heatproof container, discarding the milky sediment in the pan. When set, discard any solids from the base, reheat and repeat the process, straining through muslin or cheesecloth.

CHAPATTIS
Sift 3 cups (450 g/14 oz) wholemeal plain flour and 1 teaspoon salt into a large bowl. Return the husks. Add 40 g (1¼ oz) ghee and rub with your fingertips until the mixture resembles fine breadcrumbs. Make a well and pour in 1 cup (250 ml/ 8 fl oz) warm water. Mix with a flat-bladed knife until the dough comes together. Turn onto a lightly floured surface and knead for 10 minutes. Place in a lightly oiled bowl, cover and leave for 1 hour. Knead again for 5 minutes, or until smooth. Roll tablespoons of dough into thin circles. Heat a little oil in a large frying pan and cook 2 chapattis at a time for 1 minute each side. Remove and drain on paper towels. Makes 35.

PURIS
Sift 3 cups (450 g/14 oz) wholemeal plain flour and 1 teaspoon salt into a large bowl. Return the husks. Stir in 2 teaspoons cumin seeds. Add 40 g (1¼ oz) ghee and rub in with your fingertips until the mixture resembles fine breadcrumbs.

Make a well and pour in 1 cup (250 ml/ 8 fl oz) warm water. Mix with a flat-bladed knife until the dough comes together. Turn onto a lightly floured surface and knead for 10 minutes. Place in a lightly oiled bowl, cover and leave for 1 hour. Knead for 5 minutes, or until smooth. Roll tablespoons of dough out into thin circles. Heat 3 cm (1¼ inch) oil in a large frying pan. Cook 1 round of dough at a time, turning over until puffed and golden. Drain on paper towels. Makes 35.

GARLIC NAAN

Combine 2½ teaspoons dry yeast, 2 teaspoons sugar and ¾ cup (185 ml/ 6 fl oz) warm water in a small bowl, cover and leave in a warm place for 10 minutes, or until foamy. Sift 3 cups (375 g/12 oz) plain flour and 1 teaspoon salt into a bowl. Make a well and pour in 60 g (2 oz) melted ghee, 2 tablespoons yoghurt and the yeast mixture. Mix with

a flat-bladed knife to a soft dough, gather into a ball then turn out onto a lightly floured surface and knead for 15 minutes, or until smooth and elastic. Place in a large oiled bowl, cover loosely and leave in a warm place for 1 hour, or until it has doubled in size. Punch down the dough, then turn onto a lightly floured surface and knead for 1 minute. Divide into 4 and divide each portion into 8. Roll each piece of dough out to a 7 cm (2¾ inch) circle and place on a greased baking tray. Brush with melted ghee and sprinkle with crushed garlic and finely chopped fresh parsley. Bake in a moderate 180°C (350°F/Gas 4) oven for 5–8 minutes, or until lightly golden. Serve. Makes 32.

PARATHAS

Sift 1 cup (150 g/5 oz) wholemeal plain flour and 1 teaspoon salt into a large bowl. Return the husks to the bowl. Make a well and add 30 g (1 oz) melted

ghee and ⅔ cup (170 ml/5½ fl oz) water. Mix with a flat-bladed knife to a soft dough, gather into a ball, then turn onto a lightly floured surface and knead for 10 minutes. Place in an oiled bowl, cover loosely and leave in a warm place for 1 hour. Knead for 1 minute, divide into four, then cut each portion into four. Roll out each piece on a lightly floured surface until 2 mm (⅛ inch) thick. Melt an extra 90 g (3 oz) ghee and brush some over each circle. Fold the circle in half to make a semi-circle, brush with ghee and fold in half again to make a triangle. Roll to a thin triangle. Brush some ghee in a large frying pan and heat. Brush each triangle with ghee and cook for 1–2 minutes each side, or until puffed and golden brown. Serve. Makes 16.

FROM LEFT: Chapattis; Puris; Parathas; Garlic naan

SIDE DISHES
A spoonful of fruit chutney or vegetable pickle provides extra spice and flavour to Indian food. Alternatively, serve a selection as dips to have with flatbreads or pappadums.

SWEET MANGO CHUTNEY
Slice the flesh of 3 large mangoes and sprinkle with salt. Finely chop 2 seeded red chillies. Blend 1/2 teaspoon garam masala with 1 1/2 cups (330 g/11 oz) raw sugar and place in a large pan with 1 cup (250 ml/8 fl oz) white vinegar. Bring to the boil, reduce the heat and simmer for 5 minutes. Add the mango, chilli, a finely grated 5 cm (2 inch) piece of fresh ginger and 1/2 cup (95 g/3 1/4 oz) finely chopped pitted dates. Simmer for 1 hour, or until the mango is tender. Spoon into warm sterilized jars and seal. Store in the fridge for a week before using. Keeps for up to 1 month. Fills three 250 ml (8 fl oz) jars.

INDIAN LIME PICKLE
Cut 10 ripe yellowed limes into eight wedges each. Place in a large glass bowl, sprinkle with 2 tablespoons cooking salt and stir well. Cover with plastic wrap and leave for 48 hours in a cool dark place, stirring occasionally. Drain, rinse well and mix with 200 g (6 1/2 oz) raisins and 150 g (5 oz) sultanas. Process in batches in a food processor until coarsely chopped. Heat 3 tablespoons peanut oil in a large heavy-based pan, add 2 teaspoons ground cumin, 1 teaspoon ground coriander, 1 teaspoon black mustard seeds, 1/2 teaspoon ground chilli powder, 1/2 teaspoon ground black pepper, 5 finely

chopped cloves of garlic and a 5 cm (2½ inch) piece of fresh ginger, grated. Don't overcook the ginger or it will be bitter. Cook over medium heat for 2–3 minutes, or until very aromatic. Add the lime mixture, 1¼ cups (315 ml/10 fl oz) malt vinegar and 500 g (1 lb) soft brown sugar. Bring to the boil, stirring until the sugar dissolves. Reduce the heat and simmer for 1–1½ hours, stirring occasionally. Pour into warm, sterilized jars and seal. Refrigerate after opening. Makes about 2½ cups (600 ml/20 fl oz).

CUCUMBER WITH YOGHURT

Mix 1 finely diced small tomato, ½ finely chopped onion, ½ coarsely grated cucumber, 1 tablespoon cumin seeds and 1½ tablespoons plain yoghurt. Season, to taste. Cover and refrigerate until ready to use. Makes about ¾ cup (185 ml/6 fl oz).

BANANA WITH COCONUT

Finely dice 2 bananas, add ⅔ cup (35 g/1¼ oz) flaked coconut and ½ cup (125 ml/4 fl oz) lemon juice and stir well. Cover and refrigerate until ready to use. Makes about 1 cup (250 ml/8 fl oz).

CUCUMBER AND CORIANDER

Peel a telegraph cucumber, discard the seeds, then dice finely. Mix with 1 tablespoon lemon juice and 2 tablespoons chopped fresh coriander leaves. Season with salt, cover and refrigerate until ready to use. Makes about ¾ cup (185 ml/6 fl oz).

PAPAYA WITH MINT

Peel a papaya, slice thinly, then cut into small dice. Mix with 3 tablespoons fresh orange juice and 1 tablespoon chopped fresh mint. Cover and chill until ready to use. Makes about 1 cup (250 ml/8 fl oz).

CHILLI EGGPLANT (AUBERGINE) PICKLE

Slice 3 eggplants (aubergines) into 1 cm (½ inch) thick slices, put in a colander and sprinkle with salt. Leave for 1 hour, then rinse and pat dry. Bring 2 cups (500 ml/16 fl oz) white wine vinegar to the boil, add a few slices of eggplant at a time and cook for 4 minutes each batch. Layer the eggplant, 10 peeled cloves garlic, 2 sliced red chillies, some fresh curry leaves and a sliced lemon, in sterilized jars. Pour in enough olive oil to cover the eggplant. Seal and leave for a week in the fridge before using. Fills five 250 ml (8 fl oz) jars.

CLOKWISE, FROM TOP LEFT: Sweet mango chutney; Indian lime pickle; Banana with coconut; Cucumber and coriander; Chilli eggplant pickle (2 jars); Papaya with mint; Cucumber with yoghurt

97

CORN AND POTATO FRITTERS

Preparation time: 15 minutes
Total cooking time: 20 minutes
Makes about 40

★

2 large potatoes
260 g (8 oz) can corn kernels, drained
4 eggs, lightly beaten
6 spring onions, chopped
1/2 cup (50 g/1 3/4 oz) dry breadcrumbs
1 teaspoon garam masala
3 tablespoons oil

Dipping sauce
2/3 cup (160 g/5 1/2 oz) natural yoghurt
2 tablespoons chopped fresh mint leaves
2 teaspoons sweet chilli sauce

1 Peel and coarsely grate the potatoes. Drain on paper towel and squeeze out the excess moisture. Combine in a bowl with the corn, eggs, spring onion, breadcrumbs and garam masala. Mix well.
2 Heat 2 tablespoons of the oil in a heavy-based frying pan. Cook heaped tablespoons of mixture over medium heat for 2 minutes each side, or until golden. Drain on crumpled paper towel and keep warm. Repeat until all the mixture is used, adding extra oil to the pan if necessary.
3 For the dipping sauce, combine all the ingredients in a bowl.

CRISPY CHEESE AND CURRY LENTIL BALLS

Preparation time: 15 minutes
Total cooking time: 20 minutes
Makes about 30

★ ★

1 cup (250 g/4 oz) red lentils
4 spring onions, chopped
2 cloves garlic, crushed
1 teaspoon ground cumin
1 cup (80 g/2 3/4 oz) fresh breadcrumbs
1 cup (125 g/4 oz) grated Cheddar
1 large zucchini (courgette), grated
1 cup (150 g/5 oz) cornmeal (polenta)
oil, for deep-frying

1 Place the lentils in a pan and cover with water. Bring to the boil, reduce the heat, cover and simmer for 10 minutes, or until tender. Drain.
2 Combine half the lentils in a food processor or blender with the spring onion and garlic. Process until smooth. Transfer to a large bowl, then stir in the remaining lentils, cumin, breadcrumbs, cheese and zucchini until well combined. Roll level teaspoons of mixture into balls and toss lightly in cornmeal to coat.
3 Fill a heavy-based pan one third full of oil and heat the oil to 180°C (350°F). The oil is ready when a cube of bread dropped into the oil turns golden brown in 15 seconds. Cook small batches of the lentil balls in the oil for 1 minute each batch, or until golden brown, crisp and heated through. Carefully remove with tongs or a slotted spoon and drain on crumpled paper towels. Serve hot.

TANDOORI LAMB CUTLETS

Preparation time: 25 minutes + overnight marinating
Total cooking time: 10–15 minutes
Makes 24

★ ★

24 lamb cutlets
2 cups (500 g/16 oz) natural yoghurt
2/3 cup (30 g/1 oz) chopped fresh coriander leaves
2 tablespoons ground cumin
4 cloves garlic, crushed
2 tablespoons grated fresh ginger
1 teaspoon ground turmeric
1–2 red chillies, seeded and finely chopped

1 Clean the bones of the cutlets by scraping down the bone with sharp knife. Put the cutlets in a large shallow dish.
2 To make the marinade, combine the yoghurt, coriander leaves, cumin, garlic, ginger, turmeric and chilli in a bowl. Pour over the cutlets, mix to coat, then cover and refrigerate overnight.
3 Leave a coating of the marinade on the cutlets and barbecue on a hot barbecue plate, or grill, until tender.
IN ADVANCE: The cutlets can be marinated up to 2 days ahead. This marinade is also delicious with chicken.

ZUCCHINI
(COURGETTE)
The zucchini, a species of summer squash that originated in America, is now used in many cuisines. The most common zucchini is green, but there is also a yellow one. Zucchini don't need much preparation, just a trim on both ends and a rinse, nor do they take long to cook. They are delicious in salads, either grated or thinly sliced. Available all year, zucchini should be firm and evenly coloured when bought and should be kept in the crisper in the refrigerator.

OPPOSITE PAGE: Corn and potato fritters (top); Crispy cheese and curry lentil balls

ABOVE: Tandoori prawns

2 Combine the yoghurt with the fresh coriander, mint and salt, to taste. Pour over the prawns, mix well and leave for 5 minutes.
3 Mix the ginger, garlic, chilli powder, turmeric, coriander, garam masala and food colouring in a large bowl, add the prawns and marinate for 10 minutes.
4 Thread the prawns onto metal skewers and barbecue or grill for about 5 minutes. Turn the skewers once, so the prawns cook evenly. They are ready when they start to curl and turn opaque. Serve on skewers or loose with lemon wedges and side dishes (see page 96).

HERBED NAAN BREAD

Preparation time: 35 minutes + rising
Total cooking time: 20 minutes
Makes 32

✷ ✷

2 packets naan bread mix
90 g (3 oz) sweet potato, finely diced
90 g (3 oz) pumpkin, finely diced
90 g (3 oz) frozen peas, thawed
30 g (1 oz) chopped fresh coriander
2 tablespoons mango chutney
1 teaspoon curry powder
1/2 teaspoon garam masala
1 teaspoon crushed fennel seeds
1/4 teaspoon chilli powder
1 egg, lightly beaten

1 Prepare each packet of naan bread, according to the instructions, up to the rising stage. Knead lightly. Be careful not to overwork the dough or it will be tough.
2 Boil or steam the sweet potato and pumpkin until just tender and combine with the peas, coriander, chutney, curry powder, garam masala, fennel seeds and chilli powder in a bowl. Preheat the oven to moderately hot 200°C (400°F/Gas 6).
3 Divide each quantity of dough into 4 portions, roll each out on a lightly floured surface and cut 4 circles from each with an 8 cm (3 inch) cutter.
4 Spoon a heaped teaspoon of the filling on half of each circle, brush the edges with beaten egg, fold over and seal. Place on lightly greased baking trays, brush the tops with the remaining egg and bake for 20 minutes, or until crisp and golden brown.
IN ADVANCE: Can be made 2 days ahead or frozen for up to 2 months.

TANDOORI PRAWNS

Preparation time: 20 minutes + marinating
Total cooking time: 5 minutes
Makes 24

✷

1 kg (2 lb) raw king prawns (about 24)
1/2 cup (125 g/4 oz) natural yoghurt
1/3 cup (20 g/3/4 oz) finely chopped fresh coriander
2 tablespoons finely chopped fresh mint
1 tablespoon chopped fresh ginger
2 cloves garlic, crushed
1 teaspoon chilli powder
1 teaspoon ground turmeric
1 teaspoon ground coriander
1 teaspoon garam masala
few drops red food colouring, optional
2 lemons, cut into wedges, for serving

1 Peel and devein the prawns, leaving the tails intact. Rinse and pat dry with paper towels.

SPICY KOFTAS

Preparation time: 25 minutes
Total cooking time: 25 minutes
Makes 45

✦

500 g (1 lb) lamb mince
1 small onion, finely chopped
1 clove garlic, crushed
1 teaspoon ground coriander
1 teaspoon ground cumin
1/4 teaspoon ground cinnamon
1/2 teaspoon finely chopped red chilli
1 teaspoon tomato paste (tomato purée)
1 tablespoon chopped fresh mint
1 tablespoon chopped fresh coriander
oil, for frying

Yoghurt dip
1 small tomato, peeled, seeded and finely
   chopped
1/2 Lebanese cucumber, peeled and finely
   chopped
1 clove garlic, crushed
1 tablespoon chopped fresh mint
1/2 cup (125 g/4 oz) natural yoghurt

1 Combine the mince, onion, garlic, coriander, cumin, cinnamon, chilli, tomato paste and mint and coriander leaves in a large bowl and mix well with your hands. Season well, then roll into small balls (about 1 1/2 teaspoons each).
2 Place a large heavy-based frying pan over moderate heat and heat a little oil. Cook the koftas in batches until well browned all over and cooked through. Drain on crumpled paper towels.
3 Mix together the dip ingredients and place in a small bowl.
4 Skewer each kofta with a cocktail stick and serve with the dip.
IN ADVANCE: You can freeze the cooked koftas. When required, defrost, cover with foil and reheat in an ovenproof dish in a moderate 180°C (350°F/Gas 4) oven for 5–10 minutes. The dip can be made several hours ahead.

BELOW: Spicy koftas

POTATOES

Potatoes originated in South America and have been cultivated for centuries. In the 16th century, the Portuguese and Spanish transported potatoes to Europe, and probably India. They served as a staple for the poor as they contain protein, starch and vitamins. If they have to be peeled, peel thinly as the vitamins are just under the skin. There are many varieties, some versatile and suitable for all types of cooking, others best used for specific styles of cooking. There are also old and new potatoes. New ones, picked when immature, do not store well and should be refrigerated, but only for a few days. Old ones are best kept in a cool, dark place, away from onions which will make them deteriorate. If potatoes have green spots, cut them off thickly, and if very green, discard the potato.

ABOVE: Fresh herb pakoras

FRESH HERB PAKORAS

Preparation time: 30 minutes + standing
Total cooking time: 10 minutes
Makes 30

☆☆

1¹/₂ cups (165 g/5¹/₂ oz) besan flour
1 teaspoon ground turmeric
¹/₂ teaspoon chilli powder
1¹/₂ teaspoons garam masala
1 zucchini (courgette), diced
1 small orange sweet potato, diced
60 g (2 oz) cauliflower florets
50 g (1³/₄ oz) frozen peas, thawed
1 small onion, diced
2 tablespoons chopped fresh coriander
2 tablespoons chopped fresh basil
2 tablespoons chopped fresh parsley
2 cloves garlic, crushed
oil, for deep-frying
natural yoghurt and mango chutney, for serving

1 Sift the flour, turmeric, chilli powder, garam masala and 1¹/₂ teaspoons salt into a large bowl. Make a well and gradually add ¹/₂ cup (125 ml/4 fl oz) water, whisking to make a stiff lump-free batter. Cover and set aside for 30 minutes.

2 Beat the mixture again and stir in the vegetables, herbs and garlic. Fill a deep heavy-based pan one third full of oil and heat the oil to 180°C (350°F). The oil is ready when a cube of bread dropped into the oil turns golden brown in 15 seconds. Drop heaped teaspoons of mixture, in batches, into the oil and cook until golden. Drain on crumpled paper towels. Serve with bowls of yoghurt and mango chutney for dipping.

POTATO AND CORIANDER SAMOSAS

Preparation time: 1 hour
Total cooking time: 45 minutes
Makes about 24

☆☆

50 g (1³/₄ oz) butter
2 teaspoons grated fresh ginger
2 teaspoons cumin seeds
1 teaspoon Madras curry powder
¹/₂ teaspoon garam masala
500 g (1 lb) waxy potatoes, finely diced
30 g (1 oz) sultanas
80 g (2³/₄ oz) frozen baby peas

15 g (¹/₂ oz) fresh coriander leaves

3 spring onions, sliced

1 egg, lightly beaten

oil, for deep-frying

thick natural yoghurt, for serving

Samosa pastry

3³/₄ cups (465 g/15 oz) plain flour, sifted

1 teaspoon baking powder

110 g (3¹/₂ oz) butter, melted

¹/₂ cup (125 g/4 oz) thick natural yoghurt

1 Heat the butter in a large non-stick frying pan, add the ginger, cumin seeds, curry powder and garam masala and stir over medium heat for 1 minute. Add the potato and 3 tablespoons water and cook over low heat for 15–20 minutes, or until the potato is tender. Toss the sultanas, peas, coriander leaves and spring onion with the potato, remove from the heat and set aside to cool.

2 To make the samosa pastry, sift the flour, baking powder and 1¹/₂ teaspoons salt into a large bowl. Make a well in the centre, add the butter, yoghurt and ³/₄ cup (185 ml/6 fl oz) of water. Using a flat-bladed knife, bring the dough

together. Turn out onto a lightly floured surface and bring together to form a smooth ball. Divide the dough into four to make it easier to work with. Roll one piece out until very thin. Cover the rest until you are ready to use it.

3 Using a 12 cm (5 inch) diameter bowl or plate as a guide, cut out six circles. Place a generous tablespoon of potato filling in the centre of each circle, brush the edges of the pastry with egg and fold over to form a semi-circle. Make repeated folds on the rounded edge by folding a little piece of the pastry over as you move around the edge. Continue with the remaining pastry and filling.

4 Fill a deep heavy-based pan one third full of oil and heat the oil to 180°C (350°F). The oil is ready when a cube of bread dropped into the oil turns golden brown in 15 seconds. It is important not to have the oil too hot or the samosas will burn. Add the samosas two or three at a time and cook until golden. If they rise to the surface as they puff up, you may need to use a large, long-handled slotted spoon to hold them in the oil to cook the other side. Drain on crumpled paper towels. Serve with yoghurt.

NOTE: The samosa pastry becomes very tough if overworked. Use lightly floured hands when working the dough to prevent it sticking.

POTATO AND CORIANDER SAMOSAS

Cut six circles from each sheet of pastry, using a bowl or plate as a guide.

Measure a generous tablespoon of potato mixture onto the centre of each circle of pastry.

To secure the samosas, make folds on the edge, folding a piece over as you move along.

When the samosas are cooked, remove from the oil with a slotted spoon.

LEFT: Potato and coriander samosas

CURRIED CHICKEN PIES

Preparation time: 45 minutes + chilling
Total cooking time: 50 minutes
Makes 24

★ ☆

3 cups (375 g/12 oz) plain flour
1 teaspoon ground cumin
1 teaspoon ground turmeric
200 g (6¹/2 oz) butter, chopped
2 egg yolks, lightly beaten
50 g (1³/4 oz) butter, extra
1 onion, chopped
350 g (12 oz) chicken tenderloins, trimmed and cut into small dice
1 tablespoon curry powder
1 teaspoon cumin seeds
1 tablespoon plain flour, extra
1 cup (250 ml/8 fl oz) chicken stock
2 tablespoons mango chutney (mango chopped)
3 tablespoons chopped fresh coriander
milk, for glazing

1 Sift the flour, cumin and turmeric into a bowl. Rub in the butter using just your fingertips, until the mixture resembles fine breadcrumbs. Make a well and add the egg yolks and 5–6 tablespoons water. Mix with a flat-bladed knife using a cutting action, until the mixture comes together. Lift onto a floured surface and gather into a ball. Wrap in plastic wrap and chill for 30 minutes.
2 Lightly grease two deep 12-hole patty tins. Roll out two-thirds of the pastry to 2 mm (¹/8 inch) thick, and cut 8 cm (3 inch) rounds to fit the tins. Roll out the remaining pastry and cut 24 tops with a 5.5 cm (2¹/4 inch) cutter. Chill.
3 Heat the extra butter in a large pan and cook the onion until soft. Add the chicken and, when browned, stir in the curry powder and cumin seeds for 2 minutes. Add the extra flour and stir for 30 seconds. Remove from the heat and gradually stir in the stock. Return to the heat and stir until the sauce boils and thickens. Reduce the heat and simmer for 2–3 minutes, until reduced and very thick. Stir in the chutney and coriander leaves. Season and cool.
4 Preheat the oven to moderate 180°C (350°F/ Gas 4). Divide the filling among the pies and brush the edges with water. Join the tops by pressing around the edges with the tip of a sharp knife. Slash each top to allow steam to escape. Brush with milk and bake for 30 minutes. Cool slightly before removing from tins. Serve warm.

LAMB KORMA PIES

Preparation time: 30 minutes + chilling
Total cooking time: 1 hour 20 minutes
Makes 24

★ ☆

3 cups (375 g/12 oz) plain flour, sifted
2 tablespoons caraway seeds
180 g (6 oz) butter, chopped
1 tablespoon olive oil
1 small onion, finely chopped
1 clove garlic, crushed
2 tablespoons bottled mild curry paste
250 g (8 oz) lamb fillets, trimmed, finely diced
1 small potato, finely diced
¹/4 cup (40 g/1¹/4 oz) frozen baby peas
¹/4 cup (60 g/2 oz) natural yoghurt
1 egg, lightly beaten
2 tablespoons chopped fresh coriander

1 Combine the flour and caraway seeds in a large bowl. Rub in the butter using just your fingertips, until the mixture resembles fine breadcrumbs. Make a well, add 4 tablespoons water and mix with a flat-bladed knife, using a cutting action, until the mixture comes together in beads. Lift onto a floured surface and gather into a ball. Flatten slightly into a disc, wrap in plastic wrap and chill for 20 minutes.
2 Heat the oil in a heavy-based pan, add the onion and garlic and stir over medium heat for 3–4 minutes, or until the onion is soft. Add the curry paste and stir for 1 minute. Increase the heat to high and add the lamb, potato and peas, stirring for 5 minutes, or until the lamb is well browned all over. Add the yoghurt, bring to the boil, then reduce the heat and simmer, covered, for 30 minutes, or until the lamb is tender. Uncover and simmer for 10 minutes, or until the sauce thickens. Remove from the heat and allow to cool.
3 Preheat the oven to 180°C (350°F/Gas 5). Lightly grease two 12-hole mini muffin tins. Roll two-thirds of the dough between baking paper to 2 mm (¹/8 inch) thick. Cut 24 rounds with a 7 cm (2³/4 inch) cutter and ease into the tins. Spoon the lamb into the cases. Roll out the remaining pastry into a rectangle. Cut 24 strips 1 x 20 cm (¹/2 x 8 inches) and twist onto the top of each pie. Brush with the egg and bake for 25–30 minutes, or until golden brown. Cool slightly before removing from the tins. Serve warm, sprinkled with fresh coriander.

PEAS
This popular vegetable is used throughout the world. The juicy seeds, encased in a pod, are removed, except in varieties such as snow peas (mangetout) and sugar snap peas, which both have tender, edible pods. Frozen peas, including sweet-flavoured baby peas, are commonly used for convenience. Fresh peas take longer to cook than frozen.

OPPOSITE PAGE: Curried chicken pies (left); Lamb korma pies

INDIAN TEMPURA

Preparation time: 20 minutes + standing
Total cooking time: 25 minutes
Serves 8

★ ★

Batter

1 1/3 cups (145 g/5 oz) besan flour
75 g (2 1/2 oz) rice flour
1 teaspoon ground turmeric
1 teaspoon chilli powder
1/4 teaspoon kalonji (nigella) seeds

2 potatoes
300 g (10 oz) pumpkin
300 g (10 oz) eggplant (aubergine)
2 small onions
15 baby English spinach leaves
oil, for deep-frying
besan flour, for dusting
sweet chilli sauce, for serving

1 Sift the besan flour, rice flour, turmeric, chilli powder and 1/2 teaspoon salt into a large bowl and make a well in the centre. Gradually add 1 cup (250 ml/8 fl oz) water, whisking to make a smooth, thick batter. Stir in the kalonji seeds, cover and leave for 10 minutes.
2 Cut the potatoes and pumpkin into batons about 8 cm (3 inches) long. Cut the eggplant into thin slices and each slice into quarters. Cut the onions into quarters and separate the sections into individual pieces, discarding the centre. Wash and pat dry the baby spinach leaves.
3 Check the consistency of the batter. It should be like cream so, if it is too thick, add a little extra water. Fill a heavy-based pan one third full of oil and heat to 180°C (350°F). Test the oil by cooking 1/4 teaspoon of batter. If it keeps its shape and sizzles while rising to the top, the oil is ready. Make sure the oil stays at the same temperature and does not get too hot. The tempura should cook through as well as brown.
4 Dip batches of the vegetables in the besan flour, shake well, then dip in the batter and fry until golden brown. The cooking time will vary for each type of vegetable. Drain each batch on crumpled paper towel, sprinkle with salt and keep warm in a slow 150°C (300°F/Gas 2) oven. Serve immediately with sweet chilli sauce.
NOTE: Kalonji (nigella) seeds are available where Indian and Lebanese ingredients are sold.

ABOVE: Indian tempura

PURIS WITH CORIANDER RELISH

Preparation time: 40 minutes
Total cooking time: 10–15 minutes
Makes 32

★★

3/4 cup (90 g/3 oz) plain flour

3/4 cup (110 g/3½ oz) wholemeal plain flour

1 teaspoon salt

1 tablespoon cracked black pepper

3 tablespoons oil or ghee

1 teaspoon kalonji (nigella) seeds

oil, for deep-frying

Coriander relish

60 g (2 oz) fresh coriander leaves

20 g (3/4 oz) fresh mint leaves

1/2 small onion

1 green chilli

2 tablespoons lemon juice

1 Sift the flours and salt and pepper into a large bowl. Add the oil or ghee and rub it into the flour with your fingertips until it resembles fine breadcrumbs. Stir in the kalonji seeds. Make a well, add 3–4 tablespoons hot water and mix with a flat-bladed knife. It should be rough but hold together. Form into a ball.

2 Divide the dough into 4 and then each portion into 8 pieces, making 32 altogether. On a lightly floured surface, roll one piece at a time into a 6 cm (2½ inch) round. Keep the rest covered with a damp tea towel or plastic wrap. Don't worry about the cracked edges.

3 Heat 2.5 cm (1 inch) of oil in a wok or large heavy-based frying pan to 180°C (350°F). The oil is ready when a cube of bread dropped into the oil turns golden brown in 15 seconds. Fry 3 or 4 puris at a time, turning them halfway through. They will only take a few seconds to turn golden on each side. Remove from the oil and drain on crumpled paper towel while you fry the remainder.

4 For the coriander relish, process all the relish ingredients together in a food processor until smooth. Serve with the puris.

ABOVE: Puris with coriander relish

107

LEMON GRASS PRAWN SATAYS

Preparation time: 20 minutes + chilling
Total cooking time: 15 minutes
Makes 24

1 tablespoon oil
1 clove garlic, crushed
1 tablespoon grated fresh ginger
1 tablespoon finely chopped lemon grass,
    white part only
1 onion, finely chopped
1 tablespoon tandoori curry paste
4 kaffir lime leaves, finely shredded
1 tablespoon coconut cream
2 teaspoons grated lime rind
600 g (1 1/4 lb) raw prawns, peeled
    and deveined
12 stems lemon grass, cut into 15 cm (6 inch)
    lengths, halved lengthways

1 Heat the oil in a frying pan, add the garlic, ginger, lemon grass and onion and stir over medium heat for 3 minutes, or until golden.
2 Add the tandoori paste and kaffir lime leaves to the pan and cook for 5 minutes, or until the tandoori paste is fragrant. Allow to cool slightly. Transfer to a food processor, add the coconut cream, lime rind and prawns and mix until finely minced. Divide into 24 portions and, with wet hands, shape one portion around each piece of lemon grass stem, leaving about 3 cm (1 1/4 inches) uncovered at each end. The mixture is quite soft, so take care when handling it. Using wet hands makes the mixture easier to manage. Refrigerate for 1 hour.
3 Grill the satays under a medium heat for 5 minutes, or until cooked through.
IN ADVANCE: The prawn mixture can be frozen up to a month ahead. Thaw in the refrigerator and mould onto the lemon grass. The satays can be prepared a day ahead.

LEMON GRASS

This fresh herb is popular for its distinct lemon fragrance and flavour. The white base of the long stem is used in curries and the leaves make a refreshing cup of tea. To prepare lemon grass for cooking, cut off all the green top and a few of the tough outer leaves, rinse the white bulb and slice or chop according to the recipe. Store in the crisper section in the refrigerator.

RIGHT: Lemon grass prawn satays

MINI SPICY BURGERS

Preparation time: 30 minutes
Total cooking time: 15 minutes
Makes 24

★

6–8 rounds of naan bread

600 g (1 1/4 lb) lean beef mince

1 green chilli, chopped

1 tablespoon curry powder

3 cloves garlic, crushed

2 teaspoons finely chopped fresh ginger

1 tablespoon peanut oil

3 tablespoons thick natural yoghurt

3 tablespoons mango chutney

24 fresh mint leaves

1 Heat the oven to warm 160°C (315°F/ Gas 2–3). Using a 6 cm (2 1/2 inch) round cutter, mark the naan bread into 48 rounds, then cut with scissors. Loosely wrap in foil and warm in the oven while you make the patties.

2 In a bowl, combine the beef mince, chopped chilli, curry powder, garlic and ginger. Season with salt and black pepper. With wet hands, form the meat into 24 patties, about 6 cm (2 1/2 inches) in diameter.

3 Heat the oil in a large frying pan and cook the burgers in batches, for 2–3 minutes each side, or until done to your liking. Drain on crumpled paper towels.

4 Place 24 of the warm rounds of naan on a serving platter, top each with a beef patty, then some yoghurt, mango chutney and a mint leaf. Top with the remaining rounds of naan and serve immediately.

NOTE: Prepared naan bread can be bought at most supermarkets where you find pita bread and lavash bread. These can be substituted if naan is unavailable.

IN ADVANCE: The burger mixture can be made a day ahead and formed into patties, then stored, covered, in the refrigerator. Alternatively, the patties can be frozen in a single layer on a baking tray and, when frozen, transferred to a plastic bag, sealed and returned to the freezer. Thaw in a single layer in the refrigerator before cooking.

NAAN BREAD
This traditional Indian bread is slightly puffed, flattish and teardrop-shaped. Traditionally, the leavened dough is shaped, then slapped on the sides of a tandoor oven where it cooks quickly. However, it can be baked in a normal oven, then grilled lightly until brown. It is usually served warm or hot.

ABOVE: Mini spicy burgers

109

EASTERN APPETIZERS

When the chefs of Sung Dynasty China created a vast array of succulent bite-sized morsels to titillate the pampered palates of their Imperial rulers, little did they know that they were inventing the tradition of yum cha. These tiny snacks have survived the centuries and are now served with tea and much loved throughout China and in Chinatowns the world over. And the other countries of Asia are not standing back shyly, letting China take all the culinary glory... Japanese sushi, Thai fish cakes and Indonesian gado gado all have their place at the table of Eastern favourites.

bread dropped into the oil turns brown in 15 seconds. Add the bread and cook, prawn-side-down, for 2–3 minutes. Turn over and cook the other side for 1 minute, or until crisp. Drain on crumpled paper towels. Serve immediately.

WARM DUCK AND CORIANDER TARTS

Preparation time: 35 minutes + chilling
Total cooking time: 20 minutes
Makes 24

★

1¹/₂ cups (185 g/6 oz) plain flour
125 g (4 oz) chilled butter, chopped
3 tablespoons sesame seeds
2 tablespoons chopped fresh coriander, plus
    extra sprigs to garnish

Filling

1 large Chinese roasted duck
2 tablespoons orange marmalade
1 tablespoon kecap manis
2 teaspoons sesame oil
1 tablespoon grated fresh ginger
5 finely sliced green spring onions

1 Lightly grease two 12-hole round-based patty tins. Sift the flour and ¹/₂ teaspoon salt into a large bowl and add the butter. Rub in with your fingertips until the mixture resembles fine breadcrumbs. Stir in the sesame seeds. Make a well and add up to 2 tablespoons iced water and mix with a flat-bladed knife until the dough just comes together. Turn out onto a lightly floured surface and gather into a ball.
2 Preheat the oven to hot 210°C (415°F/ Gas 6–7). Roll the pastry out thinly on a lightly floured work surface until 3 mm (¹/₈ inch) thick. Prick lightly all over. Cut 24 rounds with a 6 cm (2¹/₂ inch) fluted cutter. Re-roll the pastry if necessary. Line the tins with pastry. Bake for 10 minutes, or until the pastry is golden brown, remove from the tins and allow to cool.
3 For the filling, remove the duck meat from the bones and shred the meat. Put the marmalade in a pan and stir over low heat until smooth. Add the remaining ingredients, including the shredded duck, and mix well. Stir until warmed through.
4 Arrange the pastry shells on a warm serving platter and add the warm filling. Garnish with

PRAWN AND CORIANDER TOASTS

Preparation time: 25 minutes
Total cooking time: 15 minutes
Makes 32

★

500 g (1 lb) peeled raw prawns
8 spring onions, chopped
1 stem lemon grass, white part only, chopped
1 clove garlic, crushed
1 egg white
1 tablespoon oil
1 tablespoon chopped fresh coriander
1 tablespoon fish sauce
2 teaspoons chilli sauce
1 teaspoon lemon juice
8 slices of stale bread, crusts removed
oil, for shallow-frying

1 Finely chop the prawns, spring onion, lemon grass, garlic, egg white, oil, coriander, sauces and lemon juice together in a food processor.
2 Spread the mixture over the bread, right to the edge, and cut each slice into 4 triangles.
3 Heat 2 cm (³/₄ inch) of oil in a pan to 180°C (350°F). The oil is hot enough when a cube of

ABOVE: Prawn and coriander toasts

the fresh coriander and serve immediately.
NOTE: The skin from the duck can also be used in the filling. However, all visible fat should be removed. Kecap manis is an Indonesian sweet soy sauce, available in most supermarkets.

COMBINATION DIM SIMS

Preparation time: 1 hour + chilling + standing
Total cooking time: 30 minutes
Makes about 30

✸

6 dried Chinese mushrooms
200 g (6¹/₂ oz) lean pork mince
30 g (1 oz) pork fat, finely chopped
100 g (3¹/₂ oz) peeled raw prawns, finely chopped
2 spring onions, finely chopped
1 tablespoon sliced bamboo shoots, finely chopped
1 celery stick, finely chopped
3 teaspoons cornflour
2 teaspoons soy sauce

1 teaspoon caster sugar
30 won ton or egg noodle wrappers
chilli or soy sauce, for serving

1 Put the mushrooms in a small heatproof bowl, cover with boiling water and leave for 10 minutes. Drain, discard the stems, and finely chop.
2 Mix the mushrooms, pork mince, pork fat, prawns, spring onion, bamboo shoots and celery in a bowl. Combine the cornflour, soy, sugar and salt and pepper into a smooth paste in another bowl. Stir into the pork mixture, cover and refrigerate for 1 hour.
3 Work with 1 wrapper at a time, keeping the rest covered with a tea towel. Place 1 tablespoon of filling in the centre of each, then moisten the edges with water and gather the edges into the centre, pressing together to seal. Set aside on a lightly floured surface.
4 Line the base of a bamboo steamer with a circle of baking paper. Arrange the dim sims on the paper, spacing them well (they will need to be cooked in batches). Cover the steamer and cook over a pan of simmering water for 8 minutes, or until the filling is cooked. Serve with chilli or soy sauce.

COMBINATION DIM SIMS

Soak the dried mushrooms in hot water for 10 minutes, to rehydrate them.

Gather the wrapper up to the centre to enclose the filling, then press together to seal.

Arrange a circle of baking paper in the base of a bamboo steamer.

LEFT: Combination dim sims

VIETNAMESE FRESH SPRING ROLLS

Preparation time: 50 minutes + soaking
Total cooking time: 25 minutes
Makes about 20

★

20 large cooked prawns
100 g (3½ oz) dried mung bean vermicelli
  (cellophane noodles)
20–25 rice paper wrappers, about 16 cm
  (6½ inches) round
40 fresh mint leaves
10 garlic chives, cut in halves

Dipping sauce

2 tablespoons satay sauce
3 tablespoons hoisin sauce
1 red chilli, finely chopped
1 tablespoon chopped roasted unsalted peanuts
1 tablespoon lemon juice

*BELOW: Vietnamese
fresh spring rolls*

1 Peel the prawns and gently pull out the dark vein from the backs, starting at the head end. Cut all the prawns in half.

2 Soak the vermicelli for 5 minutes in a bowl with enough hot water to cover. Drain well and use scissors to roughly chop the noodles into shorter lengths.

3 Working with one rice paper wrapper at a time, dip into a bowl of warm water, leave for about 30 seconds, or until the wrapper becomes soft and pliable, then remove. Be careful as the wrappers can tear easily when softened.

4 Place 1 softened wrapper on a work surface and spoon about 1 tablespoon of the noodles along the bottom third of the wrapper, leaving enough space at the sides to fold the wrapper over. Top with 2 mint leaves and 2 prawn halves. Fold in the sides towards each other and firmly roll up the wrapper, adding the piece of garlic chive as you roll so it points out of one side. Repeat with the remaining wrappers and ingredients and place the spring rolls, seam-side-down, on a serving plate.

5 For the dipping sauce, mix the ingredients in a small bowl. Serve with the spring rolls.

PORK AND LEMON GRASS WON TONS

Preparation time: 40 minutes + chilling
Total cooking time: 20 minutes
Makes 56

★ ★

400 g (13 oz) pork mince
1 teaspoon finely chopped fresh ginger
1 stem lemon grass, white part only, finely
    sliced
230 g (7¹/₂ oz) can water chestnuts, drained and
    finely chopped
2 tablespoons finely chopped fresh garlic chives
¹/₂ teaspoon chilli paste
2 tablespoons plum sauce
1 teaspoon chilli oil
1 teaspoon sesame oil
1 tablespoon cornflour
56 x 8 cm (3 inch) won ton wrappers
    (about 2 packets)
oil, for deep-frying

Dipping sauce
¹/₂ cup (125 ml/4 fl oz) light soy sauce
¹/₄ cup (60 ml/2 fl oz) balsamic vinegar
1 teaspoon finely grated fresh ginger
1 teaspoon chilli oil

1 Put the mince, ginger, lemon grass, water chestnuts, garlic chives, chilli paste, plum sauce, chilli and sesame oils and cornflour in a bowl. Mix with your hands. Cover; chill for 1 hour.
2 For the dipping sauce, combine the ingredients in a jug.
3 Work with 1 won ton wrapper at a time, keeping the rest covered. Spoon 2 teaspoons of the filling onto the centre of each wrapper and lightly brush the edges of the wrapper with water. Gather up the ends, bring the edges together in the centre and press firmly to seal. Repeat with the remaining wrappers and filling.
4 Fill a deep heavy-based pan one third full of oil. Heat the oil to 180°C (350°F). The oil is ready when a cube of bread dropped into the oil turns golden brown in 15 seconds. Deep-fry batches of won tons for 3–4 minutes, until lightly browned. Remove with a slotted spoon, drain on crumpled paper towels and serve hot with the sauce.

ABOVE: Pork and lemon grass won tons

COCONUT RICE
IN BANANA LEAVES

Preparation time: 40 minutes
Total cooking time: 1 hour 30 minutes
Makes about 12

★★

2–3 young banana leaves, or foil

2 cups (400 g/13 oz) glutinous rice

3/4 cup (185 ml/6 fl oz) coconut milk

Chicken filling

2 tablespoons oil

2–3 cloves garlic, crushed

6 curry leaves

1 teaspoon dried shrimp paste

2 teaspoons ground coriander

2 teaspoons ground cumin

1/2 teaspoon turmeric

250 g (8 oz) chicken mince

3 tablespoons coconut milk, extra

1 teaspoon lemon juice

*ABOVE: Coconut rice
in banana leaves*

1 With a sharp knife, cut away the central ribs of the banana leaves. The leaves will split into large pieces—cut into pieces about 15 cm (6 inches) square. Blanch in boiling water briefly to soften them, then spread out on a tea towel and cover.
2 Wash the rice, drain and put in a large heavy-based pan with 1 3/4 cups (440 ml/14 fl oz) water. Bring slowly to the boil, reduce the heat to very low, cover tightly and cook for 15 minutes.
3 Put the coconut milk and 1/2 cup (125 ml/ 4 fl oz) water in a small pan and heat without boiling. Stir through the rice with a fork. Transfer to a bowl and set aside to cool.
4 For the chicken filling, heat the oil in a large heavy-based frying pan, add the garlic and curry leaves and stir for 1 minute over medium heat. Add the shrimp paste, coriander, cumin and turmeric and cook for another minute. Add the chicken mince and cook and break up with a fork for 3–4 minutes, or until the chicken changes colour. Add the extra coconut milk and continue to cook over low heat for 5 minutes, or until absorbed. Remove the curry leaves. Add the lemon juice and salt and pepper, to taste. Cool.
5 Place 1 heaped tablespoon of rice in the centre of each piece of banana leaf and flatten to a

4 cm (1½ inch) square. Top with a heaped teaspoon of filling. Roll the leaf into a parcel and place, seam-side-down, in a steamer lined with leftover banana leaf scraps. Steam, in batches, for 15 minutes. Serve at room temperature with chopsticks or small forks.
NOTE: Banana leaves are used throughout Asia to wrap foods for steaming or baking. They keep the food moist and impart a mild flavour. They can be bought at Asian food stores if you don't have access to fresh leaves from a plant.
IN ADVANCE: Can be made in advance and refrigerated for up to 2 days.

CHICKEN WITH NORI

Preparation time: 25 minutes + marinating
Total cooking time: 20 minutes
Makes about 30 pieces

★★

400 g (13 oz) chicken breast tenderloins
¼ cup (60 ml/2 fl oz) Japanese soy sauce
¼ cup (60 ml/2 fl oz) mirin
4 cm (1½ inches) fresh ginger, very
   finely grated
1 sheet nori, finely chopped or crumbled into
   very small pieces
⅓ cup (40 g/1¼ oz) cornflour
1 cup (250 ml/8 fl oz) oil, for frying

1 Carefully trim and discard any sinew from the chicken, then cut the chicken into bite-sized pieces and put them in a bowl.
2 Combine the soy sauce, mirin and ginger in a small jug, pour over the chicken and toss until evenly coated. Marinate in the refrigerator for 15 minutes, then drain off any excess marinade.
3 Mix the nori with the cornflour and, using your fingertips, lightly coat the chicken.
4 Heat the oil in a heavy-based pan to 180°C (350°F). The oil is ready when a cube of bread dropped into the oil turns golden brown in 15 seconds. Fry 6–7 pieces of chicken at a time until golden, turning regularly. Drain on crumpled paper towels. Garnish with extra strips of nori, if desired.
NOTE: Nori is the most common form of dried seaweed used in Asian cookery. It is available in speciality stores. Use scissors or a very sharp knife to cut it.

CRISPY VERMICELLI CAKES WITH SESAME VEGETABLES

Preparation time: 20 minutes
Total cooking time: 15 minutes
Makes about 12

★

400 g (13 oz) rice vermicelli
oil, for shallow-frying
2 teaspoons sesame oil
2 carrots, cut into matchsticks
1 red pepper (capsicum), cut into matchsticks
2 zucchini (courgettes), cut into julienne strips
4 spring onions, cut into julienne strips
½–1 tablespoon oyster sauce

1 Soak the vermicelli for 3 minutes in a bowl with enough boiling water to cover, then drain thoroughly until very dry.
2 Heat the oil in a large heavy-based frying pan over medium heat. Shape tablespoons of the noodles into flat discs and shallow-fry in batches for 3 minutes, or until crisp and golden. Drain on crumpled paper towels.
3 Heat the sesame oil in a wok and stir-fry the vegetables for 3 minutes until softened slightly. Stir in the oyster sauce and cook for 2 minutes. Serve the cakes topped with the vegetables.

ABOVE: Chicken with nori

SATAYS & KEBABS

If you are using wooden skewers, soak them in water for 30 minutes beforehand so that they don't burn before the food is cooked. The ends can be wrapped in foil.

LIME PRAWNS
Using 12 canned sugar canes, cut into 5 mm (¼ inch) thick strips 10 cm (4 inches) long. Peel and devein 48 raw king prawns. Thread 2 prawns onto each sugar cane skewer. You may need to make small cuts in the prawns to make it easier. Brush lightly with some lime juice and cook on a lightly oiled preheated chargrill pan for 2–3 minutes each side, or until cooked through. Makes 24.

BEEF WITH BLACK BEAN SAUCE
Cut 1 kg (2 lb) rump steak into 2 cm (¾ inch) cubes and make small slits in the meat with a sharp knife. Trim bay leaf stems of leaves and thread the meat onto the stems. Brush lightly with ⅓ cup (80 ml/2¾ fl oz) black bean sauce. Cook on a preheated oiled chargrill pan for 2–3 minutes on each side, brushing with any remaining black bean sauce during cooking. Makes 28.

GARLIC LAMB
Cut 600 g (1¼ lb) trimmed lamb steaks into 2 cm (¾ inch) cubes and 6 cloves of garlic into thick slices. Thread 2 pieces of lamb and 2 slices of garlic alternately onto 35 small metal skewers. Mix together 1 chopped red chilli, 2 crushed cloves garlic and 3 tablespoons oil. Heat a chargrill pan and lightly brush with oil. Cook the skewers for 2–5 minutes, brushing occasionally with the garlic and chilli marinade. Makes 35.

CHILLI VEGETABLES

Halve 12 shiitake mushrooms, 12 baby corn cobs and 12 snow peas (mangetout). Thread alternately onto 24 small wooden skewers. Combine 2 tablespoons oil with 1 crushed clove garlic and 1 tablespoon sweet chilli sauce in a bowl and mix well. Brush over the skewers and cook the skewers in a preheated chargrill pan for 1–2 minutes, brushing with the sauce during cooking. Makes 24.

SALMON AND TUNA

Cut 600 g (1¼ lb) salmon fillet and 500 g (1 lb) fresh tuna into 2 cm (¾ inch) cubes and season with salt and pepper. Thread alternately onto small wooden skewers, using 3 pieces on each. Heat a chargrill or frying pan and brush lightly with oil. Cook the skewers for 3–4 minutes, turning frequently and squeezing with a little lime or lemon juice as they cook. Makes 18–20.

CHICKEN AND LEMON GRASS

Cut 1 kg (2 lb) chicken thigh fillets into 2 cm (¾ inch) cubes. Trim the leaves off 6 lemon grass stems. Cut the thicker ends of the stems into 10 cm (4 inch) lengths, then into quarters lengthways. Cut 12 spring onion bulbs into quarters. Make a small slit in the centre of each chicken cube and through the onion pieces, to make threading easier. Thread pieces of chicken and onion onto the lemon grass stems alternately, using 2 pieces of each for each stem. Mix together 3 tablespoons soy sauce, 3 tablespoons mirin and 2 tablespoons sugar. Heat a chargrill or frying pan and cook the skewers for 3–5 minutes. Brush with half the soy mixture as they cook, turning frequently. Add 1 finely sliced stem lemon grass (white part only) and 1 seeded and finely chopped red chilli to the remaining soy mixture and serve with the skewers, for dipping. Makes 24.

MUSHROOMS AND PROSCIUTTO

Wipe 48 Swiss brown mushrooms (sometimes called chestnut mushrooms) with a damp cloth, then cut them in half. Melt 80 g (2¾ oz) butter in a frying pan and add the mushrooms and a pinch of salt. Cook, stirring, over medium heat for 1 minute. Add ½ cup (125 ml/4 fl oz) port and cook, stirring, until it evaporates completely. Remove from the heat and set aside. Cut 18 slices of prosciutto into 4 pieces each. Thread 4 pieces of mushroom and 3 rolled pieces of prosciutto alternately onto wooden skewers and serve. Makes 24.

FROM LEFT: Lime prawns; Centre plate: Beef with black bean sauce; Chilli vegetables; Garlic lamb; Right-hand plate: Chicken and lemon grass; Mushrooms and prosciutto; Salmon and tuna

SCALLOPS

Sold in their half shells, scallops are generally still attached to their shells with a muscle. To remove from the shell, slip a small sharp knife between the shell and the scallop and gently cut away. Trim off the dark vein and white muscle before cooking. Scallops should be cooked for a short time only, otherwise they will become tough. They will turn white when cooked.

DIM SUM SCALLOPS

Preparation time: 10 minutes
Total cooking time: 10 minutes
Makes 24

★

24 scallops in the half shell

Marinade
2 tablespoons teriyaki sauce
1 tablespoon soy sauce
1 tablespoon dry sherry
2 spring onions, finely chopped
2 teaspoons lemon or lime juice
2 teaspoons oyster sauce
1 teaspoon sesame oil
1 clove garlic, crushed
1/2 teaspoon grated fresh ginger

1 Preheat the oven to moderate 180°C (350°F/Gas 4). Place the scallops, in the shells, on a baking tray.
2 Combine the marinade ingredients together in a bowl and drizzle some of the mixture over each scallop. Put the scallops on a baking tray and bake for 5–10 minutes, or until the scallops are tender and white.
NOTE: If you prefer, the scallops can be cooked under a preheated hot grill for 5 minutes instead.
IN ADVANCE: The marinade can be made a day ahead, covered and refrigerated.

SATAY SAUCE

Heat 1 tablespoon oil in a pan. Add 1 finely chopped large onion and 1 finely chopped garlic clove and stir for 8 minutes over low heat. Add 2 finely chopped red chillies and 1 teaspoon shrimp paste and cook for 1 minute. Remove from the heat. Add 250 g (8 oz) peanut butter, return to the heat and stir in 1 cup (250 ml/8 fl oz) each of coconut milk and water. Bring to the boil over low heat, stirring so that it does not stick. Add 2 teaspoons kecap manis or thick soy sauce and 1 tablespoon tomato sauce; simmer for 1 minute. Cool. Serve with skewers of chicken, meat or vegetables.

ABOVE: Dim sum scallops

STUFFED PRAWNS IN CRISPY WON TON

Preparation time: 40 minutes
Total cooking time: 10 minutes
Makes 24

★ ★

30 won ton wrappers

24 large raw prawns

400 g (13 oz) raw prawn meat

8 spring onions, very finely chopped

100 g (1¾ oz) pork fat, finely chopped

2 egg whites

1 cup (125 g/4 oz) cornflour

2 eggs, lightly beaten

oil, for deep-frying

1 Using a very sharp knife, finely shred the won ton wrappers. Place on a plate and cover with a damp tea towel until required. Peel the prawns, leaving the tails intact. Discard the heads. Using the tip of a small sharp knife, pull out the dark vein. Cut a shallow pocket along the inside of each prawn.

2 Combine the prawn meat, spring onion and pork fat on a chopping board. Using a large sharp knife, chop the mixture until very smooth. (Alternatively, you can use a food processor.) Place the mixture in a bowl and add the egg white, 3 teaspoons of the cornflour and a little salt and pepper and mix together well with your fingertips.

3 Using a knife, spread about 1 tablespoon of the prawn mixture along each prawn, pressing as much mixture as possible into the pocket. With wet hands, press any remaining mixture around the prawn. Coat the prawns in the remaining cornflour, lightly dip in egg, then loosely sprinkle with won ton shreds, pressing on very firmly.

4 Heat 4 cm (1½ inches) oil in a wok or pan to 180°C (350°F). The oil is hot enough when a cube of bread dropped into the oil turns golden brown in 15 seconds. Add the prawns in batches and cook for 4 minutes or until golden brown. Drain on crumpled paper towels and serve immediately.

NOTE: Pork fat is available in the refrigerator section of Asian supermarkets.

IN ADVANCE: The prawns can be cleaned and filled with stuffing up to a day in advance. Store in the refrigerator. Coat the prawns with shredded won ton just before frying.

STUFFED PRAWNS IN CRISPY WON TON

Finely shred the won ton wrappers with a sharp knife.

Cut a shallow incision along the underside of each prawn to make room for the stuffing.

LEFT: Stuffed prawns in crispy won ton

CRISPY CHICKEN AND FISH WRAPS WITH SWEET AND SOUR SAUCE

Preparation time: 30 minutes
Total cooking time: 4 minutes per batch
Makes 30

★ ★

Sweet and sour sauce
1/2 cup (125 g/4 oz) sugar
1/2 cup (125 ml/4 fl oz) white vinegar
1 tablespoon tomato sauce
1 tablespoon cornflour

30 won ton wrappers
oil, for deep-frying

Filling
100 g (3 1/2 oz) chicken, finely chopped
100 g (3 1/2 oz) fish fillets, finely chopped
1/2 stalk celery, finely chopped
1 small spring onion, finely chopped
2 teaspoons light soy sauce

1 To make the sauce, combine the sugar, vinegar and tomato sauce with 3/4 cup (185 ml/ 6 fl oz) water in a small saucepan. Blend the cornflour with 1 tablespoon of water in a small bowl. Add to the saucepan and stir over low heat until the mixture boils and thickens and the sugar has dissolved.
2 Combine the filling ingredients with 1/4 teaspoon salt. Place 1 teaspoon of mixture onto each won ton wrapper. Brush the edges lightly with water. Fold to form a triangle. Dab water onto the left front corner of the triangle. Fold the two bottom corners across, one on top of the other, and press together lightly with your finger.
3 Fill a deep heavy-based pan one third full of oil. Heat the oil to 180°C (350°F). The oil is hot enough when a cube of bread dropped into the oil turns golden brown in 15 seconds. Deep-fry in batches until crisp and golden brown. Shake off the excess oil and drain on crumpled paper towel. Serve with the sauce.

PORK DUMPLINGS

Preparation time: 30 minutes
Total cooking time: 45 minutes
Makes 50

★

250 g (4 oz) pork mince
125 g (4 oz) raw prawn meat, finely chopped
60 g (2 oz) bamboo shoots, chopped
3 spring onions, finely chopped
3 mushrooms, finely chopped
1 stick celery, finely chopped
1/2 pepper (capsicum), finely chopped
1 tablespoon dry sherry
1 tablespoon soy sauce
1 teaspoon sesame oil
1/2 teaspoon chopped chilli
50 won ton wrappers
soy sauce, for dipping

1 Put the mince, prawn, bamboo shoots, spring onion, mushrooms, celery, pepper, dry sherry, soy sauce, sesame oil and chilli in a bowl and mix well. Place a heaped teaspoon of the filling in the centre of each won ton wrapper. Brush the edges with a little water, then gather the wrapper around the filling to form a pouch, slightly open at the top.
2 Steam in a bamboo or metal steamer over a pan of simmering water for 15 minutes, or until cooked through. Serve with soy sauce.

CHICKEN DUMPLINGS

Preparation time: 30 minutes
Total cooking time: 45 minutes
Makes 50

★

375 g (12 oz) chicken mince
90 g (3 oz) ham, finely chopped
4 spring onions, finely chopped
1 stick celery, finely chopped
3 tablespoons bamboo shoots, chopped
1 tablespoon soy sauce
1 clove garlic, crushed
1 teaspoon grated fresh ginger

1 Combine all the ingredients in a bowl, then use to fill 50 won ton wrappers as above.

Lightly brush the edges of the won ton with water, then fold it over the filling to form a triangle.

Fold the two bottom corners across, one on top of the other, and press together lightly.

OPPOSITE PAGE: Crispy chicken and fish wraps with sweet and sour sauce (top); Dumplings

123

EGGS

Eggs, apart from being enjoyed boiled, poached, fried and scrambled, are an essential ingredient used to thicken or aerate many dishes such as soufflés, omelettes, frittata and mayonnaise. They are also used to glaze or bind and in many other ways. To successfully hard-boil eggs for dishes such as gado gado, first bring them to room temperature, then put them in a saucepan, cover with cold water and bring to the boil over high heat. Simmer over low heat for 7–8 minutes. Stirring the eggs in the first few minutes helps centre the yolk. When cooked, stand the eggs under cold running water to stop them cooking any further. If boiled eggs have dark rings around the yolk, they have been cooked too long. Keep fresh eggs refrigerated until you need them, then bring them to room temperature before using them.

ABOVE: Gado gado

GADO GADO

Preparation time: 30 minutes
Total cooking time: 35 minutes
Serves 6-8

☆

6 new potatoes
2 carrots, cut into batons
250 g (8 oz) snake beans, cut into 10 cm
    (4 inch) lengths
2 tablespoons peanut oil
250 g (8 oz) firm tofu, cubed
100 g (3¹/₂ oz) baby English spinach leaves
2 Lebanese cucumbers, cut into thick strips
1 large red pepper (capsicum), cut into
    thick strips
100 g (3¹/₂ oz) bean sprouts
5 hard-boiled eggs

Peanut sauce
1 tablespoon peanut oil
1 onion, finely chopped
²/₃ cup (160 g/5¹/₂ oz) peanut butter

¹/₄ cup (60 ml/2 fl oz) kecap manis
2 tablespoons ground coriander
2 teaspoons chilli sauce
³/₄ cup (185 ml/6 fl oz) coconut cream
1 teaspoon grated palm sugar
1 tablespoon lemon juice

1 Cook the potatoes in boiling water until tender. Drain, cool slightly, then cut into quarters. Cook the carrots and beans separately until just tender. Drain, plunge into iced water, then drain thoroughly.
2 Heat the oil in a non-stick frying pan and cook the tofu all over in batches until crisp. Drain on crumpled paper towels.
3 To make the peanut sauce, heat the oil in a pan over low heat and cook the onion for 5 minutes, or until golden. Add the peanut butter, kecap manis, coriander, chilli sauce and coconut cream. Bring to the boil, reduce the heat and simmer for 5 minutes. Stir in the sugar and juice, stirring until dissolved.
4 Arrange all the vegetables and tofu on a plate. Cut the eggs in half and place in the centre around the bowl of sauce.

FISH TEMPURA

Preparation time: 10 minutes
Total cooking time: 20 minutes
Makes 24

★ ☆

500 g (1 lb) boneless fish
1 sheet nori
1 tablespoon tempura flour

Tempura batter

1 cup (250 ml/8 oz) iced water
2 cups (250 g/8 oz) tempura flour
oil, for deep-frying

1 Cut the fish into bite-sized pieces and set aside. Using scissors, cut the nori into tiny squares and combine on a plate with the tablespoon of tempura flour.

2 For the batter, quickly mix the iced water with the tempura flour. It will be slightly lumpy. If it is too thick, add more water. Fill a heavy-based pan one third full of oil and heat to 180°C (350°F). The oil is ready when ¼ teaspoon of batter dropped into the oil keeps its shape, sizzles and rises to the top. Make sure the oil stays at the same temperature and does not get too hot. The fish should cook through.

3 Dip the fish in batches into the nori and flour, then in the batter. Fry until golden, then drain on crumpled paper towels. Season with salt and keep warm in a single layer on a baking tray in a very slow 120°C (240°F/Gas 1) oven. The fish can be served with shoyu (Japanese soy sauce), for dipping.

NOTE: Tempura flour is available at Asian supermarkets. If unavailable, substitute with 1½ cups (185 g/6 oz) plain flour and ½ cup (90 g/3 oz) rice flour. This recipe can also be made using chicken or vegetable pieces.

TEMPURA
Tempura was introduced to Japan by Portuguese and Spanish traders in the sixteenth century. However, chefs in Japan improved the batter, resulting in the special crispness with which it is associated today. The very light thin batter is made with iced water to ensure that it puffs up as soon as it hits the oil. Special tempura flour also ensures a light batter.

BELOW: Fish tempura

GINGER

If ginger is fresh when you buy it, the flesh should be juicy, not shrivelled or dried out. To prepare it for cooking, just peel with a vegetable peeler or sharp knife and cut. You can rub the skin off some very fresh ginger with your fingers. For grating, don't fuss about the irregular-shaped knob, just peel as much as you need from any part, grate on a ginger grater and return the rest to the crisper in the refrigerator. Ceramic ginger graters have little sharp teeth that grate the ginger off as you rub it up and down. Bamboo graters look like small versions of old-fashioned washboards, made with angled strips of bamboo for rubbing the ginger against.

ABOVE: Yakitori

YAKITORI
(SKEWERED CHICKEN)

Preparation time: 20 minutes + soaking
Total cooking time: 10 minutes
Makes about 25 skewers

☆

1 kg (2 lb) chicken thigh fillets
1/2 cup (125 ml/4 fl oz) sake
3/4 cup (185 ml/6 fl oz) Japanese soy sauce
1/2 cup (125 ml/4 fl oz) mirin
2 tablespoons sugar
1 cup (65 g/2 1/4 oz) spring onions, cut diagonally into 2 cm (3/4 inch) pieces

1 Soak 25 wooden skewers for about 30 minutes in water, then drain and set aside.
2 Cut the chicken fillets into bite-sized pieces. Combine the sake, soy sauce, mirin and sugar in a small pan, bring to the boil, then remove the pan and set aside.
3 Thread 3 chicken pieces onto wooden skewers, alternating with pieces of spring onion. Place the skewers on a foil-lined tray and cook under a preheated grill or barbecue, turning and brushing frequently with the sauce for about 7–8 minutes, or until the chicken is cooked through. Serve.
NOTE: The yakitori can be served with a bottled Asian dipping sauce.

THAI NOODLE BALLS WITH ASIAN DIPPING SAUCE

Preparation time: 20 minutes + soaking
Total cooking time: 20 minutes
Makes 40

☆ ☆

Asian dipping sauce
1/4 cup (60 ml/2 fl oz) sweet chilli sauce
1/4 cup (60 ml/2 fl oz) lime juice
2 tablespoons fish sauce
1 teaspoon soft brown sugar
2 teaspoons kecap manis
4 cm (1 1/2 inch) piece fresh ginger, cut into julienne strips

500 g (1 lb) Hokkien noodles
75 g (2½ oz) snake beans, finely chopped
3 spring onions, finely chopped
2 cloves garlic, crushed
50 g (1¾ oz) fresh coriander leaves, chopped
¼ cup (60 ml/2 fl oz) sweet chilli sauce
2 tablespoons fish sauce
2 tablespoons fresh lime juice
250 g (8 oz) pork mince
3 eggs, lightly beaten
1 cup (125 g/4 oz) plain flour
oil, for deep-frying

1 Mix the dipping sauce ingredients in a bowl.
2 Break up the noodles and cut with scissors into short lengths. Soak in a bowl of boiling water for 2 minutes, then drain well. Combine with the beans, spring onion, garlic, coriander, sauces, lime juice, mince, eggs and flour and mix well.
3 Fill a deep heavy-based pan one third full of oil and heat the oil to 180°C (350°F). The oil is ready when a cube of bread dropped into the oil turns golden brown in 15 seconds. Roll heaped tablespoons of mixture into balls and deep-fry in batches for 2 minutes, or until deep golden. Drain on crumpled paper towels. Serve with sauce.
IN ADVANCE: The dipping sauce can be made several days ahead and the noodle mixture the day before required. Fry close to serving time.

PRAWN PARCELS

Preparation time: 30 minutes
Total cooking time: 20 minutes
Makes 24

★★

1 tablespoon oil
2 cloves garlic, crushed
1 tablespoon grated fresh ginger
2 spring onions, chopped
500 g (1 lb) raw prawns, peeled and chopped
½ teaspoon fish sauce
½ teaspoon sugar
1 tablespoon lemon juice
2 tablespoons chopped fresh coriander
6 large spring roll wrappers, cut into quarters
oil, for deep-frying
fresh chives, for serving
sweet chilli sauce, for serving

1 Heat the oil in a frying pan, add the garlic and ginger and cook over low heat for 2 minutes. Add the spring onion and cook for 2 minutes. Increase the heat to high, add the prawns and stir-fry for 2 minutes, or until the colour just changes. Be careful not to overcook the prawns or they will become tough once deep-fried.
2 Add the fish sauce, sugar, lemon juice and coriander to the pan. Toss with the prawns for 1 minute. Remove from the heat; cool slightly.
3 Divide the cooled mixture into 24 portions. Place one portion in the centre of each piece of spring roll wrapper. Brush the edges with water and fold to form a parcel.
4 Fill a deep heavy-based pan one third full of oil. Heat the oil to 180°C (350°F). The oil is hot enough when a cube of bread dropped into the oil turns golden brown in 15 seconds. Deep-fry the parcels one at a time, holding them with tongs for the first few seconds to keep them intact. Cook until golden brown. Drain on crumpled paper towels. Tie with lengths of chives. Serve with sweet chilli sauce.
NOTE: If the spring roll wrappers are very thin, you may need to use two together.

ABOVE: Prawn parcels

RICE

Apart from various colours, tastes and textures, different types of rice are preferred for certain recipes because of their behaviour when cooked. Short-grain rice, with small oval grains, is high in starch and is used in recipes such as sushi where you want a rice that sticks together. It is also easier to eat using chopsticks, so is popular in some Asian countries. Other recipes are better with rices whose grains stay separate when cooked.

SCALLOP POCKETS

Preparation time: 40 minutes
Total cooking time: 15 minutes
Makes 25

★ ★

25 large scallops
1 tablespoon oil
5 cm (2 inch) piece fresh ginger, grated
4 spring onions, finely chopped
1 tablespoon Shaosing (Chinese) wine or
    dry sherry
2 teaspoons sesame oil
1 teaspoon cornflour
25 won ton or egg noodle wrappers
oil, for shallow frying
15 g (1/2 oz) garlic chives, blanched, for serving

1 Carefully slice or pull off any vein, membrane or hard white muscle from the scallops, leaving any roe attached.
2 Heat the oil in a pan, add the ginger and spring onion and cook over medium heat for 2 minutes, stirring occasionally. Increase the heat and, when the pan is very hot, add the scallops and stir-fry, tossing quickly, for 30 seconds. Remove the pan from the heat.
3 Blend the wine, sesame oil, cornflour and a little salt and pepper in a small bowl until it forms a smooth paste. Pour over the scallops, return to the heat and toss over high heat for 30 seconds or until the liquid has thickened. Cool completely.
4 Working with one wrapper at a time and keeping the rest covered, brush the edge of each lightly with water. Place a scallop in the centre, bring up the sides and pinch together to form a pouch with a frill at the top. Put on a paper-covered baking tray and repeat with the remaining wrappers and filling.
5 Heat 2 cm (3/4 inch) oil in a pan to 180°C (350°F). The oil is hot enough when a cube of bread sizzles and turns golden brown in 15 seconds. Cook the scallop pouches, in batches if necessary, for 5 minutes, or until golden brown. Drain on paper towels. Tie a blanched garlic chive around each and serve immediately.
IN ADVANCE: The scallop pockets can be filled a day ahead, covered and refrigerated. Don't deep-fry until just before serving.

PORCUPINE BALLS

Preparation time: 40 minutes + soaking
Total cooking time: 30 minutes each batch
Makes 24

★

1 cup (220 g/7 oz) short-grain rice
5 dried Chinese mushrooms
250 g (8 oz) beef mince
250 g (8 oz) pork mince
60 g (2 oz) finely chopped water chestnuts
4 spring onions, finely chopped
1–2 cloves garlic, crushed
1 teaspoon grated fresh ginger
1 tablespoon soy sauce
1 egg, lightly beaten

Dipping sauce
3 tablespoons light soy sauce
2 tablespoons soft brown sugar
2 tablespoons grated fresh ginger

1 Soak the rice in cold water in a large bowl for at least 2 hours, then drain and spread to dry on paper towels.
2 Place the mushrooms in a heatproof bowl and cover with boiling water. Leave for 20 minutes, squeeze dry, discard the stems and chop the mushrooms finely. Combine in a large bowl with both minces, water chestnuts, spring onion, garlic, ginger, soy sauce, egg and 1/2 teaspoon salt. Mix with your hands.
3 Divide the mixture into 24 portions and with wet hands, shape into small balls. Roll each in the rice until well coated. Line a bamboo steamer base with baking paper and put the balls in the steamer, leaving room for the rice to swell (cook in batches, depending on the size of the steamer). Place the steamer over a wok half-filled with boiling water. Steam for 30 minutes, or until the rice and meatballs are cooked through, adding more water to the wok when necessary. Serve immediately with dipping sauce.
4 For the dipping sauce, mix the ingredients with 3 tablespoons water. Serve in a small bowl.
IN ADVANCE: The mince mixture can be made a day ahead or frozen for 2 months. Roll in rice close to cooking time.

OPPOSITE PAGE:
Scallop pockets (left);
Porcupine balls

SUSHI
These rolls of nori (dried seaweed) with rice and savoury fillings are ideal for serving as finger food. Sushi looks difficult and impressive but is not hard once you have mastered the basic technique.

TO MAKE SUSHI RICE

The rice in sushi is not just plain rice. It has been cooked, then specially dressed for use. To make good sushi, you must first prepare good sushi rice. Use white short-grain rice—in Japan they use Japonica rice. Wash 2½ cups (550 g/1 lb 2 oz) short-grain rice under cold running water until the water runs clear, then leave in the strainer to drain for an hour. Put the rice in a pan with 3 cups (750 ml/24 fl oz) water and bring to the boil. Cook for 5–10 minutes, or until tunnels form on the surface of the rice, then reduce the heat to low, cover and cook the rice for 12–15 minutes, or until tender. Remove from the heat, remove the lid from the pan, cover the rice with a clean tea towel and leave for 15 minutes. To make the dressing, mix 5 tablespoons rice vinegar, 1 tablespoon mirin, 3 tablespoons sugar and 2 teaspoons salt and stir until the sugar has dissolved. Spread the rice over the base of a hangiri (a flat shallow wooden bowl) or a non-metallic dish or bowl, pour the dressing over the top and use a rice paddle or spatula to mix the dressing through the rice, separating the grains. Fan the rice until it cools to room temperature. Cover with a clean tea towel until ready to use. One quantity is enough to make each of the following sushi recipes. To prevent rice sticking to your hands when assembling sushi, dip your fingers in a bowl of warm water with a few drops of rice vinegar added.

MAKI ZUSHI

Maki zushi is probably the most well-known sushi roll—the one that you will usually find in a Japanese lunchbox. It is ideal for serving as finger food and can be filled with a variety of ingredients such as strips of sashimi tuna or salmon (available from good fishmongers), cucumber, pickled daikon, dried mushrooms (soaked in hot water for 20 minutes, so they swell up), kampyo (dried gourd), pickled ginger, omelette or sesame seeds. Place one sheet of nori on a bamboo mat with the shiny side facing down. (You will need 8 sheets of nori for this recipe. Nori is the most common form of seaweed used in Japanese and Korean cooking. It comes in paper-thin sheets, plain or roasted. If you toast it lightly over an open flame before use it will have a good nutty flavour.) Spread cooled sushi rice about 1 cm thick over the nori, leaving a 1 cm (½ inch) border on each side. Make

a shallow groove down the centre of the rice towards one short end. Spread a small amount of wasabi (an extremely hot paste, also known as Japanese horseradish) along the groove in the rice. Place a selection of strips of your filling ingredients on top of the wasabi. Lift up the edge of the bamboo mat and roll the sushi, starting from the edge nearest to you. When you've finished rolling, press the mat to make either a round or square roll. Push in any rice that may be escaping from the ends. Wet a sharp knife, trim the ends and cut the roll in half and then each half into three. Repeat with the remaining seven sheets of nori, sushi rice and fillings. Makes 48.

NOTE: Bamboo mats are not expensive and are available at Asian grocery stores. There isn't really a substitute, if you want to make successful sushi.

INSIDE OUT ROLLS

These are made with the same technique and ingredients as the maki zushi, but with the rice on the outside. Use 8 sheets of nori and one quantity of sushi rice. Place a sheet of nori on the bamboo mat and spread 1 cm (½ inch) rice over the top of it, leaving a 1 cm (½ inch) border. Cover with a sheet of plastic wrap, slightly larger than the nori. In one quick motion, turn the whole thing over, then place it back on the mat, so the plastic wrap is under the rice and the nori on top. Spread a little wasabi along the short end of the rice, about 4 cm (1½ inches) from the edge. Lay strips of cucumber, avocado and crab on top of the wasabi, then roll up from this end, using the plastic as a guide. Rewrap in plastic, then roll up in the mat to make a neat roll. Remove the plastic and roll in sesame seeds. Cut in half, trim the ends, and cut each half into three. Serve with shoyu.

SUSHI

NIGIRI ZUSHI

Trim 250 g (8 oz) sashimi tuna or salmon into a neat rectangle, removing any blood or connective tissue. Using a sharp knife, cut paper-thin slices of fish from the trimmed fillet, cleaning your knife in a bowl of water and lemon juice after cutting each slice. Form a tablespoon of your sushi rice into an oval about the same length and width as your rectangles of fish. Place a piece of fish on the open palm of your left hand, then spread a small dab of wasabi over the centre of the fish. Place the rice on the fish and gently cup your palm to make a curve. Using the middle and index fingers of your right hand, press the rice onto the fish, firmly pushing with a slight upward motion to make a neat shape. Turn over and repeat the shaping process, finishing with the fish on top of the rice. Nigiri zushi can be served with a strip of seaweed tied around the centre. Makes 16–20.

INARI ZUSHI

Combine 1 cup (250 ml/8 fl oz) dashi stock, 220 g (7 oz) sugar, 1/3 cup (90 ml/ 3 fl oz) shoyu and 1/4 cup (60 ml/2 fl oz) sake in a pan and stir over low heat until the sugar has dissolved. Bring to the boil, reduce the heat and add 16 half inari pouches (these are also known as tofu pouches and are thin slices of tofu that have been fried). Simmer for 5 minutes, allow to cool and then drain. Open the braised pouches and fill with sushi rice. Serve, cut-side-down, as they are, or tied with a blanched chive. Makes 16.

HAND ROLLS

These are small cone-shaped rolls of nori filled with rice and selected fillings. Your choice of fillings could include strips of pickled daikon, strips of cucumber,

CHILLI PRAWN SKEWERS

Preparation time: 25 minutes
Total cooking time: 10 minutes
Makes 30

★

30 large raw prawns
60 g (2 oz) butter
1 clove garlic, crushed
2 teaspoons soft brown sugar
2 tablespoons lemon or lime juice
2 tablespoons fresh coriander sprigs, finely
    chopped
2 tablespoons fresh basil leaves, finely chopped
1 tablespoon sweet chilli sauce

1 Remove the heads from the prawns, then peel, leaving the tails intact. With a sharp knife, slit each prawn down the back and devein.
2 Heat the butter in a large frying pan or wok. Add the garlic, sugar, juice, coriander, basil and sweet chilli sauce. Mix thoroughly, add the prawns in batches, then cook over medium heat for 5 minutes, or until the prawns turn pink and are cooked through.
3 Thread the prawns onto bamboo skewers or strong toothpicks. Serve warm.

BELOW: Chilli prawn skewers

IN ADVANCE: Prepare the prawns several hours ahead. Cook just before serving. They are also delicious grilled. Thread onto skewers and grill for 2–3 minutes. Brush with butter mixture during cooking. Scallops or oysters can be used instead of prawns, or alternate pieces of fish with prawns. You can use other fresh herbs such as dill and parsley.

THAI CHICKEN CAKES

Preparation time: 15 minutes
Total cooking time: 20 minutes
Makes 36

★

4 eggs, lightly beaten
2 tablespoons finely chopped fresh coriander
1 tablespoon fish sauce
2 tablespoons oil
500 g (1 lb) chicken mince
3 stalks lemon grass, white part only,
    finely chopped
2 cloves garlic, crushed
4 spring onions, chopped
1/4 cup (60 ml/2 fl oz) fresh lime juice
30 g (1 oz) coriander leaves and stems,
    chopped, extra
2 tablespoons sweet chilli sauce
1 tablespoon fish sauce
1 egg, extra, lightly beaten
1/2 cup (125 ml/4 fl oz) coconut milk
6 red chillies, seeded and finely sliced,
    to garnish

1 Preheat the oven to moderately hot 200°C (400°F/Gas 6). Lightly grease three 12-hole shallow patty tins.
2 In a bowl combine the eggs, coriander and fish sauce. Heat the oil in a large 25–28 cm (10–11 inch) frying pan and pour in the egg mixture. Cook over medium heat for about 2 minutes each side, or until golden. Roll up and shred finely. Set aside.
3 Mix the chicken mince, lemon grass, garlic, spring onion, lime juice, extra coriander, sauces, extra egg and coconut milk in a food processor until fine but not smooth. Spoon into the patty tins and top with a little shredded omelette. Bake for 15 minutes, or until cooked through. Rotate the trays once to ensure the chicken cakes all cook through. Serve hot, garnished with chilli.

LIMES
This citrus fruit is smaller than a lemon and has a fresh tart taste. In many Asian countries, the juice from limes is more commonly used than lemon juice. It is used in much the same way as lemons, for its unique flavour and as a tenderizer, and can be used as a substitute for lemons in most recipes. The juice is favoured as a beverage, often sweetened and added to soda. The rind is also grated into some dishes, as with lemons.

THAI FISH CAKES

Preparation time: 25 minutes
Total cooking time: 5–10 minutes
Makes about 24

☆

500 g (1 lb) firm white fish fillets
4 kaffir lime leaves, finely shredded
1 tablespoon chopped fresh Asian basil
2 tablespoons red curry paste
100 g (3½ oz) green beans, very
    finely sliced
2 spring onions, finely chopped
oil, for shallow-frying

Cucumber dipping sauce
1 Lebanese cucumber, finely chopped
3 tablespoons sweet chilli sauce
2 tablespoons rice vinegar
1 tablespoon chopped unsalted roasted peanuts
1 tablespoon chopped fresh coriander

1 Briefly chop the fish in a food processor until smooth. Add the lime leaves, basil and curry paste and process for 10 seconds. Transfer to a large bowl, add the beans and spring onion and mix well. Wet your hands and form level tablespoons of the mixture into small, flattish patties.
2 Mix all the sauce ingredients in a bowl.
3 Heat the oil in a heavy-based frying pan over medium heat. Cook the fish cakes, in batches, until golden brown on both sides. Drain on paper towels and serve with the dipping sauce.

ABOVE: Thai fish cakes

PEKING DUCK WITH MANDARIN PANCAKES

Preparation time: 1 hour + drying
Total cooking time: 1 hour
Makes 20

✯ ✯ ✯

1.7 kg (3 1/2 lb) duck
1 tablespoon honey
1 small Lebanese cucumber
12 spring onions
2 tablespoons hoisin sauce

Mandarin pancakes

2 1/2 cups (310 g/10 oz) plain flour
2 teaspoons caster sugar
1 tablespoon sesame oil

1 Wash the duck and remove the neck and any large pieces of fat from inside the carcass. Hold the duck over the sink (wear thick rubber gloves to protect your hands) and very carefully and slowly pour 3 litres of boiling water over it, rotating the duck so the water scalds all the skin. You may need another lot of boiling water.
2 Put the duck on a cake rack placed over a baking dish. Mix the honey and 1/2 cup (125 ml/4 fl oz) hot water and brush two coats of this glaze over the duck, ensuring it is entirely covered. Dry the duck, preferably hanging it up in a cool, airy place. (Alternatively, use an electric fan on a cool setting, positioned a metre or so away.) The skin is sufficiently dry when it is papery to touch. This may take 2–4 hours.
3 Remove the seeds from the cucumber and slice the flesh into matchsticks. Take an 8 cm (3 inch) section from each spring onion and make fine parallel cuts from the centre towards the end. Place in iced water—the spring onions will open into 'brushes'.
4 Preheat the oven to hot 210°C (415°F/ Gas 6–7). Bake the duck on the rack over a baking dish for 30 minutes. Turn the duck over carefully, without tearing the skin, then bake for another 30 minutes. Remove and leave for a minute or two. Place on a warm dish.
5 To make the mandarin pancakes, combine the flour and sugar in a bowl and pour in 1 cup (250 ml/8 fl oz) boiling water. Stir a few times to just combine and leave until lukewarm. Knead the mixture on a lightly floured surface to make a smooth dough, cover and set aside for 30 minutes.

6 Roll two level tablespoons of dough at a time into balls, then roll out to 8 cm (3 inch) rounds. Lightly brush one round with sesame oil and place another on top. Re-roll to make a thin pancake about 15 cm (6 inches) in diameter. Repeat with the remaining dough and oil to make about 10 'double' pancakes.
7 Heat a frying pan and cook the pancakes one at a time. When small bubbles appear on the surface, turn over and cook the second side, pressing the surface with a clean tea towel. The pancakes should puff up when done. Transfer to a plate. When cool enough to handle, peel each pair into two, stack on a plate and cover at once to prevent them drying out.
8 To serve, remove the crisp skin from the underside of the duck and cut into thin strips. Thinly slice the breast and leg meat and place on a warm serving plate. Arrange the cucumber sticks and spring onion brushes on a serving plate. Pour the hoisin sauce into a small dish. Place the pancakes and finely sliced duck on separate plates. Each person takes a pancake, spreads a little sauce on it, using the spring onion brush, and adds a couple of pieces of cucumber, a spring onion brush and finally a piece of duck and crisp duck skin. The pancake is then folded over into an envelope shape to hold the filling. Follow the same procedure with the remaining pancakes and duck.
NOTE: Traditionally, these pancakes are paper-thin. Once you have mastered the technique of making them, use 1 level tablespoon of the dough for each and proceed as before. Barbecued ducks are available at Asian barbecue shops and ready-made pancakes are also available where you buy the duck.
IN ADVANCE: The pancakes can be made a few hours ahead and kept covered in a cool place. Reheat briefly just before serving—either steam in a colander lined with a clean tea towel or wrap securely in foil and heat in a moderate 180°C (350°F/Gas 4) oven for 2 minutes.

PEKING DUCK
In traditional Chinese restaurants, Peking Duck is made by a master chef with years of experience. To obtain the required crispness, the duck skin is gently loosened from the flesh by massaging back and forth, making sure there are no holes in the skin. A small tube is used to blow air between the skin and carcass, which is then sealed. When the boiling water is poured over the duck, the skin plumps up and then becomes crisp when cooked. Some restaurants require 24 hours notice for serving Peking Duck.

OPPOSITE PAGE: Peking duck with mandarin pancakes

SUSHI CREPES

Pour enough egg mixture into a pan to lightly cover the base.

Cook the short-grain rice until small tunnels begin to appear on the surface.

Roll the crepe up firmly around the filling, using a sushi mat or greaseproof paper to help you.

ABOVE: Sushi crepes

SUSHI CREPES

Preparation time: I hour
Total cooking time: 30 minutes
Makes about 40

★★

4 eggs

Sushi

1 cup (220 g/7 oz) short-grain rice

2 tablespoons rice vinegar

1 tablespoon sugar

1 tablespoon mirin or dry sherry

a little wasabi paste

125 g (4 oz) sashimi tuna, cut into thin strips

1 small cucumber, peeled and cut into matchsticks

1/2 avocado, peeled and cut into matchsticks

3 tablespoons pickled ginger, cut into thin strips

soy sauce, for dipping

1 To make the egg crepes, gently whisk the eggs with 2 tablespoons cold water and a pinch of salt in a bowl until combined. Heat and lightly oil a small crepe pan, and pour enough of the egg mixture into the pan to lightly cover the base. Cook over low heat for 1 minute, being careful not to allow the crepe to brown. Turn the crepe over and cook for 1 minute. Transfer to a plate and cook the remaining mixture.

2 To make the sushi, put the rice in a pan with 2 cups (500 ml/16 fl oz) water, bring to the boil, then reduce the heat and simmer for 5 minutes, or until small tunnels begin to appear in the rice. If using gas, cover and turn the heat to very low, and continue cooking for 7 minutes, or until all the liquid is absorbed. If using an electric stovetop, remove the pan from the heat, cover and leave the rice to steam for 10–12 minutes (this prevents the rice from catching on the bottom of the pan and burning).

3 Combine the rice vinegar, sugar, mirin and 1 teaspoon salt in a jug and gently stir through the rice until well coated. Spread the rice evenly over a baking tray and cool at room temperature.

4 Place one egg crepe on a sushi mat or a piece of baking paper. Spread 4 tablespoons of the sushi rice over a third of the crepe, using a spatula or the back of a spoon.

5 Spread a tiny amount of wasabi along the

centre of the rice, taking care when doing this as the wasabi is extremely hot. Place some tuna, cucumber, avocado and ginger over the wasabi.
6 Using the sushi mat or paper to help you, fold the crepe over to enclose the filling and roll up firmly in the mat or paper. Trim the ends with a sharp knife and cut the crepe roll into 2 cm (³/4 inch) rounds with a sharp knife. Serve with soy sauce for dipping.

NOTE: Sashimi tuna is the freshest, highest quality tuna and is available from good seafood outlets. If you find the rice sticking to your hands, keep them moist by dipping in a small bowl of warm water with a squeeze of lemon added to it.

IN ADVANCE: Crepes can be made ahead and stored in an airtight container in the refrigerator. Do not slice until serving or they may dry out.

GRILLED MUSHROOMS WITH SESAME SEEDS

Preparation time: 15 minutes
Total cooking time: 10 minutes
Makes 30–35

★

1 tablespoon sesame seeds
400 g (13 oz) medium, flat mushrooms or
　shiitake mushrooms
2 tablespoons teriyaki sauce
2 tablespoons mirin or sweet sherry
1 tablespoon sugar
1 tablespoon finely chopped chives
1 teaspoon sesame oil
10 chives, cut into short lengths

1 Preheat the oven to moderate 180°C (350°/ Gas 4). Sprinkle the sesame seeds on a baking tray and bake for 10 minutes, or until golden. Remove from the tray.
2 Wipe the mushrooms with a damp cloth and discard the stalks. Put the mushrooms in a shallow dish. Combine the teriyaki sauce, mirin, sugar, chives and sesame oil, pour over the mushrooms and leave for 5 minutes.
3 Put the mushrooms on a greased baking tray, brush with half the marinade and grill under a preheated hot grill for 5 minutes. Turn the mushrooms over, brush with the remaining marinade and grill for another 5 minutes or until browned. Garnish the mushrooms with the roasted sesame seeds and chopped chives.

SPICY WON TON STRIPS

Cut fresh won ton wrappers into 1 cm (¹/2 inch) strips with scissors. Fill a deep heavy-based pan one third full of oil and heat to 180°C (350°F), or until a cube of bread dropped into the oil turns golden brown in 15 seconds. Deep-fry the won ton strips quickly in batches until golden brown, remove with a slotted spoon and drain on crumpled paper towels. While hot, sprinkle with a mixture of Chinese five-spice powder and salt. When cold, store in an airtight container. The quantity you make will depend on the number of people you are entertaining. Serve with drinks.

ABOVE: Grilled mushrooms with sesame seeds

FAR EASTERN PANTRY

Pickled ginger/red ginger: used in Japanese cooking. It has a sweet/salty sharp taste. Available in brine or sweet vinegars, in various shades of red to pale orange.

Tamarind: an essential flavour in many Asian dishes. It is available as a rich brown liquid or compressed blocks of pulp that must be soaked, kneaded and seeds removed before use.

Shrimp paste (blachan): made from shrimps that have been dried, salted and pounded to form a paste. It is sold in a block or in jars. Store in an airtight container.

Wasabi paste: also known as Japanese horseradish. An extremely hot paste made from the knobbly green root of the wasabi, native to Japan. Also comes in powdered form.

Rice paper: edible paper-thin dry rounds made from rice flour, water and salt. Only available in dry form. Must be moistened before use to make them pliable.

Spring roll wrappers: square or round and made from wheat flour and water dough. Also called egg roll wrappers.

Gow gee wrappers: rounds of dough made from wheat flour and water.

Won ton wrappers: thin squares of wheat flour and egg dough.

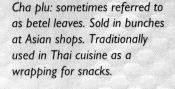

Asian basil: three varieties of aromatic basil are used in Asian cooking, all with their own distinct flavour, but fresh sweet basil is a good all-purpose one.

Cha plu: sometimes referred to as betel leaves. Sold in bunches at Asian shops. Traditionally used in Thai cuisine as a wrapping for snacks.

Water spinach: grown extensively throughout Asia. Not related to the spinach family, though English spinach can be used in its place. Requires only minimal cooking.

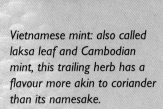

Vietnamese mint: also called laksa leaf and Cambodian mint, this trailing herb has a flavour more akin to coriander than its namesake.

Asian/golden shallots: small mild members of the onion family. Coppery brown and about the size of a large walnut. Prepare as onions.

Galangal: pinkish in colour with a distinctive peppery flavour. Available fresh (peel and slice as you would fresh ginger) or sliced, dried (must be soaked in hot water before use).

Daikon: a large elongated Asian carrot-shaped radish with quite a sweet flavour. Similar in taste and texture to ordinary radish. Also available pickled in jars.

Kampyo: thinly shaved dried strips of gourd, soaked until pliable and used as a filling in sushi or to tie wrapped food.

Bean curd skins: the skin that forms on heated soya bean milk and is then dried. Brush with water to soften. Comes in large sheets to cut to size. Use to wrap food before deep-frying, steaming or braising.

Star anise: dried star-shaped seed pod of a tree native to China. Adds aniseed taste to simmered meat and poultry. Available whole or ground.

Shiitake mushrooms: have a rich smoky flavour and are available fresh and dried. The dried variety must be soaked in boiling water for at least 20 minutes to soften before use.

Tempura flour: Available in packets in Asian grocery stores. Made up with iced water. Plain flour can be substituted but the batter won't be quite as light.

SPRING ROLLS

Preparation time: 45 minutes + soaking
Total cooking time: 20 minutes
Makes 20

★★

4 dried Chinese mushrooms
1 tablespoon oil
2 cloves garlic, crushed
1 tablespoon grated fresh ginger
150 g (5 oz) fried bean curd, cut into strips
1 large carrot, cut into very fine matchsticks
70 g (2¼ oz) water chestnuts, chopped
6 spring onions, chopped
150 g (5 oz) Chinese cabbage, shredded
1 tablespoon soy sauce
1 tablespoon cornflour
10 large spring roll wrappers
oil, for deep-frying

1 Soak the dried mushrooms in boiling water for 20 minutes. Drain and squeeze to remove any excess liquid. Slice the mushroom caps and discard the hard stems.

2 Heat the tablespoon of oil in a large wok, swirling gently to coat the base and side. Stir-fry the garlic, ginger, bean curd, carrot and water chestnuts for 30 seconds, over high heat. Add the spring onion and cabbage and cook for 1 minute, or until the cabbage is just softened. Add the soy sauce and some salt, white pepper and sugar, to taste; cool. Add the sliced mushroom caps.

3 Mix the cornflour with 2 tablespoons of water to form a paste. Keep the spring roll wrappers covered with a clean damp tea towel while you work. Place two wrappers on a board, one on top of the other. (The rolls are made with two layers of wrappers.) Cut the large square into four squares. Brush the edges of each square with a little cornflour paste. Place about 1 tablespoon of the filling in the centre of one square. With a corner facing you, roll up the wrapper firmly, folding in the sides as you roll. Repeat with the remaining wrappers and filling.

4 Fill a deep heavy-based pan one third full of oil and heat the oil to 180°C (350°F). The oil is ready when a cube of bread dropped into the oil turns golden brown in 15 seconds. Deep-fry the spring rolls, about four at a time, for 3 minutes, or until golden. Drain on crumpled paper towels.

SPRING ROLLS

Many culinary names hint at the time of year a food is usually enjoyed. *Spring rolls* are a typical example as they are traditionally eaten in Southeast Asia and China during New Year celebrations which, of course, are held in the spring.

ABOVE: Spring rolls

BABY SQUASH WITH RICE STUFFING

Preparation time: 20 minutes
Total cooking time: 10 minutes
Makes 24

★

24 baby yellow squash
1 tablespoon oil
2 teaspoons Thai red curry paste
1 spring onion, finely chopped
1 small red pepper (capsicum), finely chopped
1 cup (185 g/6 oz) cooked jasmine rice
1 tablespoon finely chopped fresh coriander
2 kaffir lime leaves, finely shredded
24 fresh coriander leaves, to garnish

1 Blanch or steam the squash for 5 minutes, or until just tender.
2 Cut a thin slice off the base of each squash to allow it to stand upright, then slice a thin piece off the top to make a lid. Set aside.
3 Using a melon baller, scoop out the flesh from the squash, leaving a thin shell. Discard the flesh.
4 Heat the oil in a wok, then add the curry paste, spring onion and red pepper and stir-fry for 2–3 minutes. Add the rice and stir-fry for another 2–3 minutes. Add the chopped coriander and kaffir lime leaves and toss to combine.
5 Remove from the heat and spoon 1 teaspoon of rice into each of the yellow squash. Garnish each with a coriander leaf and gently arrange the lids on top. Arrange on a platter and serve.
NOTE: For 1 cup (185 g/6 oz) jasmine rice, you will need to cook ⅓ cup (65 g/2¼ oz) of rice in boiling water for about 10 minutes.
IN ADVANCE: The filling and squash can be prepared a day ahead. Cover and store separately in the refrigerator. Assemble several hours before you are serving.

BELOW: Baby squash with rice stuffing

GARLIC

Although some people love the pungent flavour of garlic, while others hate it, it is indispensable as a flavouring for many recipes. It has been used for thousands of years and is renowned for its medicinal properties. It was used as an antiseptic before antibiotics. A member of the onion family, the bulb consists of a cluster of cloves surrounded by a thin skin. The cloves, with their skin on, are easily separated as required. The cloves are easier to peel if you lay them on a board and squash them slightly with the flat side of a broad knife. Crush or chop the clove with a knife or a garlic crusher. To add a subtle flavour to salads, cut a clove and rub round the inside of the salad bowl, or add a whole peeled clove to the salad dressing, then remove before serving.

OPPOSITE PAGE: Crusted tuna crisps (left); Pork gyoza dumplings

CRUSTED TUNA CRISPS

Preparation time: 45 minutes + chilling
Total cooking time: 15 minutes
Makes 24

☆☆

Wasabi cream
1/4 cup (60 ml/2 fl oz) cream
2 tablespoons sour cream
1 tablespoon wasabi powder
1/2 tablespoon lemon juice
1 tablespoon rice wine vinegar
1/2 teaspoon sugar

12 round gow gee wrappers
oil, for deep-frying
500 g (1 lb) tuna steaks, 2.5 cm (1 inch) thick
1/2 cup (80 g/2 3/4 oz) sesame seeds

Salad
125 g (4 oz) watercress
1 Lebanese cucumber
3 radishes
1 teaspoon grated fresh ginger
3 teaspoons rice wine vinegar
1 tablespoon sesame oil
1 tablespoon peanut or corn oil

1 For the wasabi cream, whisk the cream until it thickens, then gently stir in the sour cream, wasabi powder, lemon juice, rice wine vinegar and sugar. Season with salt and pepper. Refrigerate for at least 30 minutes.
2 Cut each gow gee wrapper in half. Fill a deep heavy-based saucepan one third full of oil and heat the oil to 180°C (350°F). The oil is ready when a cube of bread dropped into the oil turns golden brown in 15 seconds. Fry batches of gow gee wrappers until slightly brown and crisp, about 30 seconds per side. Drain on crumpled paper towels.
3 Cut the tuna steaks into 4 cm (1 1/2 inch) wide strips (about 2 or 3 pieces). Lightly brush with 2 teaspoons of oil, season with salt and pepper and toss in the sesame seeds. Refrigerate.
4 Divide the watercress into small sprigs. Use a vegetable peeler to slice the cucumber into thin strips. Rotate the cucumber and stop when you get to the seeds. Use the peeler to slice the radishes into thin pieces. Combine the cucumber, radish and watercress and set aside. Combine the ginger, rice wine vinegar, sesame and peanut oils

in a small non-metallic bowl. Season; set aside.
5 Heat 1 tablespoon oil in a heavy-based pan over medium heat. Sear the tuna on all sides for 1 minute per side. The sesame seeds should be golden brown and the centre of the tuna pink. Slice the tuna crossways into 24 pieces.
6 When ready to serve, stir the ginger dressing, then toss through the watercress, cucumber and radish. Place a small pile of salad on the wrappers, followed by a piece of tuna and some wasabi cream. Serve at room temperature.

PORK GYOZA DUMPLINGS

Preparation time: 40 minutes
Total cooking time: 10 minutes per batch
Makes 40

☆☆

Filling
400 g (13 oz) minced pork
15 garlic chives, chopped
2 cloves garlic, crushed
1 teaspoon sesame oil

40 gyoza or round gow gee wrappers
1/2 cup (125 ml/4 fl oz) soy sauce
1 tablespoon sesame seeds
oil, for frying

1 To make the filling, place all the ingredients in a bowl, mix well and season, to taste.
2 Place a teaspoon of filling in the centre of each wrapper, dampen the edges with water, fold over and pleat to seal. Place on a lightly oiled tray and repeat with the remaining wrappers and filling. Before steaming, lightly brush the dumplings with a little oil.
3 Half fill a wok or pan with water, cover and bring to the boil. Place batches of dumplings, not touching each other, in a bamboo steamer lined with lightly oiled baking paper. Steam for 10 minutes.
4 Combine the soy sauce and sesame seeds in a small serving dish.
5 Heat the oil in a large frying pan. Cook the gyoza dumplings in batches for about 2 minutes on one side, or until golden brown. Do not turn over. Remove from the pan and serve hot with soy sauce for dipping.
NOTE: These are quick and easy if you use a dumpling press, available at kitchen shops. You can buy the wrappers at Asian supermarkets.

FRIED SPICY TEMPEH

Preparation time: 30 minutes + standing
Total cooking time: 40 minutes
Serves 4-6

✷✷

4 small red chillies, seeded
2 stalks lemon grass, white part only
2 fresh kaffir lime leaves
1/2 cup (125 ml/4 fl oz) oil
10 Asian red or golden shallots, finely sliced
2 large cloves garlic, finely chopped
500 g (1 lb) tempeh, sliced into matchsticks
4 cm (1 1/2 inch) piece fresh galangal, peeled and thinly sliced
3 teaspoons tamarind purée
1 teaspoon salt
60 g (2 oz) palm sugar, grated

1 Slit the chillies lengthways and remove the seeds and membrane. Finely slice the chillies diagonally. Bruise the lemon grass and lime leaves with the back of a large knife.

2 Heat 2 tablespoons of the oil in a wok or pan and fry the shallots and garlic in batches over medium-low heat for 2–3 minutes, or until crisp. Drain on crumpled paper towels. Heat the remaining oil and fry the tempeh in batches for 3–4 minutes, or until very crisp (you may need to add a little more oil). Drain on crumpled paper towels. Discard all the oil except 2 teaspoons.

3 Heat the reserved oil in the wok and add the chilli, lemon grass, galangal and lime leaves. Cook over medium heat for 2 minutes, or until fragrant. Add the tamarind purée, salt, palm sugar and 1 tablespoon water. Cook for 2–3 minutes, or until the sauce is thick and has caramelized.

4 Add the crispy shallots, garlic and tempeh and stir-fry for 1–2 minutes, or until all the liquid has evaporated. Turn off the heat, spread the mixture in the wok and leave to cool. Remove and discard the lemon grass, galangal and lime leaves. Store in an airtight container for up to 5 days.

NOTE: Soft brown sugar can be used instead of palm sugar. Tempeh is an easily digestible source of protein made from soya beans. It is available at Asian speciality stores and some supermarkets.

ABOVE: Fried spicy tempeh

THAI BEEF SALAD IN CUCUMBER CUPS

Preparation time: 25 minutes + marinating
Total cooking time: 5–10 minutes
Makes 30

✷

Marinade
1/3 cup (80 ml/2¾ fl oz) kecap manis
1/3 cup (80 ml/2¾ fl oz) lime juice
1 red chilli, finely sliced
1 tablespoon sesame oil

250 g (8 oz) piece beef eye fillet
7 Lebanese cucumbers

Salad
1/2 stem lemon grass, white part only, finely chopped
1/4 cup (60 ml/2 fl oz) lime juice
1–2 fresh red chillies, finely sliced
20 g (¾ oz) fresh mint leaves, finely chopped
20 g (¾ oz) fresh coriander leaves, finely chopped
1 tablespoon fish sauce

1 Mix together the marinade ingredients. Put the beef eye fillet in a non-metallic bowl, pour in the marinade and refrigerate for 2 hours, or overnight. Allow the meat to come back to room temperature before cooking.
2 Heat a barbecue or chargrill pan and cook the beef. For medium, cook for 7 minutes. Cook less for rare and longer for well-done. Allow to cool, then finely slice into thin strips and mix with the rest of the salad ingredients.
3 Cut off the ends of the cucumber and slice about 3 cm (1¼ inches) thick. Using a melon baller, scoop out the flesh from each slice to make a 'cup' about 1 cm (½ inch) thick. Fill each cup with the Thai beef salad.
IN ADVANCE: Prepare the salad and scooped out cucumber slices separately, refrigerate, then fill at the last minute.

THAI BEEF SALAD IN
CUCUMBER CUPS

Trim the Lebanese cucumbers at both ends, then cut the cucumbers into short pieces.

Use a melon baller to scoop out the flesh, leaving a border of flesh on the base and sides to make a cup for the filling.

LEFT: Thai beef salad in cucumber cups

SPINACH AND WATER CHESTNUT DUMPLINGS

Preparation time: 1 hour 30 minutes + cooling
Total cooking time: 50 minutes
Makes 30

★★

Filling

1 tablespoon peanut oil

1 teaspoon sesame oil

1 clove garlic, crushed

2.5 cm (1 inch) piece fresh ginger, grated

2 tablespoons chopped fresh garlic chives

30 g (1 oz) water spinach, chopped into
  1 cm (1/2 inch) lengths

120 g (4 oz) can water chestnuts, drained,
  finely chopped

1 tablespoon soy sauce

Pastry

2 cups (350 g/11 oz) rice flour

2/3 cup (85 g/3 oz) tapioca starch

2 tablespoons arrowroot flour

1 tablespoon glutinous rice flour

*ABOVE: Spinach and
water chestnut dumplings*

Dipping sauce

1/2 teaspoon sesame oil

1/2 teaspoon peanut oil

1 tablespoon soy sauce

1 tablespoon lime juice

1 small red chilli, seeded and finely chopped

tapioca flour, for dusting

1 For the filling, heat the oils over medium-low heat in a wok. Add the garlic and ginger and cook, stirring, for 1 minute, or until fragrant but not brown. Add the chives, water spinach, water chestnuts and soy sauce and cook for 2 minutes. Remove from the pan and cool for about 5 minutes. Drain away any liquid.

2 Combine the pastry ingredients in a large pan with 2 1/2 cups (600 ml/20 fl oz) water, stirring to remove any lumps. Stir over low heat for 10 minutes, or until thick. Cook stirring, for another 5 minutes, or until the liquid is opaque. Turn onto a work surface dusted liberally with tapioca flour and cool for 10 minutes. (You will need to use the tapioca flour to continually dust the surface and your hands while kneading.) With floured hands, knead the dough for

10 minutes. Divide into two, covering one half with plastic wrap.

3 Roll out the dough to 2 mm (⅛ inch) thick. Cut out 9 cm (3½ inch) rounds with a cutter. Place a heaped teaspoon of filling in the centre of each circle, dampen the edge, fold over and pleat to seal. This is very easy with a dumpling press. Place on a lightly floured board or tray and repeat with the remaining dough and filling. Do not re-roll any pastry scraps. Before steaming, lightly brush the dumplings with oil.

4 Half fill a wok or pan with water, cover and bring to the boil. Place the dumplings, leaving a gap between each, in a bamboo steamer lined with lightly oiled baking paper. Cover and steam for 10 minutes, or until the pastry is opaque. Repeat until all the dumplings are done, then serve with the dipping sauce on the side.

5 For the sauce, whisk all the ingredients together in a small bowl.

NOTE: Water spinach, also known as kangkung, is available at Asian greengrocers. Rice flour, tapioca starch, arrowroot flour and glutinous rice flour are available from large Asian food stores and some supermarkets.

THAI CHICKEN ROLLS

Preparation time: 25 minutes
Total cooking time: 10 minutes
Makes 30

★ ★

600 g (1 ¼ lb) chicken mince

4 stalks lemon grass, finely chopped

4 red chillies, seeded and finely chopped

6 Asian red shallots, finely chopped

2 tablespoons finely chopped fresh
　Vietnamese mint

3 tablespoons finely chopped fresh coriander

2 tablespoons fish sauce

2 tablespoons fresh lime juice

100 g (3½ oz) packet bean curd skin

oil, for deep frying

4 kaffir lime leaves, finely shredded,
　to garnish

1 Mix the chicken mince, lemon grass, chopped chilli, shallots, mint, coriander, fish sauce and lime juice (this can be done with sharp knives or in a food processor). Cut thirty 10 x 16 cm (4 x 6½ inch) rectangles from the bean curd skin. Brush the bean curd skin lightly with water to soften it for rolling. Roll 1 tablespoon of chicken mixture into a log and place on each bean curd rectangle. Roll up from the short end, folding in the ends as you roll.

2 Fill a deep heavy-based pan one third full of oil and heat to 180°C (350°F). The oil is ready when a cube of bread dropped into the oil turns golden brown in 15 seconds. Deep-fry the chicken rolls for 1 minute, or until golden brown and cooked through. If the bean curd skin is browning before the chicken is cooked, turn the heat down. Drain well on crumpled paper towels. Serve garnished with finely shredded kaffir lime leaves. Serve immediately to retain crispness.

ABOVE: Thai chicken rolls

153

BEEF CHA PLU PARCELS

Preparation time: 25 minutes
Total cooking time: 10 minutes
Makes about 45

★ ★

1 medium leek, trimmed
250 g (8 oz) lean beef mince
1 Lebanese cucumber, finely chopped
1/2 red onion, finely chopped
5–6 fresh Vietnamese mint leaves, finely
  chopped
2 tablespoons lime juice
2 tablespoons fish sauce
2 tablespoons desiccated coconut, toasted
500 g (1 lb) cha plu (betel leaves)
1 cup (250 ml/8 fl oz) sweet chilli sauce,
  for dipping

1 Cut the leek in half lengthways, wash
thoroughly and discard the outer layers and any
hard core. Put the leek in a bowl, pour boiling
water over it and soak for 5 minutes, or until
softened. Drain well and set aside.
2 Heat 1 tablespoon of oil in a frying pan and
cook the beef mince, breaking up any lumps
with the back of a fork, for 5–8 minutes, until
cooked through and browned. Remove from
the heat and cool slightly.
3 Combine the mince with the cucumber,
onion, mint, lime juice, fish sauce and coconut.
Toss well and set aside.
4 Cut the base off the leek and cut the leek
lengthways into thin strips about 5 mm (1/4 inch)
wide. Trim the required amount of betel leaves
(larger ones are better for making into parcels),
wash and dry well.
5 Place 1 teaspoon of mixture in the centre of
each leaf and fold in the sides to form a parcel, or
draw up the sides to form a pouch. Carefully tie
with pieces of leek. Repeat with all the leaves.
Arrange on a platter with sweet chilli sauce to
dip and serve immediately.
NOTE: Betel leaves and Vietnamese mint can be
found in Asian fruit and vegetable stores as well
as in some greengrocers. If unavailable, use
blanched Chinese cabbage leaves instead of the
betel leaves and normal mint to replace the
Vietnamese mint.

BLACK SATIN CHICKEN

Preparation time: 15 minutes + soaking
Total cooking time: 1 hour
Makes about 25 pieces

★

3 dried Chinese mushrooms
1/2 cup (125 ml/4 fl oz) dark soy sauce
1/4 cup (45 g/1 1/2 oz) soft brown sugar
2 tablespoons Shaosing (Chinese) wine
1 tablespoon soy sauce
1 teaspoon sesame oil
1/4 teaspoon Chinese five-spice powder
1.4 kg (2 lb 13 oz) chicken drumettes
4 cm (1 1/2 inch) piece fresh ginger, grated

1 Put the mushrooms in a small heatproof bowl,
cover with boiling water and leave to soak for
20 minutes, or until softened. Drain, reserving
the liquid. Combine the liquid with the dark soy
sauce, sugar, wine, soy sauce, sesame oil and
five-spice powder in a small pan and bring to the
boil, stirring continuously.
2 Rub the chicken with ginger and 1 teaspoon
salt and put in a large pan. Cover with the soy
marinade and mushrooms, turning to coat
evenly. Cover and cook over low heat, turning
regularly, for 20 minutes or until the juices run
clear when pierced with a skewer. Remove the
chicken and allow to cool briefly. Boil the sauce
over high heat until thick and syrupy. Discard
the mushrooms.
3 Arrange the chicken on a platter, brush lightly
with the syrupy sauce and serve the remaining
sauce for dipping.
NOTE: Dark soy sauce is thicker in consistency
than regular soy and is available from Asian food
speciality stores. Drumettes are the meaty part of
the wing with the two smaller joints cut off.

BEEF CHA PLU PARCELS

Spoon 1 teaspoon of mixture into the centre of the underside of each leaf.

Draw up the sides of each leaf to form a pouch, or fold to form a parcel, then tie with strips of leek.

OPPOSITE PAGE: Beef cha plu parcels (top); Black satin chicken

155

and pour the lemon juice over. Cover and refrigerate for 15 minutes. Drain and pat dry.
2 Combine the cornflour, salt, pepper and sugar in a bowl. Dip the squid into the egg white and dust with the flour mixture, shaking off any excess. Fill a deep heavy-based pan one third full of oil and heat to 180°C (350°F), or until a cube of bread dropped into the oil turns golden brown in 15 seconds. Deep-fry the squid, in batches, for 1–2 minutes, or until the squid turns white and curls. Drain on crumpled paper towels. Serve immediately.

STEAMED CHINESE MUSHROOMS WITH PRAWNS

Preparation time: 40 minutes + soaking
Total cooking time: 40 minutes
Makes about 20

☆

60 g (2 oz) dried shiitake mushrooms
2 tablespoons soy sauce
3 tablespoons sesame oil
1 tablespoon grated palm sugar
1 kg (2 lb) large raw prawns, peeled and deveined
6 spring onions, finely chopped
1/2 large celery stick, finely chopped
2 tablespoons finely chopped fresh coriander
2.5 cm (1 inch) piece fresh ginger, grated
1/2 teaspoon fish sauce
1 red chilli, finely chopped
1/4 teaspoon sesame oil

1 Soak the mushrooms in boiling water for 20 minutes, then drain, reserving the liquid. Remove and discard the stems. To 1 cup (250 ml/4 fl oz) of the reserved liquid, add the soy sauce and 1 tablespoon of the sesame oil.
2 Heat the remaining sesame oil in a wok or frying pan and cook the mushrooms, on the pale side only, until lightly browned. Sprinkle with the palm sugar and cook for another minute. Add the reserved seasoned liquid and cook, covered, for about 15 minutes over low heat. Drain, reserving any remaining liquid, and cool.
3 Roughly chop the prawn meat in a food processor, then transfer to a bowl and mix with the spring onion, celery, coriander, ginger, fish sauce, chilli and sesame oil.
4 To assemble, put 1 dessertspoon of paste on each mushroom and smooth into a dome shape. Place in a steamer. Bring the reserved liquid to

SALT AND PEPPER SQUID

Preparation time: 30 minutes + marinating
Total cooking time: 10 minutes
Serves 10

☆ ☆

1 kg (2 lb) squid tubes, halved lengthways
1 cup (250 ml/8 fl oz) lemon juice
2 cups (250 g/8 oz) cornflour
1 1/2 tablespoons salt
1 tablespoon ground white pepper
2 teaspoons caster sugar
4 egg whites, lightly beaten
oil, for deep-frying
lemon wedges, for serving
fresh coriander leaves, to garnish

1 Open out the squid tubes, wash and pat dry. Lay on a chopping board with the inside facing upwards. Score a fine diamond pattern on the squid, being careful not to cut all the way through. Cut into pieces about 5 x 3 cm (2 x 1 1/4 inches). Place in a flat non-metallic dish

ABOVE: Salt and pepper squid

the boil in a pan and steam the mushrooms over the liquid, adding water if necessary, for about 15 minutes, or until the filling is cooked through.

MIXED TEMPURA

Preparation time: 20 minutes
Total cooking time: 10 minutes
Makes about 30

★ ★

12 raw king prawns
1 sheet nori, cut into 12 thin strips
2 cups (250 g/8 oz) tempura flour or
    plain flour
2 cups (500 ml/16 fl oz) iced water
2 egg yolks, lightly beaten
oil, for deep-frying
flour, for coating
60 g (2 oz) broccoli florets
100 g (3¹/₂ oz) button mushrooms
1 red pepper (capsicum), cut into thin strips
soy sauce, for serving

1 Peel and devein the prawns, leaving the tails intact. Cut a slit in the underside of each prawn (this will prevent them curling) and wrap a piece of nori around the base of the tail.
2 Sift the flour into a bowl, make a well in the centre and add the iced water and egg yolk. Stir with chopsticks until just combined. The batter should be slightly lumpy.
3 Fill a deep heavy-based pan one third full of oil and heat to 180°C (350°F), or until a cube of bread dropped into the oil turns golden in 15 seconds.
4 Dip the prawns in flour to coat, shake off any excess, then dip in the batter. Cook the prawns in batches until crisp and light golden. Drain on crumpled paper towels. Repeat with the vegetables. Serve the tempura immediately with soy sauce for dipping.
NOTE: Tempura should have a very light batter and needs to be served as soon as it is cooked. Be sure that the water is ice cold as this helps to lighten the batter. If you are unsure, add a few ice cubes. If you use plain flour, add a little extra water to help thin the batter.

BELOW: Mixed tempura

STEAMED PORK BUNS

Flatten the dough portions slightly, making them slightly thinner around the edges.

Pull the dough up around the pork filling to enclose, pinching firmly to seal.

Place each bun on a piece of greaseproof paper and place in a steamer.

STEAMED PORK BUNS

Preparation time: 40 minutes
Total cooking time: 15 minutes
Makes about 24

✦ ✦

3 cups (450 g/14 oz) char sui pork bun flour
1 cup (250 ml/8 fl oz) milk
1/2 cup (125 g/4 oz) caster sugar
1 tablespoon oil

Filling
2 teaspoons oil
1 clove garlic, crushed
2 spring onions, finely chopped
3 teaspoons cornflour
2 teaspoons hoisin sauce
1 1/2 teaspoons soy sauce
1/2 teaspoon caster sugar
150 g (5 oz) Chinese barbecued pork,
    finely chopped

1 Set aside two tablespoons of flour. In a small pan, combine the milk and sugar and stir over low heat until dissolved. Sift the remaining flour into a large bowl and make a well in the centre. Gradually add the milk, stirring until it just comes together. Lightly dust a work surface with some of the reserved flour. Turn out the dough and knead for 10 minutes, or until smooth and elastic. Gradually incorporate the tablespoon of oil by kneading it into the dough a little at a time, kneading for about 10 minutes. Cover with plastic wrap and refrigerate for 30 minutes.
2 For the filling, heat the oil in a pan, add the garlic and spring onion and stir over medium heat until just soft. Blend the cornflour with 1/3 cup (80 ml/2 3/4 fl oz) water, the sauces and sugar and add to the pan. Stir over medium heat until the mixture boils and thickens, remove from the heat and stir in the pork. Allow to cool.
3 Divide the dough into 24 portions and flatten slightly, making the edges slightly thinner than the centre. Place teaspoons of filling in the centre of each and pull up the edges around the filling to enclose, pinching firmly to seal. Place each bun on a small square of greaseproof paper and place 3 cm (1 1/4 inches) apart on a bamboo or metal steamer. Place over a large pan of simmering water and steam in batches for 15 minutes, or until the buns have risen and are cooked through.
NOTE: Char sui pork bun flour is available at Asian food stores. It gives a finer, lighter texture.

*ABOVE: Steamed
pork buns*

STIR-FRIED NOODLES WITH CORN AND PEANUTS

Preparation time: 25 minutes
Total cooking time: 10 minutes
Makes 35

★ ★ ★

1/2 cup (90 g/3 oz) roasted peanuts
1/4 cup (60 ml/2 fl oz) coconut milk
2 tablespoons lime juice
1/2 teaspoon ground turmeric
1/4 cup (60 ml/2 fl oz) oil
3 eggs, lightly beaten
125 g (4 oz) dried rice vermicelli
3 cloves garlic, crushed
1 tablespoon finely chopped fresh ginger
2 teaspoons shrimp paste (blachan)
6 spring onions, thinly sliced
400 g (13 oz) can baby corn, drained,
    quartered lengthways
150 g (5 oz) bean shoots
500 g (1 lb) Chinese cabbage, hard stems
    removed, thinly sliced
1/2 small red pepper (capsicum), thinly sliced
10 g (1/4 oz) fresh coriander leaves
1 1/2 tablespoons fish sauce
2–3 large banana leaves, for serving
1/2 cup (90 g/3 oz) roasted peanuts, extra,
    chopped, to garnish
lime wedges, for serving

1 Mix the peanuts, coconut milk, lime juice and turmeric in a food processor until combined, but so the peanuts are only roughly chopped.
2 Heat 1 tablespoon of the oil in a large wok. Add the eggs and tilt the uncooked egg to the outside edge of the wok. Cook until firm, then remove from the wok and roll up firmly. Cut into thin slices.
3 Place the vermicelli in a bowl, cover with boiling water and soak for 5 minutes. Drain and cut into short lengths with scissors.
4 Heat the remaining oil in the wok. Add the garlic, ginger and shrimp paste and stir-fry for 30 seconds, or until aromatic. Add the vegetables and stir-fry until tender. Add the vermicelli and stir-fry until heated through. Stir in the peanut mixture and stir-fry until well combined and heated through. Turn off the heat and gently stir in the omelette and coriander leaves and fish sauce.

5 Cut the banana leaves into 11 cm (4 1/2 inch) squares and blanch them in hot water for 10–15 seconds. Hold one corner of a square down on a flat surface with your finger, then fold one side of the banana leaf across, overlapping it into a cone shape. Secure down the side through to the base with a toothpick. Repeat to make 35 cones.
6 Spoon the filling into the cones, sprinkle with the extra peanuts and serve with lime wedges.
NOTE: Banana leaves are available in the fruit and vegetable section of most supermarkets or in Asian or Pacific Island stores.

ABOVE: Stir-fried noodles with corn and peanuts

TAPAS & MEZE

Tapas and meze are those delicious little appetizers served throughout the balmy Mediterranean. Tapas are at the heart of the gregarious Spanish social life. The word comes from *tapa*, 'to cover', and at first this is exactly what tapas were—slices of bread or ham placed on top of glasses of sherry in a bar to keep off the flies. Thankfully tapas have evolved somewhat since then and are often now the main reason to visit a Spanish tavern. Meze is directly translated from the Greek for 'tasty morsels' and celebrates the flavours of Greece, Turkey and the Middle East. Originally served before the main meal, a meze platter is now recognised as a magnificent feast in its own right.

PRAWN FRITTERS

Preparation time: 20 minutes
Total cooking time: 10 minutes
Makes about 30

★★

²/3 cup (85 g/3 oz) plain flour
¹/3 cup (40 g/1¹/4 oz) self-raising flour
2 spring onions, chopped
2 tablespoons chopped fresh flat-leaf parsley
pinch of cayenne pepper
³/4 cup (185 ml/6 fl oz) soda water
125 g (4 oz) small cooked prawns, peeled
 and chopped
olive oil, for deep-frying

1 Sift the flours into a large bowl. Add the spring onion, parsley, cayenne pepper and some salt and mix well. Make a well in the centre and gradually add the soda water, whisking to form a smooth lump-free batter. Add enough soda water to form a batter that will drop from a spoon. Add the prawns and stir until combined.

ABOVE: Prawn fritters

2 Fill a deep heavy-based pan one third full of oil and heat to 180°C (350°F), or until a cube of bread dropped into the oil browns in 15 seconds. Drop half tablespoons of the batter into the hot oil in batches and cook for 1–2 minutes, turning, until puffed and evenly browned all over. Remove with a slotted spoon and drain on crumpled paper towels. Serve hot.

OLIVE TWISTS

Finely chop 1 tablespoon of capers and 4 anchovy fillets and mix with 2 tablespoons olive paste, some chopped fresh parsley and a drizzle of oil, to form a smooth paste. Spread 2 sheets of ready-rolled puff pastry with the paste and cut into 1.5 cm (⅝ inch) strips. Twist each strip about 4 times and bake on baking paper covered trays in a moderately hot 200°C (400°F/Gas 6) oven for about 5–10 minutes, or until golden brown. Makes about 50.

HAM AND MUSHROOM CROQUETTES

Preparation time: 35 minutes + cooling
  + chilling
Total cooking time: 20 minutes
Makes 36

★ ★

90 g (3 oz) butter
I small onion, finely chopped
110 g (3¹/₂ oz) cap mushrooms, finely chopped
³/₄ cup (90 g/3 oz) plain flour
I cup (250 ml/8 fl oz) milk
³/₄ cup (185 ml/6 fl oz) chicken stock
110 g (3¹/₂ oz) ham, finely chopped
¹/₂ cup (60 g/2 oz) plain flour, extra
2 eggs, lightly beaten
¹/₂ cup (50 g/1³/₄ oz) dry breadcrumbs
olive oil, for deep-frying

I Melt the butter in a pan over low heat and cook the onion for 5 minutes, or until translucent. Add the mushrooms and cook, stirring occasionally, over low heat for 5 minutes. Add the flour and stir over medium–low heat for 1 minute, or until the mixture is dry and crumbly and begins to change colour.

2 Remove the pan from the heat and gradually stir in the milk and stock. Return to the heat, stirring constantly until the mixture boils and becomes very thick. Stir in the ham and some black pepper, then transfer to a bowl to cool for about 2 hours.

3 When completely cool, roll tablespoons of the mixture into croquette shapes. Place the extra flour, beaten eggs and breadcrumbs in three shallow bowls. Toss the croquettes in the flour, then in the eggs, allowing the excess to drip away, then toss in the breadcrumbs. Place on a baking tray covered with paper and refrigerate for about 30 minutes.

4 Fill a deep heavy-based pan one third full of oil and heat to 180°C (350°F), or until a cube of bread dropped into the oil browns in 15 seconds. Deep-fry the croquettes, in batches, for about 3 minutes each batch, until they are browned all over and heated through. Drain each batch on crumpled paper towels. Serve the croquettes warm or hot.

BELOW: Ham and mushroom croquettes

BOREK OF ASPARAGUS

Cut the puff pastry sheets into rectangles and put one trimmed asparagus spear on each.

Fold in the short ends, then roll the pastry up like a parcel so the asparagus is sealed in.

OPPOSITE PAGE: Scallop ceviche (top); Borek of asparagus

SCALLOP CEVICHE

Preparation time: 20 minutes + marinating
Total cooking time: Nil
Makes 15

✴ ✴

15 scallops on the half shell
1 teaspoon finely grated lime rind
2 cloves garlic, chopped
2 red chillies, seeded and chopped
1/4 cup (60 ml/2 fl oz) lime juice
1 tablespoon chopped fresh parsley
1 tablespoon olive oil

1 Take the scallops off their half shells. If the scallops need to be cut off the shells, use a small, sharp paring knife to carefully slice the attached part away from the shell, being careful to leave as little scallop meat on the shell as possible. Remove the dark vein and white muscle from the scallops, and wash the shells.
2 In a bowl, mix together the lime rind, garlic, chilli, lime juice, parsley and olive oil and season with salt and freshly ground black pepper. Place the scallops in the dressing and stir to coat evenly. Cover with plastic wrap and marinate in the refrigerator for 2 hours to 'cook' the scallop meat.
3 To serve, slide each of the scallops back onto a half shell and spoon the dressing over the top. Serve cold.

BOREK OF ASPARAGUS

Preparation time: 20 minutes
Total cooking time: 25 minutes
Makes 16

✴

16 fresh asparagus spears
1/2 teaspoon salt
1/2 teaspoon black pepper
2 tablespoons finely grated lemon rind
2 sheets ready-rolled puff pastry
1 egg yolk
1 tablespoon sesame seeds

1 Preheat the oven to moderately hot 200°C (400°F/Gas 6).
2 Add the asparagus to a large pan of lightly salted boiling water and simmer for about 3 minutes, then drain and refresh under cold running water. Trim to 10 cm (4 inch) lengths.
3 Combine the salt, black pepper and lemon rind in a shallow dish and roll each asparagus spear in this mixture.
4 Cut the puff pastry sheets into 12 x 6 cm (5 x 2½ inch) rectangles and place one asparagus spear on each piece of pastry. In a bowl, combine the egg yolk with 2 teaspoons water and brush some on the sides and ends of the pastry. Roll the pastry up like a parcel, enclosing the sides so that the asparagus is completely sealed in. Press the joins of the pastry with a fork.
5 Place the parcels on lightly greased baking trays. Brush with the remaining egg and sprinkle with sesame seeds. Bake for 15–20 minutes, or until golden. These parcels are delicious served warm or cold, with tzatziki (see page 167).

BOREK OF MUSHROOM

Preparation time: 40 minutes + cooling
Total cooking time: 40 minutes
Makes 24

✴

4 rashers bacon
250 g (8 oz) mushrooms
1 tablespoon olive oil
1 onion, chopped
1/4 teaspoon paprika
6 sheets ready-rolled puff pastry

1 Chop the bacon and mushrooms into 5 mm (1/4 inch) cubes. Heat the olive oil in a frying pan over medium heat, and cook the onion and paprika for 3 minutes, without browning. Add the bacon and cook for 3 minutes. Add the mushroom and cook for another 5 minutes, or until all the ingredients are tender. Season with salt and cracked black pepper, then spoon into a bowl. Set aside and allow to cool completely.
2 Using a 10 cm (4 inch) pastry cutter, cut 4 rounds out of each sheet of pastry. Refrigerate to make handling them easier. Preheat the oven to moderately hot 200°C (400°F/Gas 6).
3 Spoon 1 tablespoon of the mushroom and bacon into the centre of each round of pastry. Draw up the pastry to form four sides. To seal, pinch the sides together with wet fingertips. Repeat with the remaining pastry and filling.
4 Bake on baking trays covered with baking paper for 20–30 minutes, or until the pastry is golden and brown. Serve hot or warm.

SPANISH-STYLE BEEF KEBABS

Preparation time: 15 minutes + marinating
Total cooking time: 5 minutes
Makes 18–20

★★

1 kg (2 lb) rump steak
3 cloves garlic, chopped
1 tablespoon chopped fresh flat-leaf parsley
1/3 cup (80 ml/2³/4 fl oz) lemon juice
1/2 teaspoon black pepper
18–20 small wooden skewers

Paprika dressing

2 teaspoons paprika
large pinch of cayenne pepper
1/2 teaspoon salt
2 tablespoons red wine vinegar
1/3 cup (80 ml/2³/4 fl oz) olive oil

1 Trim the excess fat from the rump steak and cut into 2 cm (³/4 inch) pieces. Combine the steak, garlic, parsley, lemon juice and pepper in a bowl, cover with plastic wrap and marinate for 2 hours in the refrigerator. Meanwhile, soak the skewers in water for about 1 hour to ensure they don't burn during cooking.
2 To make the paprika dressing, whisk the paprika, cayenne pepper, salt, vinegar and oil together until well blended.
3 Preheat a lightly oiled barbecue hotplate or grill. Thread the pieces of marinated meat onto the skewers, then cook the kebabs, turning occasionally for about 4–5 minutes, or until cooked through. Drizzle with the paprika dressing and serve hot with wedges of lemon.

HALOUMI

This is a firm, stretched-curd cheese that is matured in brine (salt water). It has a salty, sharp taste, similar to feta. Haloumi can be served as part of a cheese platter, together with fresh fruit. It can also be pan-fried in olive oil, or brushed with oil before grilling. It has a smooth and creamy texture when melted.

BARBECUED HALOUMI

Lightly brush 10 slices of French bread on both sides with olive oil and barbecue until brown. Cut 250 g (8 oz) haloumi cheese into 5 mm (1/4 inch) slices. Combine a little oil and crushed garlic and brush over the cheese. Barbecue on a hotplate for 1 minute, or until soft and golden underneath. Use an egg slide to remove the cheese and place some on each piece of toast. Drizzle with a little olive oil and sprinkle with chopped mint and cracked black pepper. Makes 10.

BABA GANOUJ
(EGGPLANT/AUBERGINE DIP)

Preparation time: 15 minutes + standing
Total cooking time: 35 minutes
Makes about 1 cup (250 ml/8 fl oz)

★★

2 medium eggplants (aubergines)
3–4 cloves garlic, crushed
2 tablespoons lemon juice
2 tablespoons tahini
1 tablespoon olive oil
sprinkle of paprika, to garnish

1 Halve the eggplants (aubergines) lengthways, sprinkle with salt and leave to stand for 15–20 minutes. Rinse and pat dry with paper towels. Preheat the oven to moderate 180°C (350°F/Gas 4).
2 Place the eggplants on a baking tray and bake for 35 minutes, or until soft. Peel away the skin and discard. Place the flesh in a food processor with the garlic, lemon juice, tahini and olive oil and season, to taste, with salt and pepper. Process for 20–30 seconds. Sprinkle with paprika and serve with pieces of Lebanese bread.
NOTE: The reason eggplants are sprinkled with salt and left to stand before using is that they can have a bitter taste. The salt draws out the bitter liquid from the eggplant. Slender eggplants do not need to be treated in this way before you use them. Tahini is a paste made from crushed sesame seeds and is available at the supermarket.

TZATZIKI
(MINTED CUCUMBER DIP)

Finely grate 1 Lebanese cucumber and squeeze out the excess moisture. Mix together in a bowl with 2 crushed cloves of garlic, 250 g (8 oz) natural yoghurt, 1 teaspoon white vinegar and a teaspoon each of chopped dill and mint. Add salt and black pepper, to taste. Serve with pitta or Turkish bread or crudités.

BELOW: Baba ganouj

BAKED POLENTA
WITH SPICY RELISH

Whisk the polenta into the boiling milk, pouring the polenta in a thin stream, until it thickens.

When the mixture is thick, stir continuously with a wooden spoon for 20 minutes, or until it leaves the side of the pan.

OPPOSITE PAGE: Baked polenta with spicy relish (top); Tomato and anchovy toasts

BAKED POLENTA WITH SPICY RELISH

Preparation time: 20 minutes + chilling
Total cooking time: 1 hour
Makes 48

☆

600 ml (20 fl oz) milk
2/3 cup (100 g/3 1/2 oz) polenta
25 g (3/4 oz) butter, diced
1 tablespoon olive oil
1 tablespoon polenta, extra

Spicy relish

1 tablespoon oil
2 red onions, roughly chopped
500 g (1 lb) Roma (egg) tomatoes, roughly chopped
1 large red chilli, finely chopped
1/4 teaspoon Mexican chilli powder, or to taste
1 tablespoon soft brown sugar
1 tablespoon red wine vinegar

1 Lightly grease a 30 x 20 cm (12 x 8 inch) cake tin. Bring the milk to the boil in a pan. Reduce the heat to medium and whisk in the polenta, pouring it in a stream, until it thickens, then stir continuously with a wooden spoon for 20 minutes, or until it leaves the side of the pan. Remove from the heat and stir in the butter. Season, to taste.
2 Spread the polenta into the tin and smooth the top. Refrigerate for 2 hours, or until set.
3 To make the spicy tomato relish, heat the oil in a pan, add the onion and cook, stirring, over high heat, for 3 minutes. Add the tomato, chilli, chilli powder, sugar and vinegar. Simmer, stirring occasionally, for 20 minutes, or until thickened. Season with salt.
4 Preheat the oven to moderately hot 200°C (400°F/Gas 6). Turn the polenta out onto a board, cut into 5 cm (2 inch) squares, then into triangles. Place on a baking tray covered with paper, brush with olive oil and sprinkle with the extra polenta. Bake for 10 minutes, or until the polenta is golden and has a crust. Serve hot or warm with the warm relish.
NOTE: You can also use instant polenta which only takes about 3 minutes to cook.

TOMATO AND ANCHOVY TOASTS

Preparation time: 10 minutes
Total cooking time: 5 minutes
Makes 16

☆

16 x 1 cm (1/2 inch) thick slices Italian bread
3 cloves garlic, halved
8 ripe vine-ripened tomatoes
1/3 cup (80 ml/2 3/4 fl oz) extra virgin olive oil
2 x 45 g (1 1/2 oz) cans anchovy fillets, drained and sliced lengthways

1 Toast the bread on both sides until golden. While warm, rub both sides of the toast with the cut garlic.
2 Cut the tomatoes in half and rub each side of the toast with them, so that the juice and seeds soak well into the toast but do not saturate it. Chop the remaining tomato and pile it on the toast.
3 Drizzle each toast with the oil and top with anchovy fillets. Sprinkle with salt and ground black pepper and serve.

FETA SPREAD

Preparation time: 10 minutes
Total cooking time: Nil
Makes about 1 cup (250 ml/8 fl oz)

☆

175 g (6 oz) crumbled feta
100 g (3 1/2 oz) ricotta
3 tablespoons olive oil
15 g (1/2 oz) fresh mint, chopped
crusty bread, for serving.

1 Combine the feta, ricotta and olive oil in a bowl and mash with a fork until well combined. The mixture should still contain a few small lumps of cheese.
2 Add the mint and some cracked black pepper, to taste. Store in an airtight container in the refrigerator for up to 5 days. Toast the crusty bread and serve with the spread.
NOTE: These could be topped with slices of roasted tomato or pepper (capsicum).

GRILLED SARDINES WITH CUCUMBER

Preparation time: 20 minutes + marinating
Total cooking time: 10 minutes
Makes 30

★ ★

30 butterflied sardines, without heads
  (see Note)
2 tablespoons olive oil
2 tablespoons vegetable oil
2 tablespoons lemon juice
2 cloves garlic, sliced
1 tablespoon fresh oregano leaves
1 Lebanese cucumber
1/4 teaspoon sugar

1 Place half the sardines in a single layer in a non-metallic dish. Combine the olive and vegetable oils, lemon juice, garlic and oregano leaves and pour half over the sardines. Top with the remaining sardines and pour over the rest of the oil mixture. Cover with plastic wrap and marinate for 30 minutes in the refrigerator.
2 Meanwhile, using a wide vegetable peeler, peel strips lengthways off the cucumber, making four even sides and avoiding peeling off any cucumber with seeds. You should end up with about 15 slices of cucumber. Cut in half to make 30 strips the same length as the sardines.
3 Lay the cucumber strips flat around the sides and base of a colander and sprinkle with sugar and a little salt. Place over a bowl. Leave for 15 minutes to drain off any juices.
4 Preheat the grill. Wash the cucumber well and pat dry with paper towels. Place one strip of cucumber on the flesh side of each sardine and roll up like a pinwheel. Secure with toothpicks.
5 Place half the sardines under the grill and cook for 5 minutes, or until cooked through. Repeat with the remaining sardines. Serve warm, with tzatziki (see page 167) if desired.
NOTE: Butterflied sardines are sardines that have been gutted, deboned and opened out flat.
IN ADVANCE: The sardines can be rolled in the cucumber a day ahead. Keep covered in the refrigerator.

ABOVE: Grilled sardines with cucumber

CHICKEN ROLLS

Preparation time: 1 hour 15 minutes
Total cooking time: 1 hour 5 minutes
Makes about 40

✫ ✫

60 g (2 oz) butter

1 large onion, chopped

2 cloves garlic, crushed

2 tablespoons plain flour

1/2 cup (125 ml/4 fl oz) chicken stock

1/2 cup (125 ml/4 fl oz) milk

1 large barbecued chicken, skin removed and
   flesh shredded

1/4 cup (25 g/3/4 oz) grated Parmesan

2 teaspoons fresh thyme leaves

1/4 cup (25 g/3/4 oz) dry breadcrumbs

2 eggs, lightly beaten

13 sheets filo pastry, cut into thirds crossways

140 g (4 1/2 oz) butter, extra, melted

1 Melt the butter in a pan and add the onion.
Cook over low heat for 12 minutes, or until soft,
stirring occasionally. Increase the heat to
medium–high and add the garlic. Cook, stirring,
for 1 minute, then add the flour and cook for
1 minute. Remove from the heat and gradually
stir in the stock and milk. Return to the heat and
stir constantly until the sauce boils and thickens.
Boil for 1 minute, then remove from the heat
and add the chicken, Parmesan, thyme,
breadcrumbs, salt and pepper. Cool, then stir in
the eggs.

2 Preheat the oven to hot 220°C (425°F/Gas 7).
Lightly grease three baking trays.

3 Put one piece of filo pastry on the bench with
the short end closest to you (cover the remaining
pieces with a damp tea towel). Brush with the
extra melted butter and place a level tablespoon
of chicken mixture on the base end closest to
you. Fold in the sides, brush along the length
with butter and roll up tightly to form a roll
8 cm (3 inches) long. Put onto the baking tray
and brush the top with some of the butter.
Repeat with the remaining filo, butter and
chicken mixture.

4 Bake for 15 minutes in the top half of the
oven until well browned. Serve hot.

BELOW: Chicken rolls

STUFFED MUSSELS

Scrub the mussels with a stiff brush and pull off the hairy beard. Discard any open or broken mussels.

Spoon the mussel mixture into the shells, top with white sauce and smooth with a flat-bladed knife.

STUFFED MUSSELS

Preparation time: 40 minutes + cooling
Total cooking time: 16 minutes
Makes 18

★★

18 black mussels

2 teaspoons olive oil

2 spring onions, finely chopped

1 clove garlic, crushed

1 tablespoon tomato paste (tomato purée)

2 teaspoons lemon juice

3 tablespoons chopped fresh flat-leaf parsley

1/3 cup (35 g/1 1/4 oz) dry breadcrumbs

2 eggs, beaten

olive oil, for deep-frying

White sauce

40 g (1 1/4 oz) butter

1/4 cup (30 g/1 oz) plain flour

1/3 cup (80 ml/2 3/4 fl oz) milk

1 Scrub the mussels and remove their beards. Discard any open ones that do not close when given a sharp tap. Bring 1 cup (250 ml/8 fl oz) water to the boil in a medium saucepan, add the mussels, cover and cook for 5 minutes, shaking occasionally. Strain the liquid into a jug until you have 1/3 cup (80 ml/2 3/4 fl oz). Discard any unopened mussels. Remove the mussels from their shells and discard half the shells. Finely chop the mussels.

2 Heat the oil in a pan, add the spring onion and cook for 1 minute. Add the garlic and cook for 1 minute. Stir in the mussels, tomato paste, lemon juice and 2 tablespoons of parsley. Season with salt and pepper and set aside to cool.

3 To make the white sauce, melt the butter in a pan over low heat, add the flour and cook for 1 minute, or until pale and foaming. Remove from the heat and gradually stir in the reserved mussel liquid, the milk and some pepper. Return to the heat and stir constantly until the sauce boils and thickens and leaves the side of the pan. Transfer to a bowl to cool.

4 Spoon the mussel mixture into the shells. Top with the sauce and smooth so it is heaped.

5 Combine the crumbs and remaining parsley. Dip the mussels in the egg, then the crumbs, pressing on to cover the top.

6 Fill a deep heavy-based pan one third full of oil and heat to 180°C (350°F), or until a cube of bread dropped into the oil browns in 15 seconds. Cook the mussels in batches for 2 minutes, or until brown. Remove with a slotted spoon and drain on crumpled paper towels. Serve hot.

ABOVE: Stuffed mussels

STUFFED MUSHROOMS

Preparation time: 25 minutes + cooling
Total cooking time: 25 minutes
Makes about 30

★★

850 g (1 lb 12 oz) cap mushrooms
40 g (1 1/4 oz) butter
1 small onion, finely chopped
100 g (3 1/2 oz) pork mince
60 g (2 oz) chorizo sausage, finely chopped
1 tablespoon tomato paste (tomato purée)
2 tablespoons dry breadcrumbs
1 tablespoon chopped fresh flat-leaf parsley

1 Remove the stalks from the mushrooms, then finely chop the stalks. Set aside.
2 Melt the butter in a frying pan over low heat, add the onion and cook, stirring occasionally, for 5 minutes, or until soft. Increase the heat to high, add the pork mince, and cook for 1 minute, stirring constantly and breaking up any lumps. Add the mushroom stalks and chorizo and continue cooking for 1 minute, or until the mixture is dry and browned. Add the tomato paste and 1/2 cup (125 ml/4 fl oz) water. Bring to the boil, then reduce the heat to low and simmer for 5 minutes, or until thick. Stir in the breadcrumbs, then transfer to a bowl and cool.
3 Preheat the oven to hot 210°C (415°F/ Gas 6–7). Lightly grease a baking tray. Spoon about 1 1/2 teaspoons of the cooled meat into the mushroom caps, smoothing the top with a flat-bladed knife so that the filling is slightly domed. Place on the tray and bake in the top half of the oven for 10 minutes. Sprinkle with the parsley and serve hot.

RED PEPPER (CAPSICUM) AND WALNUT DIP

Quarter and seed 2 red peppers (capsicums). Grill skin-side-up until the skin is black and blistered. Cool in a plastic bag, then peel. Heat 1 tablespoon olive oil in a pan, add 1 chopped onion and 1 crushed clove garlic and cook until soft. Stir in 1/2 teaspoon dried chilli flakes. Process 1/2 cup (60 g/2 oz) walnuts until fine and add the peeled peppers, onion mixture, 3 tablespoons olive oil, 2 teaspoons red wine vinegar and 1/4 teaspoon salt. Process until fine and almost smooth. Can be made up to 5 days ahead and chilled in an airtight container. Makes 1 cup (250 ml/8 fl oz).

ABOVE: Stuffed mushrooms

CAULIFLOWER FRITTERS

Preparation time: 15 minutes + standing
Total cooking time: 15 minutes
Makes about 40 pieces

★ ★

600 g (1 1/4 lb) cauliflower
1/2 cup (55 g/2 oz) besan flour
2 teaspoons ground cumin
1 teaspoon ground coriander
1 teaspoon ground turmeric
pinch of cayenne pepper
1 egg, lightly beaten
1 egg yolk
oil, for deep-frying

1 Cut the cauliflower into bite-sized florets. Sift the flour and spices into a bowl, then stir in 1/2 teaspoon salt and make a well in the centre.
2 Combine 1/4 cup (60 ml/2 fl oz) water with the egg and egg yolk and gradually pour into the well, whisking to make a smooth lump-free batter. Cover and leave for 30 minutes.
3 Fill a deep heavy-based pan one third full of oil and heat to 180°C (350°F), or until a cube of bread dropped into the oil browns in 15 seconds. Holding the florets by the stem, dip into the batter, draining the excess back into the bowl. Deep-fry in batches for 3–4 minutes, or until puffed and brown. Drain, season and serve hot.

CHEESY ZUCCHINI FLOWERS

Preparation time: 1 hour 20 minutes + standing
Total cooking time: 10 minutes
Makes 24

★ ★

1 1/2 cups (185 g/6 oz) plain flour
7 g (1/4 oz) dry yeast or 15 g (1/2 oz)
   compressed fresh yeast
24 zucchini with flowers
50 g (1 3/4 oz) kefalotyri cheese or Parmesan
8 anchovy fillets in oil, drained
oil, for deep-frying

1 Sift the flour and 1 1/4 teaspoons salt into a bowl and make a well. Whisk the yeast and 1 1/4 cups (315 ml/10 fl oz) warm water in a bowl until dissolved and pour into the well. Gradually stir with the whisk to form a thick batter. Cover with plastic wrap and leave in a warm place for 1 hour, or until frothy. Do not stir.
2 Gently open the zucchini flowers and remove the centre stamens. Wash and drain. Cut the cheese into 1 cm (1/2 inch) cubes. Cut the anchovies into 1.5 cm (5/8 inch) pieces.
3 Put a cube of cheese and a piece of anchovy into the centre of each flower. Fold the petals around them. Fill a deep pan one third full of oil and heat to 180°C (350°F), or until a cube of bread dropped into the oil browns in 15 seconds. Dip the flowers into the batter, turning to coat and drain off the excess. Deep-fry in batches for 1–2 minutes, or until puffed and lightly brown. Drain on crumpled paper towel. Serve hot.

SPANISH TORTILLA

Preparation time: 20 minutes
Total cooking time: 30 minutes
Makes 16 wedges

★ ★

1/2 cup (125 ml/4 fl oz) olive oil
2 large potatoes (600 g/1 1/4 lb), peeled
   and cut into 5 mm (1/4 inch) slices
2 large onions, sliced
3 eggs
1/2 teaspoon salt
1/2 teaspoon pepper

1 Heat the oil in a 20 cm (8 inch) diameter, 5 cm (2 inch) deep non-stick frying pan. Place alternate layers of potato and onion in the pan, cover and cook for 8 minutes over low heat. Using tongs, turn the layers in sections (it doesn't matter if they break up). Cover and cook for 8 minutes, without allowing the potato to colour.
2 Place a strainer over a bowl and drain the potato mixture, reserving 1 tablespoon of the oil. (The rest can be used for cooking another time, it will have a delicately sweet onion flavour.)
3 Place the eggs, salt and pepper in a bowl and whisk to combine. Add the potato mixture, pressing down with the back of a spoon to completely cover with the egg.
4 Heat the reserved oil in the same frying pan over high heat. Pour in the egg mixture, pressing down to even it out. Reduce the heat to low, cover with a lid or foil and cook for 12 minutes, or until set. Gently shake the pan to ensure the tortilla is not sticking. Leave for 5 minutes, then invert onto a plate. Cut into wedges. Serve hot.

ANCHOVY FILLETS
The anchovy is a small saltwater fish which has been popular in Italy for centuries. Supplies from the waters of southern Europe have almost been depleted so now they often come from Africa and South America. There is also an Australian anchovy. Anchovies have a slightly oily flesh and a strong taste. If you find them too salty, they can be soaked in milk or water for about 20 minutes before use. They are commonly sold in jars and cans, preserved in and marinated in oil, or preserved in salt.

OPPOSITE PAGE:
Cauliflower fritters (top);
Cheesy zucchini flowers

STUFFED PEPPERS

Spoon filling onto the end of each pepper strip, then roll up and push a toothpick through.

Coat the peppers in flour, then dip in egg, drain off the excess and roll in the breadcrumbs to coat.

STUFFED PEPPERS (CAPSICUMS)

Preparation time: 40 minutes + cooling
Total cooking time: 25 minutes
Makes 20

★ ★

5 large red peppers (capsicums)
60 g (2 oz) butter
I small pickling onion, finely chopped
I clove garlic, crushed
¼ cup (30 g/I oz) plain flour
I cup (250 ml/8 fl oz) milk
3 x 100 g (3½ oz) cans tuna in oil, drained
I tablespoon chopped fresh flat-leaf parsley
⅔ cup (85 g/3 oz) plain flour, extra
2 eggs, lightly beaten
½ teaspoon paprika
⅔ cup (65 g/2¼ oz) dry breadcrumbs
olive oil, for deep-frying

I Preheat the grill. Cut the peppers into quarters. Cook, skin-side-up, under a hot grill until the skin is black and blistered. Place in a plastic bag and leave to cool, then peel away the skin.

2 Heat the butter in a pan over medium heat. Add the onion and cook, stirring occasionally, for 2 minutes, or until soft. Add the garlic and cook for 1 minute. Add the flour and cook, stirring, for 1 minute, or until bubbly and just beginning to change colour. Remove from the heat and gradually stir in the milk. Return to the heat and stir constantly until the mixture boils and thickens and leaves the side of the pan. Stir in the tuna, parsley and some salt. Transfer to a bowl to cool.

3 Spoon 1 tablespoon of the filling onto the base end of each pepper strip, roll up and secure the end with a toothpick. Place the extra flour in a shallow dish, the eggs in a shallow bowl and combine the paprika and breadcrumbs in another shallow dish.

4 Coat the peppers in the flour, then the eggs, allowing the excess to drip away, then toss in the crumbs.

5 Fill a deep, heavy-based pan a third full of oil and heat to 180°C (350°F). The oil is ready when a cube of bread dropped in the oil browns in 15 seconds. Cook in batches for 2 minutes, or until golden. Remove with a slotted spoon, drain on crumpled paper towels and remove the toothpicks. Serve warm or hot.

ABOVE: Stuffed peppers

TAHINI AND CHILLI PALMIERS

Preparation time: 25 minutes + chilling
Total cooking time: 20 minutes
Makes 32

☆☆

1/2 cup (135 g/4 1/2 oz) tahini
1 fresh red chilli, seeded and finely chopped
1/2 teaspoon paprika
2 sheets ready-rolled puff pastry, thawed

1 Preheat the oven to moderately hot 200°C (400°F/Gas 6).
2 Put the tahini, chilli and paprika in a bowl, season with some salt and stir to combine. Spread half the paste evenly over each pastry sheet, making sure the paste goes all the way to the edges.
3 Take one pastry sheet and fold from opposite sides until the folds meet in the middle. Then fold one side over the other to resemble a closed book. Repeat with the remaining pastry sheet and tahini mixture. Refrigerate the pastry at this stage for at least 30 minutes, to firm it up and make it easier to work with.
4 Cut the pastry into 1 cm (1/2 inch) slices. Cover two baking trays with baking paper and place the palmiers on them, making sure that the palmiers are not too close to one another as they will spread during cooking.
5 Bake the palmiers for 10–12 minutes on one side, then flip them over and bake for another 5–6 minutes, or until golden and cooked through. They are delicious served at room temperature or cold.
NOTE: To freeze the palmiers, place the sliced, uncooked palmiers on a tray and freeze until firm, then seal in plastic bags. Allow to thaw on trays and cook as above. Cooked palmiers can be stored in an airtight container for up to 1 week. If the palmiers soften, recrisp in a moderate oven for 3–5 minutes, then cool on a wire rack. Tahini is a paste made from crushed sesame seeds and is available from most supermarkets and health food stores.

TAHINI
This thick smooth paste, made from crushed sesame seeds, originated in the Middle East. Tahini is often used as an ingredient in hummus and other dips and sauces. It is also used in the making of confectionery such as halva, as well as in biscuits and cakes.

LEFT: Tahini and chilli palmiers

OLIVES
All these recipes will keep in the fridge for 3 months if stored in properly sterilized jars. Wash jars and lids thoroughly in boiling water, rinse in boiling water and dry in a slow 150°C (300°F/Gas 2) oven for 30 minutes.

OLIVES WITH HERBS DE PROVENCE

Rinse and drain 500 g (1 lb) Niçoise or Ligurian olives. Put 1 crushed clove garlic, 2 teaspoons chopped fresh basil, 1 teaspoon each chopped fresh thyme, rosemary, marjoram, oregano and mint, 1 teaspoon fennel seeds, 2 tablespoons lemon juice and 1/2 cup (125 ml/4 fl oz) olive oil in a bowl and mix together. Layer the olives and marinade in a wide-necked, 3-cup (750 ml/24 fl oz) sterilized jar, adding extra olive oil to cover the olives. Seal and marinate in the refrigerator for at least 1 week before using. Serve at room temperature.

HONEY CITRUS OLIVES

Mix together the rind of 1 lemon, lime and orange, 2 tablespoons lime juice, 4 tablespoons lemon juice, 1 tablespoon orange juice, 1 tablespoon honey, 2 teaspoons wholegrain mustard, 1/2 cup (125 ml/4 fl oz) extra virgin olive oil, 2 thinly sliced cloves garlic, 1/4 teaspoon dried oregano or 1 tablespoon chopped fresh oregano leaves and 6 thin slices of lemon and lime. Add 11/2 cups (265 g/81/2 oz) drained unpitted black olives, 11/2 cups (265 g/81/2 oz) drained unpitted green olives and 2 tablespoons chopped fresh parsley. Place in a wide-necked, 3-cup (750 ml/24 fl oz) sterilized jar, then seal and marinate in the refrigerator for at least 1 week before using. Serve at room temperature.

LEMON OLIVES WITH VERMOUTH

Combine 3 tablespoons dry vermouth, 1 tablespoon lemon juice, 2 teaspoons shredded lemon rind and 2 tablespoons extra virgin olive oil. Rinse 1 cup (170 g/5½ oz) of Spanish green or stuffed olives and pat dry. Add to the marinade and toss well. Cover and refrigerate overnight. Serve at room temperature.

DILL, GARLIC AND ORANGE OLIVES

Combine 500 g (1 lb) Kalamata olives with 3 tablespoons coarsely chopped fresh dill, 1 bruised clove garlic, 4 thin slices of orange cut into eighths and 2 torn bay leaves. Spoon into a 1-litre sterilized jar and pour in about 1¾ cups (440 ml/14 fl oz) olive oil or enough to cover the olives completely. Seal and marinate in the refrigerator for at least 2 days. Serve at room temperature.

CHILLI AND LEMON OLIVES

Combine 500 g (1 lb) cured black olives (olives with wrinkled skin) with 2 teaspoons finely grated lemon rind, 2 teaspoons chopped fresh oregano and 3 teaspoons dried chilli flakes. Transfer to a 3-cup (750 ml/24 fl oz) sterilized jar; cover with olive oil. Seal; chill for at least 2 days. Serve at room temperature.

SUN-DRIED TOMATO OLIVES

Rinse 500 g (1 lb) Spanish black olives; pat dry. Score or crack the olives. Layer in a 3-cup (750 ml/24 fl oz) sterilized jar, with 100 g (3½ oz) drained and chopped sun-dried tomatoes (reserve the oil), 2 crushed cloves garlic, 2 bay leaves, 3 teaspoons fresh thyme leaves and 2 teaspoons red wine vinegar. Pour over the reserved oil and 1 cup (250 ml/ 8 fl oz) extra virgin olive oil, or enough to cover. Seal and refrigerate overnight. Serve at room temperature.

MIXED OLIVE PICKLES

Combine 200 g (6½ oz) jumbo green olives, 4 gherkins, thickly sliced diagonally, 1 tablespoon capers, 2 brown pickling onions, quartered, 2 teaspoons mustard seeds and 1 tablespoon fresh dill sprigs in a bowl. Spoon into a 2-cup (500 ml/16 fl oz) sterilized jar and pour in ½ cup (125 ml/4 fl oz) tarragon vinegar. Top with about ½ cup (125 ml/4 fl oz) olive oil, or enough to cover completely. Seal and refrigerate for at least 2 days. Shake the jar occasionally. Serve at room temperature.

CLOKWISE, FROM TOP LEFT: Olives with herbs de provence; Honey citrus olives; Lemon olives with vermouth; Dill, garlic and orange olives; Chilli and lemon olives; Sun-dried tomato olives; Mixed olive pickles

PINE NUTS

The trees on which pine nuts grow do not yield a heavy crop until the trees are at least 70 years old. This is part of the reason they are expensive. The pine trees they come from are native to southern Europe, Mexico and some parts of the United States. Pine nuts are high in protein, iron, phosphorous and thiamin.

VEGETARIAN DOLMADES

Preparation time: 1 hour + cooling
Total cooking time: 1 hour 15 minutes
Makes about 50

★ ★ ★

1/2 cup (125 ml/4 fl oz) olive oil
6 spring onions, chopped
3/4 cup (150 g/5 oz) long-grain rice
1/4 cup (15 g/1/2 oz) chopped fresh mint
2 tablespoons chopped fresh dill
2/3 cup (170 ml/51/2 fl oz) lemon juice
1/4 cup (35 g/11/4 oz) currants
1/4 cup (40 g/11/4 oz) pine nuts
240 g (71/2 oz) packaged vine leaves (about 50)
2 tablespoons olive oil, extra

1 Heat the oil in a medium pan. Add the spring onion and cook over medium heat for 1 minute. Stir in the rice, mint, dill, half the lemon juice, and season, to taste. Add 1 cup (250 ml/8 fl oz) water and bring to the boil, then reduce the heat, cover and simmer for 20 minutes. Remove the lid, fork through the currants and pine nuts, cover with a paper towel, then the lid and leave to cool.

2 Rinse the vine leaves and gently separate. Drain, then dry on paper towels. Trim any thick stems with scissors. Line the base of a 20 cm (8 inch) pan with any torn or misshapen leaves. Choose the larger leaves for filling and use the smaller leaves to patch up any gaps.

3 Place a leaf shiny-side-down. Spoon a tablespoon of filling into the centre, bring in the sides and roll up tightly from the stem end. Place seam-side-down, with the stem end closest to you, in the base of the pan, arranging them close together in a single layer.

4 Pour in the rest of the lemon juice, the extra oil and about 3/4 cup (185 ml/6 fl oz) water to just cover the dolmades. Cover with an inverted plate and place a tin on the plate to firmly compress the dolmades and keep them in place while they are cooking. Cover with the lid.

5 Bring to the boil, then reduce the heat and simmer for 45 minutes. Cool in the pan. Serve at room temperature.

NOTE: Store, covered with the cooking liquid, in the refrigerator for up to 2 weeks.

ABOVE: Vegetarian dolmades

FELAFEL

Preparation time: 2 hours 15 minutes
  + overnight soaking
Total cooking time: 15 minutes
Makes about 16

★★

250 g (8 oz) dried chickpeas
4 spring onions, chopped
2 cloves garlic, crushed
1/2 cup (15 g/1/2 oz) chopped fresh flat-leaf parsley
1/4 cup (15 g/1/2 oz) chopped fresh mint
1/2 cup (25 g/3/4 oz) chopped fresh coriander
1/4 teaspoon cayenne pepper
2 teaspoons ground cumin
2 teaspoons ground coriander
1/2 teaspoon baking powder
oil, for deep-frying

1 Put the chickpeas in a large bowl, cover with plenty of cold water and soak overnight. Drain.
2 Combine the chickpeas, spring onion, garlic, parsley, mint, coriander, cayenne, cumin, ground coriander, baking powder and 1 teaspoon salt. Process batches in a processor for 30–40 seconds, or until finely chopped and the mixture holds together. Refrigerate, uncovered, for 2 hours.
3 Press 2 tablespoons of mixture together in the palm of your hand and form into a patty. Fill a deep heavy-based pan one third full of oil and heat to 180°C (350°F), or until a cube of bread dropped into the oil browns in 15 seconds. Deep-fry the felafel in batches for 3–4 minutes, or until well browned. Drain on crumpled paper towels and serve hot with hummus.

LABNEH

Preparation time: 20 minutes + 4 days chilling
Total cooking time: Nil
Makes 12

★★

2 cups (500 g/1 lb) thick Greek-style natural
  yoghurt
2 teaspoons sea salt
1 tablespoon dried oregano
2 teaspoons dried thyme leaves
11/3 cups (350 ml/11 fl oz) olive oil
1 bay leaf

1 Fold a 60 x 30 cm (24 x 12 inch) piece of muslin in half to make a 30 cm (12 inch) square.
2 Combine the yoghurt, salt and 1 teaspoon black pepper in a bowl. Line a bowl with the muslin and spoon the mixture into the centre. Bring the corners together and, using a piece of kitchen string, tie as closely as possible to the yoghurt, leaving a loop at the end. Thread the loop through the handle of a wooden spoon and hang over a bowl to drain in the fridge for 3 days.
3 Combine the oregano and thyme in a shallow bowl. Pour half the oil into a 2-cup (500 ml/16 fl oz) jar and add the bay leaf.
4 Roll level tablespoons of the yoghurt into balls. Toss in the combined herbs and place into the jar of oil. Pour in the remaining oil to cover the balls completely, seal and refrigerate for at least 1 day. Serve at room temperature, with chunky bread.

ABOVE: Felafel (top); Labneh

HUMMUS

Hummus means chickpeas in Arabic. You will see it spelt in many ways including homos, houmus, houmous and humus. The well-known recipe from Syria, *Hummus-bi-tahina*, has the addition of tahini. To make this classic dish, add 2 tablespoons of tahini to the recipe on this page. Add to the cooked chickpeas just before processing. Tahini, a paste made from crushed sesame seeds, is available at most supermarkets,

ABOVE: Fried chickpeas

FRIED CHICKPEAS

Preparation time: 30 minutes +overnight soaking
Total cooking time: 15 minutes
Makes about 2¹/₂ cups (600 g/20 oz)

✴ ✴

300 g (10 oz) dried chickpeas
oil, for deep-frying
¹/₂ teaspoon mild or hot paprika, to taste
¹/₄ teaspoon cayenne pepper

1 Put the chickpeas in a large bowl, cover with plenty of cold water and soak overnight. Drain well and pat dry with paper towels.
2 Fill a deep heavy-based pan one third full of oil and heat to 180°C (350°F), or until a cube of bread dropped into the oil browns in 15 seconds. Deep-fry half the chickpeas for 3 minutes. Remove with a slotted spoon. Drain on crumpled paper towel and repeat with the rest of the chickpeas. Partially cover the pan as some beans may pop. Don't leave the oil unattended.
3 Reheat the oil and fry the chickpeas again in batches for 3 minutes each batch, or until browned. Drain. Season the paprika with salt and cayenne pepper, and sprinkle over the hot chickpeas. Cool.

HUMMUS

Preparation time: 30 minutes + overnight soaking
Total cooking time: 1 hour
Makes about 2 cups (500 g/16 oz)

✴ ✴

125 g (4 oz) dried chickpeas
1 tablespoon olive oil
1 small finely chopped onion
1¹/₂ teaspoons ground cumin
pinch of cayenne pepper
2 tablespoons lemon juice
¹/₂ cup (125 ml/4 fl oz) olive oil, extra
3 cloves garlic, crushed

1 Put the chickpeas in a large bowl, cover with plenty of cold water and soak overnight. Rinse well and transfer to a pan of boiling water. Cook, covered, over medium heat for 1 hour, or until tender. Drain and return to the pan. Add the tablespoon of olive oil, onion, cumin and cayenne pepper to the pan and cook over high heat for 1 minute. Transfer to a food processor, add the lemon juice, extra olive oil and garlic, season with salt and process until smooth. Add water if you prefer a thinner consistency.

MEAT PATTIES WITH HALOUMI FILLING

Preparation time: 25 minutes + chilling
Total cooking time: 10 minutes
Makes 24

★★

8 slices (125 g/4 oz) white bread, crusts
   removed
700 g (23 oz) lamb or beef mince
1 tablespoon chopped fresh flat-leaf parsley
3 tablespoons chopped fresh mint leaves
1 onion, grated
2 eggs, lightly beaten
140 g (4^1/2 oz) haloumi cheese (see Note)
^{1}/3 cup (40 g/1 ^{1}/4 oz) plain flour
olive oil, for shallow-frying

1 Put the bread in a bowl, cover with water and then squeeze out as much water as possible. Place the bread in a bowl with the mince, parsley, mint, onion, egg, pepper and ^{1}/2 teaspoon salt. Knead the mixture by hand for 2–3 minutes, breaking up the mince and any large pieces of bread with your fingers. The mixture should be smooth and leave the side of the bowl. Cover and refrigerate for 30 minutes.
2 Cut the haloumi into 24 rectangles, 3 x 1 x 1 cm (1^1/4 x ^{1}/2 x ^{1}/2 inch). Place the flour in a shallow dish. Divide the mince mixture into level tablespoon portions. Roll a portion into a long shape and flatten in the palm of your hand. Place the cheese in the centre and top with another portion of mince. Pinch the edges together and roll into a torpedo 6 cm (2^1/2 inches) long. Repeat with the remaining mince.
3 Heat 2 cm (^{3}/4 inch) oil in a deep heavy-based frying pan to 180°C (350°F), or until a cube of bread dropped into the oil browns in 15 seconds. Toss the patties in flour, shake off the excess and fry in batches for 3–5 minutes, or until brown and cooked through. Drain on crumpled paper towels. Serve hot.
NOTE: Haloumi is a creamy white sheep's milk cheese kept in brine. It can be bought from delicatessens and supermarkets.

BELOW: Meat patties with haloumi filling

FRIED WHITEBAIT

Preparation time: 10 minutes + chilling
Total cooking time: 10 minutes
Serves 6-8

★★

500 g (1 lb) whitebait
2 teaspoons sea salt
1/3 cup (40 g/1 1/4 oz) plain flour
1/4 cup (30 g/1 oz) cornflour
2 teaspoons finely chopped fresh
   flat-leaf parsley
olive oil, for deep-frying
1 lemon, cut into wedges, for serving

1 Combine the whitebait and sea salt in a bowl and mix well. Cover and refrigerate.
2 Combine the sifted flours and chopped parsley in a bowl and season well with cracked pepper. Fill a deep heavy-based pan one third full of oil and heat to 180°C (350°F), or until a cube of bread browns in 15 seconds. Toss a third of the whitebait in the flour mixture, shake off the excess and deep-fry for 1 1/2 minutes, or until pale and crisp. Remove with a slotted spoon and drain well on crumpled paper towels. Repeat with the remaining whitebait, cooking in two batches.
3 Reheat the oil and fry the whitebait a second time in three batches for 1 minute each, or until lightly browned. Drain on crumpled paper towels and serve hot with lemon wedges.

ABOVE: Fried whitebait

TARAMASALATA

Remove the crusts from 4 slices of white bread. Put the bread in a bowl, cover with water, drain and squeeze out as much water as possible. Place in a bowl. Finely grate a small onion into the bowl and add 100 g (3 1/2 oz) tarama (cod roe), 2 tablespoons freshly squeezed lemon juice, 3 tablespoons olive oil and a pinch of black pepper. Mix with a fork until well combined. Alternatively, process the ingredients until smooth. Taramasalata can be made up to 3 days ahead and stored in an airtight container in the refrigerator. Makes about 1 cup (250 ml/8 fl oz).

BACALAO CROQUETTES WITH SKORDALIA

Preparation time: 50 minutes + 8 hours soaking
Total cooking time: 55 minutes
Makes 24

★★

400 g (13 oz) dried salt cod or bacalao
  (see Note)
300 g (10 oz) floury potatoes, unpeeled
1 small brown pickling onion, grated
2 tablespoons chopped fresh flat-leaf parsley
1 egg, lightly beaten
oil, for deep-frying

Skordalia

250 g (8 oz) floury potatoes, unpeeled
2 cloves garlic, crushed
1 tablespoon white wine vinegar
2 tablespoons olive oil

1 Remove the excess salt from the cod by placing in a large bowl, covering with cold water and leaving to soak for 8–12 hours, changing the water three times. Drain on crumpled paper towels.
2 To make the skordalia, boil or steam the 250 g potatoes until tender, peel and mash. Cool and add the garlic, vinegar and oil. Season with salt and cracked black pepper, mix well and set aside.
3 Put the cod in a pan, cover with water, bring to the boil, then reduce the heat and simmer for 15 minutes. Drain well and dry on paper towels. When cool enough to handle, remove the skin and bones from the cod and flake with your fingers into a bowl. Meanwhile, boil or steam the potatoes until tender, peel and mash well.
4 Add the mashed potato to the cod with the onion, parsley, egg and 1/2 teaspoon cracked pepper. Mix well with a wooden spoon to form a thick mixture. Taste before seasoning with salt.
5 Fill a deep heavy-based pan one third full of oil and heat to 180°C (350°F), or until a cube of bread dropped into the oil browns in 15 seconds. Drop level tablespoons of the mixture into the oil and cook in batches for 2–3 minutes, or until well browned. Drain on crumpled paper towel. Serve hot with skordalia.
NOTE: Dried bacalao or salted cod is available at delicatessens or fish markets. The skordalia can be made up to 4 days ahead and kept covered in the refrigerator until needed.

POTATOES

The texture, whether waxy or floury when cooked, is the main concern when selecting the type of potato for a recipe. Waxy potatoes, such as Desiree and Bintji, have a high moisture content and are low in starch. Most have a creamy, dense flesh and are suitable for salads and gratins as they hold together. They are not suitable for chips. Floury potatoes, such as the Russet and King Edward, have a lower moisture content and are higher in starch, with coarser flesh. This makes them good for mashing, baking and chip-making. There are more varieties of potato being sold, some of them good all-rounders.

LEFT: Bacalao croquettes with skordalia

1 Lightly oil a 3 cm (1¼ inch) deep baking tin with a base measuring 26 x 17 cm (10½ x 6½ inches).

2 Sift the flour and ½ teaspoon salt into a bowl. Rub the butter into the flour until it resembles fine breadcrumbs. Pour in the oil and rub it in by lifting the flour mixture onto one hand and lightly rubbing the other hand over the top. The mixture should clump together. Make a well in the centre and, while mixing by hand, add enough water to form a firm supple dough. Knead gently to bring the dough together—it may not be completely smooth. Cover with plastic wrap and chill for 1 hour.

3 Trim away the bottom quarter from the spinach stalks. Wash and shred the remaining leaves and stalks. Pile the spinach onto a clean tea towel, twist as tightly as possible and squeeze out as much moisture as possible. Put into a bowl with the leek, nutmeg, dill, feta, breadcrumbs and ½ teaspoon cracked black pepper.

4 Preheat the oven to hot 220°C (425°F/Gas 7). Roll out just over half the dough on a lightly floured surface until large enough to line the base and sides of the tin. Lift the dough into the tin, pressing evenly over the base and sides.

5 Add the eggs and oil to the spinach mixture. Mix with your hand, but do not overmix or the mixture will become too wet. Spoon into the pastry-lined tin.

6 Roll out the remaining pastry on a lightly floured surface until large enough to cover the tin. Lift onto the tin and press the two pastry edges firmly together to seal. Trim the excess pastry with a sharp knife from the outer edge of the tin, then brush the top with a little extra olive oil. Using a sharp knife, mark into three strips lengthways and then diagonally into diamonds. Make two or three small slits through the top layer of pastry to allow the steam to escape during cooking.

7 Bake the pie on the centre shelf for 45–50 minutes, or until well browned. Cover with foil if the pastry is overbrowning. The pie is cooked if it slides when you gently shake the tin. Turn out onto a wire rack to cool for 10 minutes, then transfer to a cutting board or back into the tin to cut into diamonds. Serve warm or cold.

SPINACH PIE DIAMONDS

Preparation time: 50 minutes + chilling
Total cooking time: 50 minutes
Makes about 15

★ ★

2 cups (250 g/4 oz) plain flour
30 g butter, chopped
¼ cup (60 ml/2 fl oz) olive oil
½ cup (125 ml/4 fl oz) warm water

Filling

420 g (14 oz) English spinach
1 leek, white part only, halved lengthways and thinly sliced
¼ teaspoon ground nutmeg
2 teaspoons chopped fresh dill
200 g (6½ oz) feta, crumbled
1 tablespoon dry breadcrumbs
3 eggs, lightly beaten
2 tablespoons olive oil

*ABOVE: Spinach
pie diamonds*

KIBBEH

Preparation time: 45 minutes + cooling + chilling
Total cooking time: 25 minutes
Makes 15

★ ★ ★

1 1/3 cups (235 g/7 1/2 oz) fine burghul wheat
150 g (5 oz) lean lamb, chopped
1 onion, grated
2 tablespoons plain flour
1 teaspoon ground allspice

Filling

2 teaspoons olive oil
1 small onion, finely chopped
100 g (3 1/2 oz) lean lamb mince
1/2 teaspoon ground allspice
1/2 teaspoon ground cinnamon
1/3 cup (80 ml/2 3/4 fl oz) beef stock
2 tablespoons pine nuts
2 tablespoons chopped fresh mint

1 Put the burghul wheat in a large bowl, cover with boiling water and leave for 5 minutes. Drain in a colander, pressing well to remove the water. Spread on paper towels to absorb the remaining moisture.

2 Process the wheat, lamb, onion, flour, and allspice until a fine paste forms. Season well, then refrigerate for 1 hour.

3 For the filling, heat the oil in a frying pan, add the onion and cook over low heat for 3 minutes, or until soft. Add the mince, allspice and cinnamon, and stir over high heat, for 3 minutes. Add the stock and cook, partially covered, over low heat for 6 minutes, or until the mince is soft. Roughly chop the pine nuts and stir in with the mint. Season well with salt and cracked pepper, then transfer to a bowl and allow to cool.

4 Shape 2 tablespoons of the wheat mixture into a sausage shape 6 cm (2 1/2 inches) long. Dip your hands in cold water, and with your finger, make a long hole through the centre and gently work your finger around to make a shell. Fill with 2 teaspoons of the filling and seal, moulding it into a torpedo shape. Smooth over any cracks with your fingers. Place on a foil-lined tray and refrigerate, uncovered, for 1 hour.

5 Fill a deep heavy-based pan one third full of oil and heat the oil to 180° (350°F), or until a cube of bread dropped into the oil browns in 15 seconds. Deep-fry the kibbeh in batches for 2–3 minutes, or until well browned. Drain on crumpled paper towels. Serve hot.

ONIONS

A member of the lily family, onions are one of the staples in the pantry. The colour, shape and intensity of flavour varies greatly. Raw onions have a strong flavour which is mellowed when cooked. Many savoury recipes, including soups, sauces, tarts, casseroles and curries, call for an onion or two to enhance their flavour. They are also used raw in salads and are fried, baked or boiled as a vegetable in their own right. Although, there are many varieties, most people choose by the colour, the brown being the most commonly used, followed by white, yellow and red.

LEFT: Kibbeh

1 Mix the yeast, sugar, 2 tablespoons of the plain flour and 1/4 cup (60 ml/2 fl oz) warm water in a bowl. Cover with plastic wrap and leave in a warm place for 10 minutes, or until frothy.

2 Sift the remaining flours and cinnamon into a large bowl, return the husks to the bowl and stir through the sesame seeds and 1/2 teaspoon salt. Pour in the oil and rub it in by lifting the flour mixture onto one hand and lightly rubbing the other hand over the top. Make a well in the centre and add the yeast mixture and about 1/4 cup (60 ml/2 fl oz) warm water, or enough to mix to a soft but not sticky dough. Knead on a floured surface for about 2 minutes, or until smooth and elastic. Place in a lightly oiled bowl, turning the dough to coat in the oil. Cover loosely with plastic wrap and leave in a warm place for 45–60 minutes, or until doubled in bulk.

3 Preheat the oven to moderately hot 200°C (400°F/Gas 6). Lightly grease a baking tray. Punch down the dough to expel the air, divide it into three portions and roll each on a lightly floured surface into a long sausage shape about 30 cm (12 inches) long. Place the first roll on the baking tray. Cut through almost to the base of the roll at 2 cm (3/4 inch) intervals with a serrated knife (about 15 portions). Repeat with the remaining rolls.

4 Cover with a tea towel and leave in a warm place for 30 minutes, or until well risen. Bake for 30 minutes, or until browned underneath and the rolls sound hollow when tapped. Reduce the oven temperature to very slow 120°C (250°F/Gas 1/2). Cool the rolls on the tray for 5 minutes. Transfer each roll to a cutting board and cut through the markings. Place cut-side-up on two baking trays. Bake for 30 minutes, or until the tops feel dry. Turn each biscuit and bake for another 30 minutes, or until completely dry and crisp. Cool. Store in an airtight container for up to 3 weeks.

5 Dunk each biscuit quickly into cold water and place on a tray. Top with the combined tomato and feta. Drizzle with the combined oil and vinegar and sprinkle with oregano. Season.
NOTE: To make another delicious topping, combine 1 sliced roasted pepper (capsicum), 10 pitted and quartered Kalamata olives and 2 tablespoons chopped flat-leaf parsley. Season. Combine 3 tablespoons of extra virgin olive oil and 1 tablespoon of red wine vinegar and drizzle over the top.

OLIVE OIL BISCUITS

Preparation time: 30 minutes + standing
Total cooking time: 1 hour 30 minutes
Makes about 45

★★★

7 g (1/4 oz) dried yeast or 15 g (1/2 oz) fresh
1 teaspoon sugar
1 1/2 cups (185 g/6 oz) plain flour
1 1/2 cups (225 g/7 oz) plain wholemeal flour
1 teaspoon ground cinnamon
1 1/2 tablespoons sesame seeds, toasted
1/2 cup (125 ml/4 fl oz) olive oil

Topping
4 ripe tomatoes, diced
160 g (5 1/2 oz) feta, crumbled
1/3 cup (80 ml/2 3/4 fl oz) extra virgin olive oil
2 tablespoons red wine vinegar
1 teaspoon dried oregano

ABOVE: Olive oil biscuits

CALAMARI ROMANA

Preparation time: 10 minutes + chilling
Total cooking time: 10 minutes
Makes about 30

⭐⭐

350 g (11 oz) cleaned small squid hoods
1/2 teaspoon salt
1/3 cup (40 g/1 1/4 oz) plain flour
1/4 teaspoon black pepper
oil, for deep-frying
lemon wedges, for serving

1 Cut the squid into 1 cm (1/2 inch) wide rings. Combine the squid rings with the salt, cover and refrigerate for about 30 minutes, then dry on crumpled paper towels.
2 Combine the flour and pepper in a bowl. Fill a deep, heavy-based pan a third full of oil and heat to 180°C (350°F). The oil is ready when a cube of bread dropped in the oil browns in 15 seconds. Flour a few squid rings and cook, turning with a long-handled spoon, for 3 minutes, or until lightly browned and crisp. Flour the remaining batches just before frying. Drain on crumpled paper towels and serve hot with the lemon wedges.

ZUCCHINI PATTIES

Preparation time: 20 minutes
Total cooking time: 15 minutes
Makes about 25

⭐⭐

2 medium zucchini, grated
1 small onion, grated
1/4 cup (30 g/1 oz) self-raising flour
1/3 cup (35 g/1 1/4 oz) grated kefalotyri cheese
  or Parmesan
1 tablespoon chopped fresh mint
2 teaspoons chopped fresh parsley
pinch of ground nutmeg
1/4 cup (25 g/3/4 oz) dry breadcrumbs
1 egg
olive oil, for shallow-frying

1 Put the zucchini and onion into the centre of a clean tea towel, twist as tightly as possible and squeeze dry. Combine the zucchini, onion, flour, cheese, mint, parsley, nutmeg, breadcrumbs and egg in a large bowl. Season well with salt and cracked black pepper, and mix with your hands to a stiff mixture that clumps together.
2 Heat the shallow-frying oil in a large pan over medium heat. Drop level tablespoons of the mixture into the pan and shallow-fry for 2–3 minutes, or until well browned all over, turning once. Drain well on paper towels and serve hot. The patties can be served plain sprinkled with salt or are delicious served with tzatziki (see page 167).
NOTE: Kefalotyri is a pale hard sheep's milk cheese originating in Greece. In this recipe, Parmesan or pecorino cheeses can be substituted.
IN ADVANCE: This recipe is best prepared close to cooking. Cooked patties can be reheated on a baking tray covered with baking paper. Heat in a moderate 180°C (350°F/Gas 4) oven for 3–5 minutes, or until warmed through.

ABOVE: Calamari Romana

FETA

Feta is a semi-hard cheese with a crumbly texture. It is not matured but preserved in a liquid made up of its whey and brine. It originated in Greece where it was made from the milk from goats or ewes and is an essential ingredient in the Greek salad, as well as being used in pies, tarts and in fillings for stuffed vegetables.

MEATBALLS

Preparation time: 25 minutes + chilling
Total cooking time: 20 minutes
Makes about 28

★ ★

4 slices white bread, crusts removed
150 g (5 oz) pork mince
150 g (5 oz) veal mince
1 tablespoon chopped fresh flat-leaf parsley
1 tablespoon chopped fresh mint
1 onion, grated
1/2 teaspoon ground cumin
1 egg
1/4 cup (25 g/3/4 oz) grated kefalotyri cheese or Parmesan
1/2 cup (60 g/2 oz) plain flour
olive oil, for shallow-frying

1 Cover the bread with water in a bowl, then squeeze out as much water as possible. Place in a large bowl with the mince, parsley, mint, onion, cumin, egg and cheese. Season. Knead the mixture by hand for 2–3 minutes until smooth. Cover and refrigerate for 30 minutes.
2 Put the flour in a shallow dish. With wet hands, roll level tablespoons of the meatball mixture into balls. Heat the oil over medium heat. Toss the meatballs in the flour. Shallow-fry in batches for 3–5 minutes, or until the meatballs are browned and cooked through. Drain on crumpled paper towels. Serve hot.

CHEESE PASTRIES

Preparation time: 40 minutes
Total cooking time: 20 minutes
Makes 16

★

160 g (5 1/2 oz) feta, grated
60 g (2 oz) ricotta
2 tablespoons chopped fresh mint
1 egg, lightly beaten
2 spring onions, finely chopped
2 tablespoons dry breadcrumbs
4 sheets ready-rolled puff pastry
1 egg, extra, lightly beaten
1 tablespoon sesame seeds

1 Preheat the oven to hot 220°C (425°F/ Gas 7). Lightly grease two baking trays.
2 Put the feta, ricotta, mint, egg, spring onion, breadcrumbs and 1/2 teaspoon cracked black

ABOVE: Meatballs

Use poultry shears to cut down the side of the backbones of the quails.

Place the quails on the work surface and gently press down to flatten them.

Cut the quails in half through the breasts, then cut that half in half again.

pepper in a bowl and mix with a fork to combine and break up the ricotta.

3 Using a pastry cutter or saucer, cut 10 cm (4 inch) rounds from the pastry sheets. Spoon level tablespoons of the cheese mixture into the centre of each round and lightly brush the edges with water. Fold over to enclose the filling, expelling any air, and firmly seal with the prongs of a fork to form a crescent shape. Brush with the extra egg and sprinkle with sesame seeds.

4 Put the crescents on the baking trays and bake for 15–20 minutes, or until well browned and puffed. Serve hot.

BARBECUED QUAIL

Preparation time: 40 minutes + chilling
Total cooking time: 10 minutes
Makes 24

★★★

6 quails
1 cup (250 ml/8 fl oz) dry red wine
2 sticks celery, including tops, chopped
1 carrot, chopped
1 small onion, chopped
1 bay leaf, torn into small pieces
1 teaspoon allspice
1 teaspoon dried thyme leaves
2 cloves garlic, crushed
2 tablespoons olive oil
2 tablespoons lemon juice
lemon wedges, for serving

1 To prepare the quails, use poultry shears to cut down either side of the backbone, then discard the backbone. Remove the innards and neck, wash the insides and pat dry with paper towels. Place breast-side-up on the bench, open out flat and gently press to flatten. Using poultry shears, cut in half through the breast then cut each half in half again into the thigh and drumstick piece and breast and wing piece.

2 In a non-metallic bowl, combine the wine, celery, carrot, onion, bay leaf and allspice. Add the quail and stir to coat. Cover and refrigerate for 3 hours, or preferably overnight, stirring occasionally. Drain and sprinkle with thyme, salt and pepper.

3 Whisk the garlic, oil and lemon juice in a small bowl.

4 Heat a lightly oiled barbecue plate until hot or heat a grill to its highest setting. Reduce the heat to medium and cook the quail breast pieces for 4–5 minutes on each side and the drumstick pieces for 3 minutes each side, or until tender and cooked through. Brush frequently with the lemon mixture. Serve hot with lemon wedges.

ABOVE: Barbecued quail

OREGANO

This herb grows along the ground on long stems. It has a small, strong-flavoured leaf which is very popular in Greek and Italian cookery. It blends well with tomatoes, eggplant and other vegetables, beef, lamb, fish, and is, of course, used in many sauces and on pizzas. Oregano is easy to grow in your own garden. Dried oregano has a full flavour if fresh is not available.

ABOVE: Pan-fried cheese slices

PAN-FRIED CHEESE SLICES

Preparation time: 10 minutes
Total cooking time: 5 minutes
Makes about 12

⭐

250 g (8 oz) kefalograviera (see Note)
2 tablespoons plain flour
1/4 cup (60 ml/2 fl oz) olive oil
1/2 teaspoon dried oregano
1/2 lemon, cut into wedges, for serving

1 Cut the cheese into 1 cm (1/2 inch) slices. The pieces can be as large as you wish, as they can be cut smaller for serving.
2 Put the flour in a shallow dish and season well with cracked pepper. Toss the cheese in the flour. Heat the oil over high heat in a frying pan until hot. Add the cheese to the pan and cook for 1 minute, or until browned and crusty underneath. Carefully turn the cheese to brown the other side. Lift onto a serving plate and sprinkle with oregano. Serve hot with lemon wedges and fresh bread.
NOTE: Kefalograviera and kefalotyri are pale hard sheep's milk cheeses originating in Greece.

TOMATO AND EGGPLANT (AUBERGINE) BOREK

Preparation time: 50 minutes + chilling
Total cooking time: 1 hour
Makes 30

⭐⭐

75 g (2 1/2 oz) butter, melted
1/3 cup (80 ml/2 3/4 fl oz) olive oil
1 1/2 cups (185 g/6 oz) plain flour

Filling
250 g (8 oz) tomatoes
2 teaspoons olive oil
1 small onion, chopped
1/2 teaspoon ground cumin
300 g (10 oz) eggplant (aubergine), cut into 2 cm (3/4 inch) cubes
2 teaspoons tomato paste (tomato purée)
1 tablespoon chopped fresh coriander
1 egg, lightly beaten

1 Put the butter, oil and 1/3 cup (80 ml/2 3/4 fl oz) water into a bowl. Season well with salt. Gradually add the flour in batches, mixing with a wooden spoon to form an oily, lumpy dough that leaves the side of the bowl. Knead gently to bring the dough together, cover with plastic wrap and refrigerate for 1 hour.

2 Core the tomatoes and cut a small cross at the base. Plunge into a pan of boiling water and leave for 1 minute. Drain, plunge into cold water, then remove the peel. Halve the tomatoes, squeeze over a bowl to remove the seeds, and finely chop the flesh.

3 Heat the oil in a frying pan, add the onion and cook, stirring, over low heat for 2–3 minutes, or until soft. Add the cumin, cook for 1 minute, then add the eggplant and cook, stirring, for 8–10 minutes, or until the eggplant begins to soften. Stir in the tomato and tomato paste. Cook over medium heat for 15 minutes, or until the mixture becomes dry. Stir occasionally. Season and stir in the coriander. Cool.

4 Preheat the oven to moderate 180°C (350°F/Gas 4). Lightly grease two baking trays.

5 Roll out half the pastry on a lightly floured surface to 2 mm (⅛ inch) thick. Using an 8 cm (3 inch) cutter, cut rounds from the pastry. Spoon 2 level teaspoons of the mixture into the centre of each round, lightly brush the edges with water and fold over the filling, expelling any air. Press firmly and crimp the edge with a fork to seal. Place on the trays and brush with the beaten egg. Bake in the top half of the oven for 25 minutes, or until golden brown and crisp.

HAM AND OLIVE EMPANADILLAS

Preparation time: 45 minutes + cooling
Total cooking time: 25 minutes
Makes about 15

✫

2 hard-boiled eggs, roughly chopped
40 g (1¼ oz) stuffed green olives, chopped
95 g (3 oz) ham, finely chopped
30 g (1 oz) Cheddar, grated
3 sheets ready-rolled puff pastry
1 egg yolk, lightly beaten

1 Preheat the oven to hot 220°C (425°F/Gas 7). Lightly grease two baking trays. Combine the eggs with the olives, ham and Cheddar in a bowl.
2 Cut the puff pastry sheets into 10 cm (4 inch) rounds (about five rounds from each sheet.) Spoon a tablespoon of the mixture into the centre of each round, fold over the pastry to enclose the filling and crimp the edges to seal.
3 Place the pastries on the trays 2 cm (¾ inch) apart. Brush with egg yolk and bake for 15 minutes, or until brown and puffed. Swap the trays around after 10 minutes. Cover loosely with foil if browning too much. Serve hot.

EGGPLANT (AUBERGINE)
Eggplants are common in the Mediterranean region and are used in many recipes. The skin varies from dark purple (almost black) to paler and even to white. Inside, the flesh is creamy-white, sometimes tending to pale green. Eggplants come in many shapes, from long and thin, to fat and round, and some the size of grapes. When you buy them, they should be quite firm. The larger eggplants can taste slightly bitter so, to draw out the bitter juices before cooking, cut or slice as required for the recipe, sprinkle generously with salt, then leave for about half an hour before rinsing, drying and cooking. The slender eggplants do not require salting.

LEFT: Ham and olive empanadillas

193

TEX-MEX

The border between Mexico and Texas may separate two very different countries but where food is concerned the line blurs. Tex-Mex cooking is as bright and colourful as sunny Texas and Mexico where it originated. While an antipasto platter or a tray of canapés might signify a certain type of calm and sophisticated gathering, an array of fiery Tex-Mex food seems to call out 'party'. It begs loud conversation, colourful characters and jugs of cold Margaritas—although you might want to persuade your guests to leave their sombreros at home. So, if you want your party to go with a sizzle, bring out the jalapenos. Olé.

SAVOURY POTATO EMPANADAS

Preparation time: 1 hour
Total cooking time: 40 minutes
Makes 32

☆ ☆

3 tablespoons olive oil
1 small onion, finely diced
2 spring onions, thinly sliced
1 clove garlic, crushed
100 g (3¹/₂ oz) beef mince
1 teaspoon ground cumin
1 teaspoon dried oregano
125 g (4 oz) potatoes, cubed
4 sheets ready-rolled puff pastry
50 g (1³/₄ oz) black olives, pitted and quartered
1 hard-boiled egg, finely chopped
1 egg, separated
pinch of paprika
pinch of sugar

1 In a heavy-based frying pan, heat 1 tablespoon of the oil, add the onion and spring onion and stir for 5 minutes. Stir in the garlic and cook for 3 minutes. Remove from the pan and set aside.

2 Heat another tablespoon of oil in the pan, add the beef mince and stir over medium heat until browned, breaking up any lumps with a fork. Add the onion mixture and stir well.
3 Add the cumin, oregano, and ¹/₂ teaspoon each of salt and pepper, and stir for another 2 minutes. Transfer to a bowl and cool. Wipe out the pan.
4 Heat another tablespoon of oil in the pan, add the potato and stir over high heat for 1 minute. Reduce the heat to low and stir for 5 minutes, or until tender. Cool slightly and then gently mix into the beef mixture.
5 Preheat the oven to moderately hot 200°C (400°F/Gas 6). Cut rounds from the pastry with an 8 cm (3 inch) cutter. Grease two baking trays.
6 Spoon heaped teaspoons of the beef mixture onto one side of each pastry round (leaving a border wide enough for the pastry to be folded over). Place a few olive quarters and some chopped egg on top of the beef mixture. Brush the border with egg white. Carefully fold the pastry over to make a half moon shape, pressing firmly to seal. Press the edges with a floured fork, to decorate, and then gently transfer to the baking trays. Stir the egg yolk, paprika and sugar together and brush over the empanadas. Bake for 15 minutes, or until golden brown and puffed.
IN ADVANCE: The puffs can be made 2 days ahead or frozen for 2 months.

EMPANADAS
These pies vary in the way they are made. Sometimes they are sold in wedges cut from large flat pies, but they are also often made as small turnovers. The fillings range from savoury to sweet, or a mixture of both. Empanadas are shallow-fried or baked.

ABOVE: Savoury potato empanadas

SPICY TORTILLA TRIANGLES

Preparation time: 20 minutes
Total cooking time: 5 minutes
Makes 24

✮ ✮

2 x 23 cm (9 inch) round flour tortillas
¼ cup (60 ml/2 fl oz) oil

Topping

1 onion, finely chopped
2 cloves garlic, crushed
2 small red chillies, finely chopped
425 g (14 oz) can pinto beans, drained,
     mashed roughly
1 cup (250 ml/8 fl oz) thick and chunky
     bottled salsa
2 tablespoons chopped fresh coriander leaves
90 g (3 oz) Cheddar, grated

1 Cut the tortillas into quarters and cut each
quarter into three triangles.
2 Heat 2 tablespoons of the oil in a frying pan.
Add a few triangles to the pan, cook for

30 seconds on each side, or until crisp and
golden brown. Remove from the pan and drain
on paper towels. Repeat with the remaining
triangles, adding extra oil as necessary.
3 For the topping, heat 1 tablespoon of oil in a
medium pan, add the onion, garlic and chilli and
stir over medium heat for 3 minutes, or until the
onion is tender. Stir in the pinto beans, salsa and
fresh coriander. Remove from the heat and leave
to cool.
4 Spread the topping on the triangles, leaving a
border around the edges, and sprinkle with
Cheddar. Grill for 1 minute, or until the cheese
has melted.
NOTES: Tortilla triangles can be cooked in the
oven instead of fried and grilled. Place the
triangles on a baking tray in a preheated
moderate 180°C (350°F/Gas 4) oven for
5 minutes or until crisp. Add the topping and
cook for another 3–5 minutes, or until the cheese
has melted.
     Red kidney beans can be used instead of
pinto beans.
IN ADVANCE: Tortilla triangles can be made a
day ahead; store in an airtight container. The
topping can be made a day ahead and stored in
the refrigerator. Assemble the triangles up to
1 hour ahead. Grill just before serving.

TORTILLAS
Mexican flour tortillas
are small flat pancakes
traditionally made from a
dough using masa harina
(cornmeal). They are
cooked on both sides and
are the basis of popular
dishes such as tacos,
burritos, enchiladas and
tostadas. For all of these,
the flour tortillas are
either rolled or folded
around a filling, or fried
until crisp, then topped or
filled with the traditional
mixtures of cooked meats,
vegetables and spices.

*ABOVE: Spicy
tortilla triangles*

2 To make the batter, sift the flour into a large bowl, stir in the cornmeal and make a well in the centre. Gradually add the combined egg, oil and 1½ cups (375 ml/12 fl oz) water, whisking to make a smooth, lump-free batter.

3 Fill a deep heavy-based pan one third full of oil and heat to 180°C (350°F). The oil is ready when a cube of bread dropped into the oil turns golden brown in 15 seconds. Dip the frankfurts into the batter a few at a time; drain off the excess batter. Using tongs, gently lower the frankfurts into the oil. Cook over medium-high heat for 1–2 minutes, or until golden and crisp and heated through. Carefully remove from the oil. Drain on crumpled paper towels and keep warm. Repeat with the remaining frankfurts. Serve with tomato sauce.

NOTE: You can add a teaspoon of chopped fresh chilli or a pinch of chilli powder to the batter.

BAKED HONEY AND GARLIC RIBS

Preparation time: 20 minutes + marinating
Total cooking time: 55 minutes
Makes about 30

★

1.5 kg (3 lb) American-style pork spare ribs
½ cup (175 g/6 oz) honey
6 cloves garlic, crushed
5 cm (2 inch) piece fresh ginger, finely grated
¼ teaspoon Tabasco
3 tablespoons chilli sauce
2 teaspoons grated orange rind

1 Cut the ribs into small pieces, with about 1 bone per piece. Place in a large dish. Combine the remaining ingredients and pour over the ribs. Stir until well coated. Refrigerate for several hours, or overnight.

2 Preheat the oven to moderately hot 200°C (400°F/Gas 6). Drain the ribs and place the marinade in a small pan. Place the ribs in one or two large shallow ovenproof dishes in a single layer.

3 Bring the marinade to the boil and simmer gently for 3–4 minutes, or until it has thickened and reduced slightly.

4 Brush the ribs with the marinade and bake for 50 minutes, basting with the marinade three or four times. Cook until the ribs are well browned and tender. Serve the ribs hot with any remaining marinade.

MINI CORN DOGS

Preparation time: 10 minutes
Total cooking time: 8–10 minutes
Makes 16

★★★

8 large frankfurts
8 wooden skewers
cornflour, for dusting
oil, for deep-frying
tomato sauce, for dipping

Batter

1¾ cups (220 g/7 oz) self-raising flour
¼ cup (35 g/1¼ oz) cornmeal
1 egg, lightly beaten
1 tablespoon oil

1 Cut the frankfurts in half crossways. Cut 8 wooden skewers in half and insert one half through each frankfurt, leaving some of the skewer sticking out for a handle. Dust the frankfurts with a little cornflour.

ABOVE: Mini corn dogs

STARS AND STRIPES BARBECUED RIBS

Preparation time: 30 minutes + overnight
  marinating
Total cooking time: 15 minutes
Makes about 30

☆

1/2 teaspoon dry mustard, or prepared
  English mustard
1/2 teaspoon ground sweet paprika
1/4 teaspoon ground oregano
1/4 teaspoon ground cumin
1 1/2 tablespoons peanut oil
1 teaspoon Tabasco sauce
1 clove garlic, crushed
1/2 cup (125 ml/4 fl oz) tomato sauce
2 tablespoons tomato paste (tomato purée)
2 tablespoons soft brown sugar
1 tablespoon Worcestershire sauce
2 teaspoons brown vinegar
1.5 kg (3 lb) American-style pork spare ribs

1 For the sauce, combine the mustard, paprika, oregano, cumin and oil in a pan. Add the remaining ingredients, except the ribs. Cook, stirring, over medium heat for 3 minutes, or until combined. Allow to cool.
2 Coat the ribs with sauce and marinate overnight. Cook on a hot barbecue grill, turning frequently, until firm and well done. Cut into individual ribs before serving.
NOTE: Get very lean pork spare ribs as fatty ones tend to flare up and burn. You can use beef spare ribs if you prefer but first simmer until tender, then drain.

FRIED CHICKEN

Mix 1 kg (2 lb) chicken drumettes in a bowl with 2 cups (500 ml/16 fl oz) buttermilk. Cover and refrigerate for 2 hours, turning occasionally. Half fill a large, deep heavy-based pan with oil and heat to 180°C (350°F). The oil is ready when a cube of bread dropped into the oil turns golden brown in 15 seconds. Place 1 1/2 cups (185 g/6 oz) plain flour in a shallow dish and season. Drain the chicken and shake off any excess buttermilk, then coat in the flour. Deep fry in batches for 6–8 minutes, making sure the oil is not too hot or the chicken won't cook through. Drain on paper towels. Makes about 20.

TOMATOES

Tomatoes are sold fresh, in cans, or processed and sold as sauces and pastes with various consistencies, sometimes with flavourings added. Tomato paste, known in the U.K. as tomato purée, is strained concentrated tomatoes which have been cooked for several hours until they form a very thick, dark paste. Salt is added, and sometimes sugar. The intense flavour is used sparingly to flavour stews, stocks, sauces and soups. Some are slightly more concentrated than others so experiment to find which you prefer. Tomato sauce is a much thinner consistency than the paste and is often blended with sugar, salt, spices and other flavourings.

LEFT: Stars and stripes barbecued ribs

199

HOT CORN CAKES WITH AVOCADO AND PRAWNS

Preparation time: 25 minutes
Total cooking time: 15–20 minutes
Makes 32

✯

3/4 cup (110 g/3 1/2 oz) frozen corn kernels, thawed, roughly chopped
1 1/2 canned chipotle peppers, roughly chopped, and 2 teaspoons of the sauce
1/2 cup (60 g/2 oz) plain flour
1/3 cup (50 g/1 3/4 oz) polenta (cornmeal)
1/2 teaspoon baking powder
1/4 teaspoon bicarbonate of soda
1 teaspoon salt
1/2 teaspoon sugar
1 cup (250 ml/8 fl oz) buttermilk
20 g (3/4 oz) butter, melted
1 egg
32 cooked medium prawns, peeled, deveined
32 fresh coriander leaves, to garnish

Avocado sauce

1 ripe avocado, roughly chopped
2 tablespoons lime juice
1 canned chipotle pepper, in sauce
1/2 cup (15 g/1/2 oz) fresh coriander leaves
1 clove garlic, chopped
1/2 teaspoon salt
1 teaspoon ground cumin
2 tablespoons sour cream

1 Roughly chop the corn and chipotle peppers, using short bursts of a food processor.
2 Combine the dry ingredients in a large bowl and make a well. Whisk the buttermilk, butter and egg together in a jug, gradually add to the dry ingredients and whisk until thoroughly incorporated. Stir in the chopped corn and chipotle pepper. (The batter should have the consistency of pancake batter.) Add a tablespoon of water to thin the batter if necessary. Set aside.
3 Purée all the sauce ingredients in a food processor until very smooth. Season.
4 Heat a lightly greased frying pan over medium heat. Spoon tablespoons of the corn cake batter into the pan, forming 5 cm (2 inch) cakes, cooking in batches. Cook until golden brown, about 1 minute per side. Remove from the pan and repeat with the remaining batter. Keep the

cakes warm until ready to serve. Alternatively, you can make the corn cakes up to 2 days ahead of time, wrap well in plastic wrap and refrigerate. Place a single layer on a baking sheet and reheat in a warm 170°C (325°F/Gas 3) oven for 5 minutes, or until warmed through. (Corn cakes can also be served at room temperature.)
4 To assemble, dollop a heaped teaspoon of avocado sauce on the warmed corn cakes. Place one cooked prawn on top of the avocado sauce. Garnish with coriander leaves.

MINI TORTILLAS WITH CHORIZO SALSA

Preparation time: 25 minutes
Total cooking time: 12–15 minutes
Makes about 30

✯

4 x 20 cm (8 inch) round flour tortillas
2 tablespoons olive oil
250 g (8 oz) chorizo sausages
1/3 cup (90 g/3 oz) Greek-style natural yoghurt
20 g (3/4 oz) finely chopped fresh coriander
1 ripe avocado
1 large tomato, seeded
1/4 red onion
2 teaspoons balsamic vinegar
1 tablespoon virgin olive oil
30 small fresh coriander leaves, to garnish

1 Preheat the oven to moderate 180°C (350°F/Gas 4). Cut 7–8 circles from each tortilla with a 5.5 cm (2 1/4 inch) cutter, or cut into triangles. Heat 1 tablespoon of the oil in a large non-stick frying pan, add one third of the mini tortillas and cook in a single layer, turning once, until crisp and golden. Drain on crumpled paper towels. Repeat with the remaining oil and tortillas.
2 Chop the sausages into small cubes and bake on a baking tray for 10 minutes, or until cooked through. Cool; drain on crumpled paper towel.
3 Meanwhile, combine the yoghurt and chopped coriander in a small bowl; set aside.
4 Chop the avocado, tomato and onion into small cubes and combine in a bowl. Add the sausage, vinegar, oil and salt and pepper, to taste, and gently stir to combine.
5 To assemble, spoon the sausage onto tortillas and top with yoghurt and coriander leaves.

OPPOSITE PAGE: Hot corn cakes with avocado and prawns (left); Mini tortillas with chorizo salsa

CHARRED PRAWNS WITH PEPPER (CAPSICUM) MAYONNAISE

Preparation time: 20 minutes + marinating
Total cooking time: 40 minutes
Makes 24

★ ★

1 kg (2 lb) large raw prawns

4 cloves garlic, crushed

3 tablespoons lime juice

1 teaspoon ground cumin

3 tablespoons chopped fresh coriander

lime wedges, for serving

Pepper (capsicum) mayonnaise

1 small red pepper (capsicum)

6 cloves garlic, unpeeled

1 tablespoon olive oil

1/3 cup (90 g/3 oz) whole-egg mayonnaise

1 tablespoon lime juice

1 Peel and devein the prawns, leaving the tails intact. Combine the garlic, lime juice, cumin and coriander in a bowl, place the prawns in the marinade and mix well. Cover and refrigerate for at least 2 hours.

2 To make the pepper mayonnaise, preheat the oven to moderately hot 190°C (375°F/Gas 5). Cut the red pepper into quarters and remove the seeds and membrane. Place on a baking tray with the garlic and drizzle with the olive oil. Cook for 20–30 minutes, or until the skin blisters on the pepper and the garlic is soft but not burnt. Place in a plastic bag until cool, then peel the red pepper and garlic.

3 Combine the red pepper and garlic in a food processor with the mayonnaise until smooth. Transfer to a bowl and stir in the lime juice. Add salt, to taste.

4 Preheat a lightly oiled chargrill or heavy-based pan until it just starts to smoke. Drain the prawns, discarding the marinade and cook in batches for 2 minutes on each side, or until cooked. Serve the prawns with the mayonnaise and a wedge of lime.

ABOVE: Charred prawns with pepper mayonnaise

EMPANADAS

Preparation time: 45 minutes + cooling
Total cooking time: 1 hour
Makes 48

★ ★

oil, for frying
1 small onion, finely chopped
1 small green pepper (capsicum), finely chopped
1 clove garlic, crushed
350 g (11 oz) beef mince
200 g (6½ oz) pork mince
¾ cup (185 ml/6 fl oz) tomato passata, or chopped canned tomatoes
110 g (3¾ oz) pitted green olives, chopped
8 frozen sheets shortcrust pastry, thawed

1 Heat a little oil in a frying pan and cook the onion over low heat for 3 minutes, or until soft. Add the green pepper, cook for 3 minutes, then add the garlic and cook for another minute. Add the minces and cook, breaking up any lumps with a fork, until browned.

2 Stir in the tomato passata and green olives and bring to the boil. Reduce the heat and simmer for 10 minutes, stirring occasionally, or until most of the liquid has evaporated. Remove from the heat, season to taste, and allow to cool completely.

3 Cut six 8 cm (3 inch) rounds from each sheet of pastry. Place 2 heaped teaspoons of the filling onto each round and fold over to enclose. Press the edges down with a fork to seal.

4 Heat 2 cm (¾ inch) of oil in a deep frying pan to 180°C (350°F). The oil is ready when a cube of bread dropped into the oil turns golden brown in 15 seconds. Cook the empanadas in batches until crisp and golden, then drain well on crumpled paper towels. Alternatively, bake in a moderately hot 200°C (400°F/Gas 6) oven for 20–25 minutes, or until puffed and golden.

IN ADVANCE: These can be made up to 2 days ahead, or frozen, uncooked.

ONIONS

Brown onions, which keep well, have a strong flavour and are best cooked, while white onions are usually milder and sweeter and hence can be used in salads as well as cooked. Red and yellow onions, which don't keep as long as other onions, are used in salads for their colour and sweetness. Chopped or sliced onions should be cooked slowly over medium-low heat to soften and sweeten them.

LEFT: Empanadas

CEVICHE

Preparation time: 20 minutes + overnight chilling
Total cooking time: Nil
Makes about 48 cubes

★

600 g (1 1/4 lb) very fresh, skinless, firm
    white-fleshed fish such as snapper fillets
1/3 cup (80 ml/2 3/4 fl oz) lime juice
1/2 red onion, very finely diced
1 teaspoon finely chopped red chilli
1 teaspoon finely chopped green chilli
1 tomato, seeded and chopped into very
    small dice
2 tablespoons finely chopped fresh parsley

1 Remove any bones from the fish with
tweezers. Cut the fish into bite-sized pieces and
place in a shallow glass bowl. Pour the lime juice
over the fish, cover with plastic wrap and
refrigerate overnight.
2 Toss the diced onion, chilli, tomato and
chopped parsley through the fish.
3 Arrange on a serving plate and serve
immediately, providing cocktail sticks for guests
to help themselves.

TEX-MEX CHEESE CRISPS

Preparation time: 20 minutes + chilling
Total cooking time: 12 minutes
Makes 80

★

1 3/4 cups (215 g/7 oz) plain flour
1 teaspoon chilli powder
1 teaspoon garlic salt
1/2 teaspoon ground paprika
200 g (6 1/2 oz) butter, chopped
1 egg, lightly beaten
200 g (6 1/2 oz) Cheddar, grated

1 Preheat the oven to hot 210°C (415°F/
Gas 6–7). Lightly brush two baking trays with
melted butter.
2 Sift the flour, chilli powder, garlic salt and
paprika into a large bowl. Rub the butter into
the flour with your fingertips until the mixture
resembles fine breadcrumbs. Add the egg and
cheese and stir until the mixture comes together.
Turn onto a lightly floured surface and gather
together into a ball. Cover the dough with
plastic wrap and refrigerate for 20 minutes.
3 Roll the dough on a lightly floured surface to
3 mm (1/8 inch) thickness. Cut into shapes with
a 6 cm (2 1/2 inch) star-shaped biscuit cutter. Place
on the trays, allowing room for spreading. Bake
for 12 minutes, or until crisp and golden brown.
Leave on the trays for 2 minutes before
transferring to a wire rack to cool.

TORTILLA FLUTES

Preparation time: 25 minutes
Total cooking time: 15 minutes
Makes 24

★ ★

1/4 cup (60 ml/2 fl oz) olive oil
2 small onions, finely chopped
2 garlic cloves, crushed
1/2 teaspoon chilli powder
2 teaspoons ground cumin
1 kg (2 lb) cooked chicken, finely chopped
2 tablespoons finely chopped fresh
    coriander
24 soft flour or corn tortillas
oil, for shallow-frying
red or green chilli sauce, for serving
1 avocado, sliced, for serving

1 Heat the olive oil in a frying pan and fry the
onion and garlic over medium heat for
2–3 minutes, or until the onion is just tender
but not soft. Add the chilli powder and cumin
and stir for 1 minute.
2 Add the chicken and mix well. Cook over
medium heat until just heated through. Stir in
the coriander and remove from the heat.
3 Soften the tortillas, one at a time, by heating
in a dry heavy-based frying pan over high heat
for about 30 seconds each side.
4 Lay a tortilla flat on a work surface and place
a large spoonful of chicken mixture along the
centre. Carefully roll up to form a flute.
5 Pour oil in a deep frying pan to 5 cm
(2 inches) deep and heat the oil to 180°C
(350°F). The oil is ready when a cube of bread
dropped into the oil turns golden brown in
15 seconds. Holding the flute together with
tongs (or fasten with toothpicks), cook one at
a time until slightly crisp. Drain on crumpled
paper towels. Serve with chilli sauce and
avocado slices.

CEVICHE
Ceviche was originally a
Peruvian dish, consisting of
small pieces of raw fish
marinated or 'cooked' in
a mixture that includes
lime or lemon juice—this
tenderises and flavours the
fish. Normally, the dish is
served cold with toast, or
in lettuce cups with
cooked sweet potato and
corn cobs.

*OPPOSITE PAGE,
CLOCKWISE FROM TOP:
Ceviche; Tortilla flutes;
Tex-Mex cheese crisps*

GUACAMOLE

This is a Mexican dip or spread made by mixing mashed ripe avocado with lime or lemon juice as well as chopped onion, tomato and chilli. Sometimes other ingredients are added. Traditionally, the dip is served with tortillas or nachos but you can have it with your favourite chips or dipping biscuits.

ABOVE: Mexican layered dip

MEXICAN LAYERED DIP

Preparation time: I hour + chilling
Total cooking time: Nil
Serves 12

★★

Guacamole

3 ripe avocados

I small tomato

1–2 red chillies, finely chopped

I small red onion, finely chopped

I tablespoon chopped fresh coriander

I tablespoon lime or lemon juice

2 tablespoons sour cream

1–2 drops habanero or Tabasco sauce

450 g (14 oz) can refried beans

35 g (1 ¼ oz) packet of taco seasoning mix

300 g (10 oz) sour cream

200 g (6½ oz) ready-made salsa sauce

60 g (2 oz) Cheddar, grated

2 tablespoons chopped pitted black olives

200 g (6½ oz) corn chips

chopped fresh coriander leaves, to garnish

1 For the guacamole, roughly chop the avocado flesh, then mash lightly with a fork. Cut the tomato in half horizontally. Using a teaspoon, scoop out the seeds and discard. Finely dice the flesh and add to the avocado. Stir in the chilli, onion, coriander, lime juice, sour cream and sauce. Season with salt and cracked black pepper. Cover and refrigerate until required.

2 Using a fork, mix the refried beans and taco seasoning together in a small bowl.

3 To assemble, spread the beans in the centre of a large platter (we used a 30 x 35 cm/12 x 14 inch dish), leaving a border for the corn chips. Spoon the sour cream on top, leaving a small border of bean mixture showing. Repeat with the guacamole and salsa sauce so that you can see each layer. Sprinkle the top with cheese and olives.

4 Arrange some of the corn chips around the edge just before serving and garnish with the coriander. Serve with the remaining corn chips.

NOTE: Tabasco and habanero sauces are both made from fiery hot chillies, so taste before adding too much.

IN ADVANCE: This dip can be made 2 hours ahead, and refrigerated, covered. Surround with corn chips close to serving time.

CORN FRITTERS

Preparation time: 15 minutes
Total cooking time: 20–25 minutes
Makes 20

★ ★

1¼ cups (155 g/4½ oz) plain flour
1½ teaspoons baking powder
½ teaspoon ground coriander
¼ teaspoon ground cumin
130 g (4½ oz) can corn kernels, well drained
130 g (4½ oz) can creamed corn
½ cup (80 ml/2¾ fl oz) milk
2 eggs, lightly beaten
2 tablespoons chopped fresh chives
½ cup (125 ml/4 fl oz) olive oil

Dipping sauce

1 tablespoon brown vinegar
3 teaspoons soft brown sugar
1 teaspoon chilli sauce
1 tablespoon chopped fresh chives
salt, to taste

1 Sift the flour, baking powder, ground coriander and cumin into a bowl and make a well in the centre. Add the corn kernels, creamed corn, milk, eggs and chives all at once. Stir until the ingredients are combined and the mixture is free of flour lumps. Season, to taste, with salt and pepper.

2 Heat the oil in a large frying pan to 180°C (350°F). The oil is ready when a cube of bread dropped into the oil turns golden brown in 15 seconds. Drop heaped tablespoons of mixture into the pan about 2 cm (¾ inch) apart and flatten slightly with the back of a spoon. Cook in batches over medium–high heat for 2 minutes, or until the underside is golden. Turn over and cook the other side. Remove from the pan and drain on crumpled paper towels. Repeat the process with the remaining mixture. Serve the fritters with the dipping sauce.

3 For the dipping sauce, heat the vinegar, sugar and chilli sauce in a small pan for 1–2 minutes, until the liquid is heated through and the sugar is dissolved. Stir in the chives and season with salt, to taste.

IN ADVANCE: The fritters can be made several hours ahead. Reheat on baking trays covered with baking paper in a moderate 180°C (350°F/ Gas 4) oven for 5 minutes.

LEFT: Corn fritters

CORNMEAL CHILLIES

Preparation time: 40 minutes + chilling
Total cooking time: 2–3 minutes each batch
Makes 24

★★

2 x 330 g (11 oz) jars mild whole chillies
125 g (4 oz) Cheddar, grated
200 g (6½ oz) cream cheese, softened
⅔ cup (85 g/3 oz) plain flour
4 eggs, lightly beaten
1¼ cups (185 g/6 oz) cornmeal
1¼ cups (125 g/4 oz) dry breadcrumbs
oil, for deep-frying
sour cream, for serving

1 Select 24 large, uniform chillies. Drain well and dry with paper towels. With a sharp knife, cut a slit down the length of one side of each chilli. Remove the seeds and membrane.

2 Combine the Cheddar and cream cheese and spoon some into each chilli. Put the flour on a large plate and the beaten egg in a small bowl. Combine the cornmeal and breadcrumbs on a flat dish. Roll each chilli in the flour, shake off the excess, dip in the egg and roll in the crumb mixture to coat thoroughly. Refrigerate for 1 hour. Re-dip in egg and re-roll in breadcrumbs. Refrigerate for another hour.

3 Fill a deep heavy-based pan one third full of oil and heat the oil to 180°C (350°F). The oil is ready when a cube of bread dropped into the oil turns golden brown in 15 seconds. Deep-fry the chillies in small batches until golden brown. Drain on crumpled paper towels. Serve with sour cream.

IN ADVANCE: These can be prepared up to 3 hours ahead.

ABOVE: Cornmeal chillies

PRAWN AND CORN CAKES WITH LIME MAYONNAISE

Preparation time: 40 minutes + chilling
Total cooking time: 10 minutes
Makes 30

★ ★ ★

500 g (1 lb) cooked prawns
1 tablespoon light olive oil
2 jalapeno chillies, seeded and finely chopped
1 teaspoon ground coriander
4 spring onions, finely chopped
20 g (3/4 oz) fresh coriander leaves, chopped
130 g (4 1/2 oz) can corn kernels, drained
130 g (4 1/2 oz) can creamed corn
1 egg, lightly beaten
1/3 cup (90 g/3 oz) sour cream
2 1/2 cups (200 g/6 1/2 oz) fresh breadcrumbs
oil, for shallow-frying

Lime mayonnaise

2 egg yolks
1 clove garlic, crushed
1/3 cup (80 ml/2 3/4 fl oz) vegetable oil
1/3 cup (80 ml/2 3/4 fl oz) olive oil
2 tablespoons lime juice
1 small green chilli, finely chopped

1 Peel, devein and finely chop the prawns. Heat the oil in a pan over medium heat. Add the chilli, ground coriander and spring onion and fry for 2–3 minutes, until soft and fragrant. Remove the pan from the heat and add the fresh coriander, prawns, corn kernels and creamed corn. Mix, then transfer to a bowl.
2 Add the egg, sour cream and 1 cup (80 g/ 2 3/4 oz) of breadcrumbs, mix and season, to taste. Cover and refrigerate for 2 hours.
3 Shape level tablespoons of mixture into patties. Coat all over with the remaining breadcrumbs and refrigerate for another 30 minutes.
4 Heat 2 cm (3/4 inch) oil in a large frying pan and cook the patties in batches for 3–4 minutes each side, or until golden brown. Drain on crumpled paper towels.
5 For the lime mayonnaise, combine the egg yolks and garlic in a bowl. Slowly add the vegetable oil, one drop at a time, whisking continuously to form a smooth mixture. When all the vegetable oil has been added, slowly add the olive oil in a thin stream, whisking continuously. Add the lime juice and chilli and mix well. Season well with salt and pepper and refrigerate, covered, until needed. Serve with the chilli prawn and corn cakes.
NOTE: The corn cake mixture is very soft and needs gentle handling. To make the cakes firmer, freeze for 30 minutes. To save time, buy whole egg mayonnaise and stir in some grated lime rind, chopped chilli and garlic.

PRAWNS
Whole unpeeled cooked prawns can be frozen in a large block. Put them in a plastic container, such as an ice cream tub, fill with icy cold water and freeze. When ready to use, thaw the prawns in a large bowl in the fridge.

LEFT: Prawn and corn cakes with lime mayonnaise

QUESADILLAS Use flour tortillas from

the bread section of your supermarket to make these Mexican snacks. And stun

your guests with your authentic pronunciation... 'kay-sah-dee-yah'.

GUACAMOLE ROLLS

Mix a 450 g (14 oz) can of refried beans with 90 g (3 oz) grated Cheddar. Cut 7 flour tortillas into rounds, using an 8 cm (3 inch) cutter. Wrap in foil and cook in a moderate 180°F (350°F/Gas 4) oven for 2–3 minutes, until warmed through. To make the guacamole, mash 2 avocados and mix with 1 small chopped red onion, 1 tablespoon mayonnaise, 1 chopped red chilli, 1 tablespoon lime juice and 1 tablespoon chopped fresh coriander. Spread a little bean mixture over the base of each tortilla and roll up like a horn. Place, seam-side-down, on a baking tray and bake for another 5 minutes, or until crisp. Spoon a teaspoon of guacamole into the open end and serve. Makes 42.

CHEESE QUESADILLAS

Roast 2 jalapeno chillies by holding with tongs over a flame until blackened and blistered. You can also roast chillies under a hot grill. Put in a plastic bag and when cool, you will find the skin peels away easily. Finely chop the chilli flesh and mix with 250 g (8 oz) grated Cheddar and 75 g (2½ oz) grated mozzarella cheese. Spread evenly over 3 flour tortillas, then top with another 3 tortillas. Cut out rounds with a 6 cm (2½ inch) cutter, then fry in a little oil for 1–2 minutes, or until golden brown on each side. Serve with home-made salsa. Makes about 25–30.

TACO CHICKEN QUESADILLAS

In a large frying pan, heat 1 tablespoon oil, add 1 finely chopped red onion and 1 finely diced red pepper (capsicum). Cook until the onion has softened. Add 2 crushed cloves garlic, ¼ teaspoon paprika, 1 teaspoon ground cumin and 1 teaspoon ground coriander and cook for 2 minutes. Add 400 g (13 oz) chicken mince and cook for 5–8 minutes, until brown, breaking up any lumps. Add a 400 g (13 oz) can chopped tomatoes and simmer for 20 minutes, or until thick. Cut 7 flour tortillas into rounds with an 8 cm (3 inch) cutter. Place a teaspoon of the mixture on one half of each round. Sprinkle with 220 g (7 oz) grated Cheddar. Bake in a moderate 180°C (350°F/Gas 4) oven for 1 minute, or until the cheese has melted. Fold over and hold for a few seconds to stick. Garnish with sliced spring onion. Makes 42.

CORN, TOMATO AND BEAN QUESADILLAS

Combine 1 finely chopped red onion, 2 chopped tomatoes, a 310 g (10 oz) can drained and rinsed corn kernels and 1 diced red pepper (capsicum). Drain and rinse a 425 g (14 oz) can pinto beans and mash with a fork. Place 3 flour tortillas on a work surface, spread the pinto beans evenly over the tortillas, top with the corn and tomato mixture and sprinkle with 90 g (3 oz) grated Cheddar. Top with 3 more flour tortillas. Heat 2 teaspoons oil in a 25 cm (10 inch) frying pan and cook the stacks for 3–4 minutes each side, until golden brown. Remove from the pan and cut into 12 triangles. Makes 36.

CHILLI BEEF QUESADILLAS

Heat 1 tablespoon oil in a frying pan and cook 1 chopped onion and 2 crushed cloves garlic for 2–3 minutes. Add 400 g (13 oz) beef mince and cook for 5–7 minutes until brown, breaking up any lumps. Stir in a 325 g (11 oz) bottle of Mexican black bean salsa. Bring to the boil, reduce the heat and simmer for 3–4 minutes, or until the mixture reduces and thickens. Season. Place 3 flour tortillas on a work surface and sprinkle with 125 g (4 oz) grated Cheddar. Spoon the mince evenly over the cheese, then top with another 3 tortillas. Heat 2 teaspoons oil in a 25 cm (10 inch) frying pan and cook the stacks for 3–4 minutes each side, or until golden brown. Remove from the pan, trim off the sides and cut into 5 cm (2 inch) squares. Makes about 36.

FROM LEFT: Guacamole rolls; Cheese quesadillas; Taco chicken quesadillas; Corn, tomato and bean quesadillas; Chilli beef quesadillas

CORNBREAD WITH BEANS

Preparation time: 1 hour
Total cooking time: 30 minutes
Makes 24

★★

1 large green chilli
1 large red chilli
1 cup (150 g/5 oz) cornmeal (polenta)
1 cup (125 g/4 oz) self-raising flour
1/2 cup (60 g/2 oz) grated Cheddar
1 egg, lightly beaten
3/4 cup (185 ml/6 fl oz) milk
310 g (10 oz) can creamed corn
Tabasco sauce, for serving
fresh coriander leaves, to garnish

Topping

1 cup (230 g/7 1/2 oz) refried beans
2 tablespoons sour cream
1/2 teaspoon ground cumin
1/2 teaspoon ground coriander
1/2 teaspoon paprika

1 Preheat the oven to moderately hot 200°C (400°F/Gas 6). Grease a 20 x 30 cm (8 x 12 inch) shallow baking tin. Roast the chillies by holding them with tongs (one at a time) over a gas flame, until well blackened. Alternatively, cut the chillies in half, remove the seeds and membrane, flatten out and grill skin-side-up until black and blistered. Place in a plastic bag until cool, then peel, cut in half and chop finely.
2 Combine the cornmeal, flour, Cheddar, chilli flesh and 1 teaspoon salt in a bowl. Make a well in the centre and add the egg, milk and creamed corn. Stir until just combined, being careful not to overbeat.
3 Pour into the tin and bake for 20 minutes, or until lightly browned and firm to touch. Turn onto a wire rack to cool.
4 For the topping, mix all the ingredients in a small bowl until well combined.
5 Using a serrated knife, trim the edges of the cornbread. Cut into 3 cm (1 1/4 inch) squares. Place on a platter and top each square with a teaspoon of topping. Sprinkle each with a drop of Tabasco and garnish with a coriander leaf.
IN ADVANCE: The topping can be made the day before and stored, covered, in the refrigerator.

REFRIED BEANS

Although you would never guess from the name, these are dried beans (pinto, red kidney or black beans) that have been boiled until tender, then fried until very soft. Refried beans actually translates as 'well-fried'.

ABOVE: Cornbread with beans

MEXICAN MEATBALLS

Preparation time: 30 minutes
Total cooking time: 35 minutes
Makes about 28

☆

2 slices white bread, crusts removed
3 tablespoons milk
250 g (8 oz) veal or beef mince
250 g (8 oz) pork mince
1 small onion, grated
1 egg, lightly beaten
1 teaspoon cumin seeds
2 tablespoons chopped fresh coriander
1 litre beef stock
2 tablespoons tomato paste (tomato purée)
sprigs of fresh coriander, to garnish

Tomato chilli sauce
3–4 red serrano chillies (or to taste)
1 small onion, finely chopped
2 cloves garlic, crushed
400 g (13 oz) can chopped tomatoes
2 teaspoons sugar

1 Roughly tear the bread into a bowl and soak in the milk for about 2 minutes. Squeeze, then break the bread into small pieces. Combine with the minces, onion, egg, cumin and fresh coriander. Season. The mixture will be sloppy. Mix well with your hands, then roll into about 28 small balls.

2 Mix the stock and tomato paste in a large saucepan and bring to the boil. Add the meatballs and return to the boil, then reduce the heat and simmer over low heat for 20 minutes, or until cooked through. Remove the meatballs with a slotted spoon, place in a warm serving bowl and provide cocktail sticks for serving. Garnish with coriander to serve. Strain and reserve the cooking liquid for another use, or freeze.

3 For the sauce, cut the chillies in half, discard the seeds, then finely chop. Heat a little oil in a pan and cook the onion over low heat for about 3 minutes, until soft and golden. Stir in the garlic and chilli for 1 minute. Stir in the tomato and sugar and simmer for 15 minutes. Cool slightly, then purée in a food processor. Season with salt and pepper and serve with the meatballs.

NOTE: Moisten your fingers with water when rolling the meatballs, to help prevent them sticking to you.

LEFT: Mexican meatballs

CHICKEN TAMALES

Preparation time: 45 minutes
Total cooking time: 1 hour 15 minutes
Makes 12

☆ ☆

Dough
100 g (3½ oz) butter, softened
1 clove garlic, crushed
1 teaspoon ground cumin
1½ cups (210 g/7 oz) masa harina
⅓ cup (80 ml/2¾ fl oz) cream
⅓ cup (80 ml/2¾ fl oz) chicken stock

Filling
1 corn cob
2 tablespoons oil
150 g (5 oz) chicken breast fillets
2 cloves garlic, crushed
1 red chilli, seeded and chopped
1 red onion, chopped
1 red pepper (capsicum), chopped
2 tomatoes, peeled and chopped

1 To make the dough, beat the butter with electric beaters until creamy. Then add the garlic, cumin and 1 teaspoon salt and mix well. Add the masa harina and combined cream and stock alternately, beating until combined.
2 To make the filling, add the corn to a pan of boiling water and cook for 5–8 minutes, or until tender. Cool, then cut off the kernels with a sharp knife. Heat the oil in a frying pan and cook the chicken until golden. Remove, cool and shred finely. Add the garlic, chilli and onion to the pan and cook until soft. Add the red pepper and corn and stir for 3 minutes. Add the chicken, tomato and 1 teaspoon salt and simmer for 15 minutes, or until the liquid has reduced.
3 Bring a large pan of water to the boil and place a large bamboo steamer over it, making sure it doesn't touch the water.
4 Cut 12 pieces of baking paper 20 x 15 cm (8 x 6 inches). Spread a thick layer of dough over each piece, leaving a border at each end. Place some filling in the centre, roll up and secure both ends with string. Cook in the steamer for 35 minutes, or until firm.
IN ADVANCE: The filling can be made a day ahead. Assemble on the day of serving.

TAMALE BEEF AND BEAN PIES

Preparation time: 1 hour
Total cooking time: 50 minutes
Makes 30

☆ ☆

1 tablespoon oil
1 small onion, finely chopped
250 g (8 oz) beef mince
1 clove garlic, crushed
¼ teaspoon chilli powder
200 g (6½ oz) canned crushed tomatoes
1½ cups (375 ml/12 fl oz) beef stock
300 g (10 oz) can red kidney beans, drained
2½ cups (360 g/11½ oz) masa harina
1 teaspoon baking powder
125 g (4 oz) butter, cut into cubes and chilled
125 g (4 oz) Cheddar, grated
sour cream, for serving

1 Heat the oil in a frying pan. Add the onion and cook over low heat for 3–4 minutes, or until soft. Increase the heat, add the mince and cook until browned all over. Add the garlic, chilli, tomato and ½ cup (125 ml/4 fl oz) stock. Bring to the boil, then reduce the heat and simmer for 35 minutes, or until the liquid has evaporated to a thick sauce. Stir in the beans and cool.
2 Lightly grease 30 holes in deep mini muffin tins. Sift the masa harina, baking powder and ½ teaspoon salt into a bowl. Rub the butter into the flour with your fingertips until it resembles fine breadcrumbs. Make a well in the centre and, with a flat-bladed knife, mix in the remaining stock, then use your hands to bring the mixture together into a ball. Divide into thirds and roll two thirds between 2 sheets of baking paper and cut out rounds with a 7 cm (2¾ inch) cutter. Line the muffin tins. Trim the edges and reserve any leftover pastry.
3 Preheat the oven to moderately hot 200°C (400°F/Gas 6). Spoon the filling into the pastry cases and sprinkle with the Cheddar. Roll out the remaining pastry and reserved pastry as above. Cut into 4 cm (1½ inch) rounds to cover the tops of the pies. Brush the edges with water and place over the filling. Trim the edges and press the pastry together to seal. Bake for 20–25 minutes, or until the pastry is crisp and lightly browned. Serve with sour cream.

CHICKEN TAMALES

Combine the dough ingredients, then beat the mixture until smooth.

Spread a thick layer of dough over each piece of baking paper.

Put some filling in the centre and roll the tamales up firmly.

Tie both ends of the paper securely with short pieces of string.

OPPOSITE PAGE: Chicken tamales (top); Tamale beef and bean pies

215

TOSTADAS WITH EGG AND CHORIZO

Preparation time: 15 minutes
Total cooking time: 10 minutes
Makes 28

☆

4 flour tortillas
25 g (³/₄ oz) butter, melted
1 teaspoon olive oil
1 chorizo sausage, peeled and finely chopped
25 g (³/₄ oz) butter
5 eggs, lightly beaten
3 tablespoons milk
1 tablespoon chopped fresh coriander,
   to garnish

1 To make the tostadas, preheat the oven to moderately hot 200°C (400°F/Gas 6). Cut the tortillas into 28 rounds with a 6 cm (2¹/₂ inch) cutter. Line two baking trays with baking paper and brush the tortilla rounds with melted butter. Bake on the trays for 5–6 minutes, or until golden and crisp. Take care not to burn. Transfer to a serving platter.

2 Meanwhile, heat the oil in a small saucepan and cook the chorizo until crispy. Drain on crumpled paper towels. Wipe out the saucepan with paper towel and gently melt the butter. Add the combined eggs and milk and cook gently over low heat, stirring constantly until soft and creamy.

3 Remove from the heat and spoon the mixture into a warm bowl. (This is to stop the eggs from cooking further.) Fold the chorizo through and season, to taste, with salt and black pepper. Pile 2–3 teaspoons of the egg and chorizo mixture onto each tostada, scatter with fresh coriander and serve immediately.

IN ADVANCE: You can cook the tostadas ahead of time. Just before serving, warm them in the oven, wrapped in foil, for a few minutes. You will have to cook the egg and chorizo at the last minute.

ABOVE: Tostadas with egg and chorizo

CHICKEN DRUMSTICKS WITH RANCH DRESSING

Preparation time: 25 minutes + marinating
Total cooking time: 10 minutes
Makes 32

★

32 small chicken drumsticks
1 tablespoon cracked black pepper
1 tablespoon garlic salt
1 tablespoon onion powder
olive oil, for deep-frying
1 cup (250 ml/8 fl oz) tomato sauce
1/3 cup (80 ml/2 3/4 fl oz) Worcestershire sauce
40 g (1 1/4 oz) butter, melted
1 tablespoon sugar
Tabasco sauce, to taste

Ranch dressing
1 cup (250 g/8 oz) whole egg mayonnaise
1 cup (250 g/8 oz) sour cream
1/3 cup (80 ml/2 3/4 fl oz) lemon juice
1/3 cup (20 g/3/4 oz) chopped fresh chives

1 Remove the skin from the chicken and use a cleaver or large knife to cut off the knuckle. Wash the chicken thoroughly and pat dry with paper towels. Combine the pepper, garlic salt and onion powder and rub some into each piece of chicken.

2 Fill a deep heavy-based pan one third full of oil and heat the oil to 180°C (350°F). The oil is ready when a cube of bread dropped into the oil turns golden brown in 15 seconds. Cook the chicken in batches for 2 minutes each batch, remove with tongs or a slotted spoon and drain on paper towels.

3 Transfer the chicken to a large non-metal bowl or shallow dish. Combine the sauces, butter, sugar and Tabasco, pour over the chicken and stir to coat. Refrigerate, covered, for several hours or overnight. Prepare and heat the barbecue 1 hour before cooking.

4 Place the chicken on a hot lightly oiled barbecue grill or flatplate and cook for 20–25 minutes, or until cooked through. Turn and brush with the marinade during cooking. Serve with the ranch dressing.

5 For the ranch dressing, mix together the mayonnaise, sour cream, juice, chives, and salt and pepper, to taste.

TABASCO
This is a very hot spicy red sauce made using red chillies grown specially in Louisiana in America. The chillies are ground with vinegar and salt, then matured for 3 years in oak barrels. The result is the peppery sauce which is used as a condiment in Tex-Mex and other cuisines, as well as for spicing some cocktails.

LEFT: Chicken drumsticks with ranch dressing

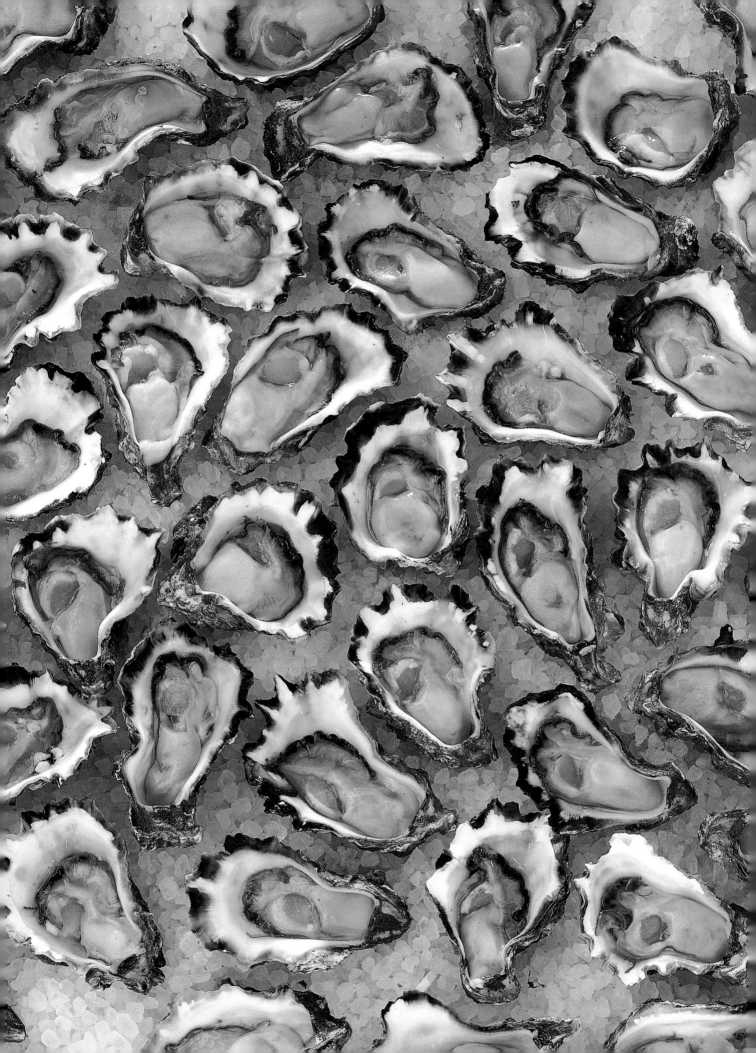

PARTY TIME

So, you've written the invitations and now there's no denying it... it's not a 'gathering', not just a 'few friends coming over', it's a fully-fledged party. And with the word 'party' comes the anticipation, the excitement and the thrill. Keep calm and don't overdo it: a selection of five or six of the following ideas (double or treble the recipes as necessary) will keep you cooler than a frenzy of twenty different dishes. Ring the changes by serving miniature versions of food your guests expect to be 'big'—tiny meat pies and mini pan-fried sandwiches. Alternatively, push the boat out and serve nothing but the best Champagne and a sophisticated range of seafood to be eaten straight from the shell.

C.

HERBS

As dried herbs have a stronger flavour than fresh, they are used more sparingly. If a recipe calls for fresh herbs that are unavailable, in many cases you can use dried if you adjust the quantity. For every tablespoon of chopped fresh herbs, substitute 1 teaspoon of dried. Store dried herbs in an airtight container in a cool dark place. When in plentiful supply, fresh herbs can be chopped, then frozen in ice cube trays with a little water. You can use the frozen cubes in sauces.

MINI MEAT PIES

Preparation time: 20 minutes
Total cooking time: 25 minutes
Makes 24

★ ★

6 sheets ready-rolled shortcrust pastry
2 small tomatoes, sliced
1/2 teaspoon dried oregano leaves

Filling

1 tablespoon oil
1 onion, chopped
2 cloves garlic, crushed
500 g (1 lb) beef mince
2 tablespoons plain flour
1 1/2 cups (375 ml/12 fl oz) beef stock
1/3 cup (80 ml/2 3/4 fl oz) tomato sauce
2 teaspoons Worcestershire sauce
1/2 teaspoon dried mixed herbs

1 Preheat the oven to moderately hot 200°C (400°F/Gas 6). Cut the pastry into 48 circles (if making traditional pies, only 24 if making uncovered pies) using a 7 cm (2 3/4 inch) round cutter. Press 24 circles into two lightly greased 12-hole patty tins.

2 To make the filling, heat the oil in a heavy-based pan, add the onion and garlic and cook over medium heat for 2 minutes, or until the onion is soft. Add the mince and stir over high heat for 3 minutes, or until well browned and all the liquid has evaporated. Use a fork to break up any lumps of mince.

3 Add the flour, stir until combined, then cook over medium heat for 1 minute. Add the stock, sauces and herbs and stir over the heat until boiling. Reduce the heat to low and simmer for 5 minutes, or until the mixture has reduced and thickened; stir occasionally. Allow to cool.

4 Divide the filling among the pastry circles. Top each with two half slices of tomato and sprinkle with oregano. Bake for 25 minutes, or until the pastry is golden brown and crisp. For traditional pies, place the remaining pastry rounds over the tomato and oregano topping and seal the edges with beaten egg before baking. Serve hot.

ABOVE: Mini meat pies

CHICKEN AND CORN BITES

Preparation time: 15 minutes
Total cooking time: 15 minutes
Makes 50

☆

1 1/2 cups (185 g/6 oz) self-raising flour
2 teaspoons chicken stock powder
1/2 teaspoon chicken seasoning salt
60 g (2 oz) butter, chopped
50 g (1 3/4 oz) corn chips, finely crushed
2 eggs, lightly beaten
chicken seasoning salt, extra

1 Preheat the oven to moderate 180°C (350°F/
Gas 4). Line a baking tray with baking paper.
2 Sift the flour, stock powder and seasoning salt
into a large bowl and add the butter. Rub into
the flour with your fingertips until the mixture
resembles fine breadcrumbs. Stir in the corn
chips. Make a well in the centre, add the eggs
and mix with a flat-bladed knife, using a cutting
action until the mixture comes together in beads.
3 Gently gather the dough together, lift out
onto a lightly floured surface and press together
into a ball. Roll out to 4 mm (1/4 inch) thickness.
Cut the dough into shapes with a plain or fluted
biscuit cutter.
4 Place on the tray and sprinkle with chicken
salt. Bake for 15 minutes, or until lightly
browned. Cool on the tray.
IN ADVANCE: Store in an airtight container for
up to 2 days or freeze.

POLENTA SQUARES WITH SMOKED TURKEY AND CRANBERRY SAUCE

Preparation time: 25 minutes + chilling
Total cooking time: 20 minutes
Makes 35

☆ ☆

1 litre chicken stock
1 1/2 cups (250 g/8 oz) instant polenta
150 g (5 oz) sliced smoked turkey breast,
  finely shredded
3/4 cup (185 g/6 oz) whole egg mayonnaise
2 tablespoons cranberry sauce
1 clove garlic, crushed
1/2 teaspoon finely grated lime rind

2 teaspoons lime juice
1 teaspoon finely chopped fresh thyme
oil, for deep-frying
thyme leaves, extra, to garnish

1 Lightly grease a 20 x 30 cm (8 x 12 inch)
shallow baking tin. Place the chicken stock in a
large pan and bring to the boil. Reduce the heat
and gradually add the polenta, stirring constantly.
Cook for 2 minutes, over medium heat, until the
polenta becomes thick. Spread into the tin and
refrigerate for 30 minutes, or until firm.
2 Combine the turkey, mayonnaise, cranberry
sauce, garlic, lime rind, juice and thyme in a
bowl, then add salt and pepper, to taste.
3 Cut the polenta into 35 squares. Fill a deep
heavy-based pan one third full of oil and heat the
oil to 180°C (350°F). The oil is ready when a
cube of bread dropped in the oil turns golden
brown in 15 seconds. Deep-fry the polenta in
several batches until lightly browned and crisp.
Drain on crumpled paper towels. Top the
polenta squares with the turkey mixture and
garnish with thyme leaves. Serve warm.
IN ADVANCE: Topping and polenta can be made
a day ahead. Cook the polenta close to serving.

*ABOVE: Chicken
and corn bites*

221

SPICY SAUSAGE ROLL-UPS

Preparation time: 20 minutes
Total cooking time: 20 minutes
Makes about 25

★

2 sheets frozen shortcrust pastry
2 tablespoons French mustard
5 sticks cabanossi
1 egg yolk, beaten

1 Preheat the oven to hot 200°C (400°F/Gas 6). Cut each pastry sheet in half. Cut triangles with bases of 6 cm (2½ inches). Place a small dob of mustard at the base of each pastry piece. Cut the cabanossi into 7 cm (2¾ inch) lengths and place across the mustard on the pastry triangles.
2 Dampen the tips of the triangles with a little water. Working from the base, roll each pastry triangle around the pieces of cabanossi. Press lightly to secure the tip to the rest of the pastry.
3 Place the roll-ups on a lightly greased baking tray and brush with a mixture of egg yolk and 2 teaspoons cold water. Bake for 15–20 minutes, or until the roll-ups are golden brown.
IN ADVANCE: These can be made up to 2 days ahead, refrigerated, then gently reheated in the oven when required.

GLAZED CHICKEN WINGS

Preparation time: 30 minutes + marinating
Total cooking time: 45 minutes
Makes about 40

★

2 kg (4 lb) chicken wings
½ cup (125 ml/4 fl oz) barbecue sauce
½ cup (160 g/5½ oz) apricot jam
2 tablespoons white vinegar
2 tablespoons soy sauce
2 tablespoons tomato sauce
1 tablespoon sesame oil
2 cloves garlic, crushed

1 Trim excess fat from the wings. Stir the barbecue sauce, jam, vinegar, soy sauce, tomato sauce, oil and garlic in a small pan over low heat until just combined. Cool slightly, pour over the chicken wings and mix well. Cover and marinate in the refrigerator for at least 2 hours.
2 Preheat the oven to moderate 180°C (350°F/Gas 4). Drain the excess marinade from the wings and reserve. Bake the wings in a lightly greased baking dish for 45 minutes. To prevent sticking, you can add a little water. Turn halfway through the cooking time, brushing occasionally with the reserved marinade.

RIGHT: Spicy sausage roll-ups (left); Glazed chicken wings; Zucchini boats

COCONUT
Used extensively in Asian and Indian cuisines, as well as many others, coconut is available in many forms including milk, cream, oil, shredded, flaked and desiccated, or powdered. High in saturated fat, it is not good if you are watching your weight.

ZUCCHINI (COURGETTE) BOATS

Preparation time: 20 minutes
Total cooking time: 10 minutes
Makes 30

☆

5 large zucchini (courgettes)
1 large tomato, finely chopped
2 spring onions, finely chopped
1 tablespoon chopped fresh parsley
2 slices salami, finely chopped
1/2 cup (60 g/2 oz) grated Cheddar

1 Cut each zucchini into three equal pieces, about 4 cm (1 1/2 inches) long. Cut each piece in half lengthways.
2 Using a teaspoon, scoop a small hollow from each piece. Add the zucchini to a pan of simmering water for about 3 minutes, or until tender; drain. Refresh under cold water, then pat dry with paper towels.
3 Combine the tomato, onion, parsley, salami and Cheddar in a small bowl. Spoon the filling into the zucchini boats. Cook under a preheated grill until the Cheddar has melted and the boats are warmed through. Serve immediately.

CHILLI PRAWNS WITH SHREDDED COCONUT

Preparation time: 40 minutes + marinating
Total cooking time: 8–10 minutes
Makes about 48

☆

1 cup (250 ml/8 fl oz) tomato sauce
3 cloves garlic, crushed
1 teaspoon ground chilli
1/4 cup (60 ml/2 fl oz) lemon juice
2 teaspoons finely grated lemon rind
2 tablespoons soy sauce
2 tablespoons honey
1 tablespoon oil
2 kg (4 lb) raw king prawns, peeled and deveined
1 cup (60 g/2 oz) shredded coconut

1 In a large bowl, mix the tomato sauce, garlic, chilli, lemon juice, rind, soy sauce and honey. Add the prawns and marinate in the refrigerator for at least 2 hours. Drain. Reserve the marinade.
2 Heat the oil in a large frying pan. Add the prawns and coconut and cook until the prawns turn pink. Stir in the marinade and cook for 2 minutes, or until heated through. Stir in the coconut. Serve on a platter.

ABOVE: Chilli prawns with shredded coconut

223

SWEET POTATO ROSTI

Preparation time: 30 minutes
Total cooking time: 45 minutes
Makes 30

★

3 sweet potatoes, unpeeled
2 teaspoons cornflour
40 g (1 1/4 oz) butter
150 g (5 oz) mozzarella cheese, cut
    into 30 cubes

1 Boil or microwave the sweet potatoes until almost cooked, but still firm. Set aside to cool, then peel and coarsely grate into a bowl. Add the cornflour and 1/2 teaspoon salt and toss lightly to combine.
2 Melt a little of the butter in a frying pan. Place teaspoons of the potato in the pan and put a cube of cheese in the centre of each mound. Top with another teaspoon of potato and gently flatten to form rough circles. Increase the heat to medium and cook for about 3 minutes each side, or until golden. Repeat with remaining potato mixture and mozzarella cubes.
IN ADVANCE: The sweet potatoes can be cooked and grated up to 2 hours ahead and set aside, covered, until serving time. Assemble and cook the rosti close to serving time.

CORN AND RED PEPPER (CAPSICUM) TARTS

Preparation time: 20 minutes
Total cooking time: 25 minutes
Makes about 36

★

3 sheets frozen puff pastry, thawed
310 g (10 oz) canned corn kernels, drained
150 g (5 oz) Red Leicester cheese, grated
1 small red pepper (capsicum), finely chopped
2 eggs, lightly beaten
1/4 cup (60 ml/2 fl oz) buttermilk
2/3 cup (170 ml/5 1/2 fl oz) thick (double) cream
1 teaspoon Dijon mustard
dash of Tabasco sauce

1 Preheat the oven to moderately hot 200°C (400°F/Gas 6). Lightly grease three 12-hole round-based patty tins. Using a 6 cm (2 1/2 inch) round pastry cutter, cut circles from the pastry sheets. Press the circles into the prepared tins and prick the bases all over with a fork.
2 Combine the corn, cheese and red pepper in a bowl and season with salt and freshly ground pepper. Whisk the eggs, buttermilk, cream, mustard and Tabasco sauce in a jug. Spoon some of the vegetable mixture into the pastry cases, then pour the egg mixture over the top until the cases are almost full. Bake for 20–25 minutes, or until well risen and set. The tarts can be served hot or cold. Garnish with herbs of your choice if you wish.
IN ADVANCE: The tarts can be made up to a day ahead and refrigerated, covered, in an airtight container, or frozen for up to 2 months.

EGGS WITH SALMON AND CAPERS

Preparation time: 20 minutes
Total cooking time: 10 minutes
Makes 24

★

12 eggs
1 tablespoon drained capers, finely chopped
1 tablespoon finely chopped fresh dill
1/2 cup (125 g/4 oz) whole egg mayonnaise
200 g (6 1/2 oz) sliced smoked salmon
extra dill, to garnish

1 Put the eggs in a saucepan, cover with cold water and slowly bring to the boil. Gently stir the eggs while boiling to centre the yolk. Cook for 7 minutes, rinse under cold water and peel. Cut the eggs in half lengthways.
2 Remove the yolk from the egg halves, press the yolks through a sieve or grate finely into a bowl, then combine with the capers, dill and mayonnaise. Mix with a fork until well combined. Season, to taste.
3 Using a 1 cm (1/2 inch) star nozzle, pipe a small rosette of the egg mixture into each of the egg halves.
4 Shred the salmon slices and pile on top of the egg halves. Garnish with dill sprigs and black pepper, to taste. Serve.

OPPOSITE PAGE: Sweet potato rosti (top); Corn and red pepper tarts

SANDWICHES Sandwiches don't have

to be ungainly chunks of bread filled with salmon paste or cheese spread. Welcome

to the sophisticated party sandwich. It could just be the star of your show.

HAM AND CORN RELISH RIBBONS

Mix 1 cup (250 g/8 oz) sour cream with ½ cup (140 g/4½ oz) corn relish and spread on 8 slices of white bread. Top each with a slice of dark seed bread. Top that with sliced ham, then sandwich with a buttered slice of white bread. Remove the crusts and slice each sandwich into three. Makes 24 ribbon sandwiches.

VEGETABLE TRIANGLES

Cut 500 g (1 lb) butternut pumpkin into chunks, put in a baking dish, drizzle with oil and bake in a moderately hot 200°C (400°F/Gas 6) oven for 1 hour, or until tender. Cool, then mash. Spread 4 slices of soy and linseed bread with 1 tablespoon of tomato salsa. Top each with sliced marinated eggplant, coriander leaves and sliced spring onion. Spread 4 more slices of bread with the mashed pumpkin and place on top. Remove the crusts and cut into triangles. Makes 16.

226

CHICKEN AND GUACAMOLE SQUARES

Mash 2 avocados with 1 tablespoon mayonnaise, 1 teaspoon chopped chilli, 1 tablespoon lemon juice, 1 small chopped tomato and 1/2 finely chopped red onion. Spread over 8 slices of wholemeal bread and top with 250 g (8 oz) sliced smoked chicken breast. Add trimmed snow pea (mangetout) sprouts. Sandwich with more bread, remove the crusts and cut into squares. Makes 32.

TURKEY AND BRIE TRIANGLES

Trim the crusts from 8 slices bread. Spread 4 with cranberry sauce. Using 120 g (4 oz) turkey breast, 120 g (4 oz) sliced brie and 4 butter lettuce leaves, make into sandwiches. Cut into triangles. Makes 16.

ROAST BEEF, PATE AND ROCKET FINGERS

Trim the crusts from 16 slices of bread. Spread 160 g (5 1/2 oz) cracked pepper paté over half the bread. Make sandwiches using 250 g (8 oz) sliced rare roast beef, 160 g (5 1/2 oz) semi-dried tomatoes and rocket leaves. Cut each into three fingers to serve. Makes 24.

LEMON SANDWICHES WITH PRAWNS

Wash and dry 1 1/2 thin-skinned lemons and slice finely. Make lemon sandwiches with 10 slices of multi-grain bread. Cut each sandwich into 8 triangles. Remove the crusts and serve with 500 g (1 lb) peeled and deveined cooked king prawns, leaving the tails intact. Makes 40.

CHICKEN, ROCKET AND WALNUT SANDWICHES

Fry 250 g (8 oz) chicken breast fillets and 500 g (1 lb) chicken thigh fillets until cooked. Cool, then chop finely. Mix with 1 cup (250 g/8 oz) mayonnaise, some finely chopped celery and chopped walnuts. Season. Make into sandwiches with 20 slices bread, adding trimmed rocket to each. Remove the crusts and cut the sandwiches into fingers. Makes 30.

CLOKWISE, FROM BOTTOM LEFT: Chicken and guacamole squares; Vegetable triangles; Ham and corn relish ribbons; Turkey and brie triangles; Roast beef, pâté and rocket fingers; Chicken, rocket and walnut sandwiches; Lemon sandwiches with prawns

MARINATED ROASTED VEGETABLE DIP

Preparation time: 55 minutes + marinating
Total cooking time: 50 minutes
Serves 8

★ ★

1 small eggplant (aubergine), sliced

2 zucchini (courgettes), sliced

3 red peppers (capsicums)

1/2 cup (125 ml/4 fl oz) extra virgin olive oil

2 cloves garlic, sliced

2 Roma tomatoes

200 g (6 1/2 oz) canned artichoke hearts, drained

7 g (1/4 oz) fresh oregano leaves

250 g (8 oz) ricotta cheese

45 g (1 1/2 oz) black olives, pitted and sliced

1 Place the eggplant and zucchini in a colander over a bowl, sprinkle generously with salt and leave for 15–20 minutes. Meanwhile, cut the red peppers into large flat pieces, removing the seeds and membrane. Cook, skin-side-up, under a hot grill until the skin is black and blistered. Cool in a plastic bag, then peel. Reserve about a quarter of the peppers to use as a garnish and place the rest in a large non-metallic bowl.

2 Place half the olive oil in a bowl, add 1 garlic clove and a pinch of salt and mix. Rinse the eggplant and zucchini and pat dry with paper towels. Place the eggplant on a non-stick or foil-lined tray and brush with the garlic oil. Cook under a very hot grill for 4–6 minutes each side, or until golden brown, brushing both sides with oil during grilling. The eggplant will burn easily, so keep a close watch. Allow to cool while grilling the zucchini in the same way. Add both to the red pepper in the bowl.

3 Slice the tomatoes lengthways, place on a non-stick or foil-lined baking tray and brush with the garlic oil. Reduce the temperature slightly and grill for 10–15 minutes, or until soft. Add to the bowl with the other vegetables.

4 Cut the artichokes into quarters and add to the bowl. Mix in any remaining garlic oil along with the remaining olive oil. Stir in the oregano and remaining garlic. Cover with a tight-fitting lid or plastic wrap and refrigerate for at least 2 hours.

5 Drain the vegetables and place in a food processor. Add the ricotta and process for 20 seconds, or until smooth. Reserve a tablespoon of olives to garnish. Add the rest to the processor. Mix in a couple of short bursts,

ABOVE: Marinated roasted vegetable dip

then transfer to a non-metallic bowl and cover with plastic wrap. Chill for at least 2 hours.
6 Slice the reserved roasted red pepper into fine strips and arrange over the top of the dip with the reserved olives.

HERBED SCALLOP KEBABS

Preparation time: 1 hour + soaking
Total cooking time: 10 minutes
Makes 24

★★

24 scallops
6 large spring onions, green part only
2 zucchini (courgettes)
2 carrots
20 g (3/4 oz) butter, melted
2 teaspoons lemon juice
1 tablespoon white wine
2 teaspoons mixed dried herbs
1/4 teaspoon onion powder

1 Soak 24 wooden skewers in cold water for 30 minutes. Wash the scallops, slice or pull off any vein, membrane or hard white muscle, then pat dry with paper towels. Cut the spring onions in half lengthways, then into 8 cm (3 inch) lengths. Line a baking tray with foil.
2 Using a vegetable peeler, slice the zucchini and carrots lengthways into thin ribbons. Plunge the vegetable strips into a bowl of boiling water, leave for 1 minute, then drain. Plunge into a bowl of iced water and leave until cold. Drain and pat dry with paper towels.
3 Roll each scallop in a strip of onion, carrot and zucchini and secure with a wooden skewer.
4 Combine the butter, juice and wine in a small bowl. Brush over the scallops. Sprinkle with the combined herbs and onion powder. Place under a hot grill for 5–10 minutes, or chargrill or barbecue until the scallops are tender and cooked through.
IN ADVANCE: Scallops can be prepared several hours ahead. Refrigerate, covered, until needed.

SCALLOPS
World-wide, there are more than 400 species of this popular bivalve mollusc. Both the roe and the muscle that opens and closes the shell are edible. The attractive fan-shaped fluted shells, which vary in colour, make ideal serving dishes.

LEFT: Herbed scallop kebabs

CRAB-STUFFED MUSHROOMS

Preparation time: 25 minutes
Total cooking time: 6 minutes
Makes 24

★

24 small cap mushrooms
30 g (1 oz) butter, softened
4 spring onions, chopped
200 g (6 1/2 oz) can crab meat, drained
2 tablespoons lemon juice
1/2 teaspoon chilli powder
1 cup (250 g/8 oz) sour cream
25 g (3/4 oz) Parmesan, grated
125 g (4 oz) Cheddar, grated
pinch of paprika

1 Preheat the oven to moderate 180°C (350°F/ Gas 4). Remove the mushroom stalks and chop finely; set aside. Place the mushroom caps on a baking tray.
2 Combine the butter, spring onion, crab, lemon juice, chilli powder and freshly ground pepper, to taste, in a bowl.
3 Mix in the mushroom stalks, sour cream and Parmesan. Spoon even amounts into the mushroom caps and sprinkle with the combined Cheddar and paprika.
4 Bake for 5–6 minutes, or until the Cheddar has melted and the mushrooms heated through. Serve warm.

CAVIAR EGGS

Preparation time: 20 minutes
Total cooking time: 7 minutes
Makes 40

★

20 eggs
1 tablespoon curry powder
1 1/2 cups (375 g/12 oz) whole egg mayonnaise
45 g (1 1/2 oz) jar red caviar
45 g (1 1/2 oz) jar black caviar

1 Put the eggs in a saucepan, cover with cold water and slowly bring to the boil. Gently stir the eggs while boiling to centre the yolk. Cook for 7 minutes, rinse under cold water and peel.
2 Cut the eggs in halves lengthways, remove the yolks and push the yolks through a fine sieve

into a bowl. Blend in the curry powder and mayonnaise, stirring until the mixture is smooth.
3 Put the filling in a piping bag fitted with a 1 cm (1/2 inch) star nozzle. Pipe the mixture into the egg cavities. Garnish with red and black caviar just before serving.
IN ADVANCE: The eggs can be prepared hours ahead, covered and refrigerated. Decorate with caviar close to serving.

SESAME CHICKEN STICKS

Preparation time: 25 minutes + overnight marinating
Total cooking time: 25 minutes
Makes about 32

★ ★

4 chicken breast fillets, cut into strips
1/4 cup (60 ml/2 fl oz) teriyaki sauce
1 tablespoon chilli sauce
1 tablespoon natural yoghurt
2 teaspoons curry powder
2 cups (100 g/3 1/2 oz) crushed cornflakes
1/4 cup (40 g/1 1/4 oz) sesame seeds
35 g (1 1/4 oz) Parmesan, grated

Sweet and sour sauce
1 tablespoon cornflour
1/2 cup (125 ml/4 fl oz) white vinegar
1/2 cup (125 g/4 oz) caster sugar
1/4 cup (60 ml/2 fl oz) tomato sauce
1 teaspoon chicken stock powder

1 Combine the chicken strips in a bowl with the teriyaki sauce, chilli sauce, yoghurt and curry powder. Mix well, cover and refrigerate overnight.
2 Preheat the oven to moderately hot 190°C (375°F/Gas 5). Combine the cornflakes, sesame seeds and Parmesan in a shallow dish. Drain the excess marinade from the chicken. Coat each chicken strip in the crumb mixture.
3 Place the strips in a single layer on a greased baking tray. Bake for 20–25 minutes, or until crisp and golden. Serve hot with the sauce.
4 To prepare the sauce, blend the cornflour with the vinegar and combine with the remaining ingredients and 1 cup (250 ml/8 fl oz) water in a small saucepan. Stir over medium heat until the mixture boils and thickens.
IN ADVANCE: Crumbed chicken strips can be frozen in a single layer for 2 months.

CAVIAR
True caviar, which is very expensive, is the roe or eggs from the sturgeon family of fish. The size of the roe varies according to the type of fish, and the colour ranges from light grey to black. Red caviar comes either from salmon, the roe of which is naturally red, or from lumpfish. Lumpfish roe is tiny and pink and is dyed black or red and sold as Danish or German caviar.

OPPOSITE PAGE, FROM LEFT: Crab-stuffed mushrooms; Caviar eggs; Sesame chicken sticks

1 Preheat the oven to moderate 180°C (350°F/ Gas 4). Spread the almonds and pecans on a large baking tray and bake for 5–10 minutes, or until they are crisp and lightly coloured. Remove and allow to cool.

2 Combine the sugar, salt and spices in a small bowl and mix well.

3 Heat a large non-stick frying pan and add the almonds and pecans. Sprinkle the spice mixture over the nuts and stir over medium heat for 5 minutes, or until the nuts turn golden. The sugar will melt and coat the nuts. Gently shake the frying pan often to ensure even cooking. If the nuts stick together, separate them with a wooden spoon. When the nuts are cooked, remove from the heat and spread them on a lightly oiled baking tray to cool.

NOTE: If you use a small frying pan, cook the nuts in batches. Cashews, macadamias or peanuts can be used or, if you prefer, just one variety.

IN ADVANCE: Transfer the cooled nuts to tightly sealed jars or containers. They will keep for a couple of weeks.

GOATS CHEESE TARTS WITH PEPPER (CAPSICUM) AND CARAMELIZED ONION

Preparation time: 20 minutes + chilling
Total cooking time: 55 minutes
Makes about 48

☆

2 cups (250 g/8 oz) plain flour

125 g (4 oz) butter, chopped

1 red pepper (capsicum)

150 g (5 oz) firm goats cheese, grated

1 cup (250 g/8 oz) sour cream or
    crème fraîche

2 eggs

1 clove garlic, crushed

2 teaspoons finely chopped fresh lemon thyme

30 g (1 oz) butter

1 large red onion, halved and finely sliced

2 teaspoons soft brown sugar

1 teaspoon balsamic vinegar

1 Preheat the oven to moderately hot 190°C (350°F/Gas 4). Lightly grease two 12-hole round-based patty tins.

2 Sift the flour with a pinch of salt into a large bowl. Add the butter and rub into the flour with

SWEET AND SALTY PARTY NUTS

Preparation time: 20 minutes
Total cooking time: 15 minutes
Serves 6-8

☆

250 g (8 oz) blanched almonds

250 g (8 oz) pecans

1/4 cup (60 g/2 oz) sugar

1 teaspoon salt

1 teaspoon ground cinnamon

pinch of ground cloves

1/2 teaspoon curry powder

1/4 teaspoon ground cumin

1/2 teaspoon ground black pepper

ABOVE: Sweet and salty party nuts

your fingertips until the mixture resembles fine breadcrumbs. Make a well in the centre and stir in up to 4 tablespoons water to form a firm dough. Gently gather together and lift onto a lightly floured surface. Press into a ball, then flatten into a disc. Wrap in plastic wrap and refrigerate for 30 minutes.

3 Roll out half the dough on a lightly floured surface to 2 mm (⅛ inch) thick and cut out 24 rounds with a 5 cm (2 inch) cutter. Place into the patty tins and refrigerate for 10 minutes.

4 Cut the pepper into quarters and remove the seeds and membrane. Cook, skin-side-up, under a hot grill until the skin is black and blistered. Place in a plastic bag until cool, then peel. Cut the flesh into thin strips.

5 Mix together the goats cheese, sour cream, eggs, garlic, thyme and salt and pepper and set aside.

6 Melt the butter in a frying pan and cook the onion for 5 minutes, or until golden brown. Add the sugar and vinegar and cook for another 5 minutes, or until caramelized.

7 Divide half the goats cheese mixture evenly onto the pastry rounds and top with half the pepper strips and half the caramelized onion. Bake for 20 minutes, or until golden brown. Repeat with the remaining pastry and filling. Serve immediately.

DEVILS ON HORSEBACK

Preparation time: 10 minutes + soaking
Total cooking time: 6 minutes
Makes 24

★

8 bacon rashers
12 pitted prunes
12 oysters, on the shell or bottled
2 tablespoons Worcestershire sauce
Tabasco sauce, to taste

1 Soak 24 wooden skewers in water for 30 minutes. Trim the rind from the bacon and cut each rasher into three pieces. Wrap a portion of bacon around each prune and secure with a skewer.

2 Remove the oysters from their shells, or drain from the bottling liquid. Sprinkle lightly with Worcestershire sauce and ground black pepper, to taste. Wrap each oyster in bacon, securing with a skewer as before.

3 Cook under a preheated grill or lightly oil the outer edge of a preheated barbecue flatplate. Cook the savouries, turning occasionally, until the bacon is crisp. Serve warm, sprinkled with a dash of Tabasco sauce.

DEVILS ON HORSEBACK
There are two versions of this party piece. One has oysters wrapped in bacon before being cooked, while the other has prunes instead of oysters. The prunes are sometimes cooked in wine, then stuffed with mango chutney or an almond. The addition of hot Tabasco sauce turns *Angels on Horseback* into little devils.

ABOVE: Devils on horseback

POTATO AND ROSEMARY PIZZETTAS

Preparation time: 25 minutes + standing
Total cooking time: 12–15 minutes
Makes 48

★ ★

1 teaspoon dried yeast
1/2 teaspoon sugar
2 1/2 cups (310 g/10 oz) plain flour
1/3 cup (80 ml/2 3/4 fl oz) olive oil
400 g (13 oz) pontiac potatoes, unpeeled
2 tablespoons olive oil, extra
1 tablespoon fresh rosemary leaves

1 Place the yeast, sugar and 1/3 cup (80 ml/ 2 3/4 fl oz) water in a small bowl, cover and leave in a warm place until foamy.
2 Sift the flour and 1/4 teaspoon salt into a large bowl. Make a well in the centre and stir in the yeast mixture, the oil and 1/3 cup (80 ml/ 2 3/4 fl oz) water; mix to a soft dough. Turn out onto a lightly floured surface and knead for 5 minutes, or until the dough is smooth and elastic. Place the dough in an oiled bowl, cover and leave in a warm place for about 1 hour, or until the dough has doubled in size.
3 Preheat the oven to hot 220°C (425°F/Gas 7). Punch down the dough to expel the air. Turn out and knead for 1 minute, or until smooth. Divide into 48 portions and roll each portion to a 5 cm (2 inch) round. Place on lightly greased baking trays.
4 Cut the potatoes into slices. Cover each dough round with a slice of potato, leaving a 1 cm (1/2 inch) border. Brush the pizzettas with the extra olive oil and sprinkle with rosemary leaves and salt. Bake on the highest shelf in the oven for 12–15 minutes, or until the pastry is crisp and lightly browned. Serve immediately.
IN ADVANCE: Best made close to serving. The dough can be prepared ahead on the day of serving and refrigerated, covered, up to the point of second kneading. Alternatively, at this stage, the dough can be frozen. When hard, remove from the trays and seal in plastic bags. Place on lightly greased baking trays to thaw. The pizzas can be baked several hours ahead and reheated in a moderate 180°C (350°F/Gas 4) oven for 5 minutes, or until warmed through.

POTATO BASKETS WITH CHEESE

Preparation time: 15 minutes
Total cooking time: 55 minutes
Makes about 40

★

20 small new potatoes
250 g (8 oz) ricotta cheese
35 g (1 1/4 oz) Cheddar, grated
25 g (3/4 oz) Parmesan, shredded
oil, for spraying or brushing
15 g (1/2 oz) fresh chives, finely chopped, to garnish

1 Preheat the oven to moderately hot 200°C (400°F/Gas 6). Boil or steam the potatoes for 10 minutes, or until just tender when tested with a skewer (do not overcook or the potatoes will fall apart when you are preparing them). Drain well and cool completely.
2 Meanwhile, in a small bowl combine the ricotta, Cheddar and Parmesan. Season, to taste, and set aside.
3 Cut the cooled potatoes in half and use a melon baller to scoop out the flesh, leaving a 5 mm (1/4 inch) border. Discard the flesh.
4 Lightly spray the potato halves with oil and bake on baking trays for 30–45 minutes, or until crisp and golden. Heat the grill to high.
5 Fill each potato shell with a teaspoon of the cheese mixture and grill for 5–8 minutes, or until the tops are lightly golden and the cheese has melted. Arrange on a serving dish and garnish each with chopped chives. Serve immediately.
IN ADVANCE: The potatoes can be cooked and filled in advance, then grilled just before serving.

CUCUMBER BITES

Cut 1 cm (1/2 inch) rounds of telegraph cucumber. You can leave as is or cut into shapes with a decorative cutter. Top with dollops of taramasalata (see page 184) or creamy salmon dip (see page 236). Sprinkle with chopped fresh dill and decorate with small pieces of sliced lemon. Cooked, peeled and deveined prawns can be put on top, or small pieces of smoked salmon. Refrigerate until ready to serve.

ROSEMARY
This fragrant herb is native to the Mediterranean region. The silvery-grey spiky leaves complement many foods including lamb, fish, tomatoes and vegetables. Because of its strong flavour the herb should be used sparingly. The leaves are also available dried or ground.

OPPOSITE PAGE: Potato and rosemary pizzettas (top); Potato baskets with cheese

DIPS
These are a favourite at any gathering. Serve them up with crudités, crackers or crusty bread and watch your guests hovering around the bowl trying not to look too greedy.

CREAMY SALMON
Combine 200 g (6½ oz) cream cheese with 100 g (3½ oz) chopped smoked salmon and 5 tablespooons cream in a food processor and mix until smooth. Season with pepper and sprinkle with a few chopped chives. Keep refrigerated until ready to use.
Makes about 1½ cups.

HOT APPLE CHUTNEY
Beat ¼ cup (60 g/2 oz) sour cream, ½ cup (125 g/4 oz) natural yoghurt, ¼ cup (70 g/2¼ oz) ready-made hot apple chutney and 1 teaspoon maple syrup together until smooth. Season, to taste, with salt and pepper and refrigerate until ready to serve.
Makes about 1½ cups.

BLUE CHEESE AND CREAM
Mix 250 g (8 oz) blue cheese in a food processor with ½ cup (125 ml/4 fl oz) cream until smooth. Transfer to a bowl, stir in another ½ cup (125 ml/4 fl oz) cream and 2 teaspoons apple cider vinegar and mix well. Season with salt and pepper, cover and refrigerate until ready to use. Makes about 1½ cups.

SWEET AND SOUR

Beat 1 cup (250 g/4 oz) natural yoghurt and ⅓ cup (80 ml/2¾ fl oz) bottled sweet and sour sauce together until smooth. Add 1 tablespoon finely chopped fresh chives and season, to taste, with salt and pepper. Cover and keep refrigerated until ready to use. Makes about 1½ cups.

CUCUMBER AND PEAR

Beat 2 tablespoons whole egg mayonnaise, 2 tablespoons natural yoghurt, 1 tablespoon sour cream and 1 teaspoon Dijon mustard together until well combined and smooth. Finely dice half a pear and ¼ of a small cucumber and stir into the mixture with 1 teaspoon of lemon juice. Season, to taste, with salt and freshly ground black pepper. Cover and keep refrigerated until ready to use. Makes about 1 cup.

REFRIED BEANS

Combine a 460 g (14 oz) can refried beans and ¼ cup (60 g/2 oz) sour cream in a food processor and mix until smooth, adding salt and pepper, to taste. Cover and keep at room temperature until ready to use. Makes about 1½ cups.

AVOCADO AND HERB

Place 1 avocado, 1 tablespoon each of sour cream, lemon juice and light olive oil, 1 small seeded tomato and ¾ cup (25 g/¾ oz) coriander leaves in a food processor and mix until smooth. Season with salt and pepper. Transfer to a glass bowl, lay plastic wrap directly onto the surface of the dip (to prevent a skin forming) and keep refrigerated until ready to use. Try to make this dip close to serving time, so it doesn't discolour. Makes about 2 cups.

CORN AND BACON

Cut the corn kernels from 2 cobs of corn and cook in boiling water, covered, for about 10 minutes, then drain. Meanwhile cook 250 g (8 oz) lean finely chopped bacon in a non-stick pan until very crispy and drain on paper towels. Put the corn in a food processor with 1 crushed clove garlic and mix until quite smooth. Add 250 g (8 oz) spreadable cream cheese and process until well combined. Spoon into a serving dish, cool to room temperature and sprinkle the bacon and some chopped chives over the top. Makes about 2 cups.

CLOKWISE, FROM TOP LEFT: Creamy salmon; Blue cheese and cream; Cucumber and pear; Avocado and herb; Corn and bacon; Refried beans; Sweet and sour; Hot apple chutney

mustard in a small bowl. Peel the eggs, and toss lightly in the flour.

3 Divide the chicken mixture into 24 even portions. Using damp hands, wrap each portion around an egg. Brush each wrapped egg with the beaten egg, and then roll in breadcrumbs, shaking off any excess.

4 Fill a deep heavy-based pan one third full of oil and heat the oil to 180°C (350°F). The oil is ready when a cube of bread dropped in the oil turns golden brown in 15 seconds. Deep-fry the coated eggs until golden brown, then drain on crumpled paper towels. Serve hot, either whole or cut in half.

IN ADVANCE: The eggs can be assembled up to 4 hours ahead and refrigerated, covered, until required. Deep-fry just before serving and garnish with fresh herb sprigs.

RATATOUILLE TRIANGLES

Preparation time: 45 minutes + chilling
Total cooking time: 40 minutes
Makes 18

✩

3 tablespoons oil
1 spring onion, finely chopped
1–2 cloves garlic, crushed
1 eggplant (aubergine), diced
1 red pepper (capsicum), diced
2 zucchini (courgettes), diced
6 button mushrooms, diced
1 tomato, peeled, seeded and chopped
1 tablespoon chopped capers
2 tablespoons chopped fresh parsley
50 g (1 3/4 oz) Parmesan, grated
2 sheets ready-rolled puff pastry

1 Heat the oil in a heavy-based frying pan, add the spring onion and garlic and stir for 2 minutes. Add the eggplant, red pepper, zucchini and mushrooms and cook, stirring, for 10 minutes, or until softened.

2 Remove from the heat and add the tomato, capers and parsley. Cool and add the Parmesan. Cut each sheet of pastry into 3 equal strips and each strip into 3 triangles. Roll up a thin border on each side of the triangle and twist the corners to seal. Place on a greased baking tray and prick all over with a fork. Cover and chill for 10–15 minutes.

3 Preheat the oven to moderately hot 190°C (375°F/Gas 5) and bake the triangles for

SCOTCH QUAIL EGGS

Preparation time: 30 minutes
Total cooking time: 20 minutes
Makes 24 whole eggs or 48 halves

✩ ✩

24 quail eggs
600 g (1 1/4 lb) chicken mince
2 teaspoons grated fresh ginger
2 tablespoons chopped fresh chives
2 teaspoons Dijon mustard
1/2 cup (60 g/2 oz) plain flour
2 eggs, lightly beaten
1 cup (100 g/3 1/2 oz) dry breadcrumbs
oil, for deep-frying

1 Place the eggs in a pan and cover with water. Place over medium heat, stirring the eggs gently until the water boils (this centres the yolks). Cook for 5 minutes once boiling. Drain, place in a bowl of cold water and set aside to cool.

2 Mix the chicken mince, ginger, chives and

ABOVE: Scotch quail eggs

15 minutes, or until crisp. Place a tablespoon of filling into each pastry triangle and reheat for 5–10 minutes.

IN ADVANCE: These ratatouille triangles can be made up to 2 days ahead. Store the pastry triangles and ratatouille separately, covered, in the refrigerator. When required, fill the triangles and reheat briefly on greased baking trays in a moderate 180°C (350°F/Gas 4) oven.

POTATO NOODLE NIBBLES

Preparation time: 30 minutes + cooling
Total cooking time: 40 minutes
Serves 6

✷✷

450 g (14 oz) floury potatoes, peeled
   and chopped
40 g (1¼ oz) butter, softened
2 tablespoons grated Parmesan or
   Pecorino cheese
100 g (3½ oz) besan (chickpea flour)
2 teaspoons ground cumin
2 teaspoons garam masala
1 teaspoon ground coriander
1 teaspoon chilli powder
1 teaspoon cayenne pepper
1½ teaspoons ground turmeric
oil, for deep-frying

1 Boil or steam the potato until tender. Drain and cool for 15–20 minutes, then mash with the butter and cheese. Add the besan, cumin, garam masala, coriander, chilli powder, cayenne, turmeric and ¾ teaspoon of salt and mix with a wooden spoon until a soft, light dough forms. Turn out and knead lightly 10–12 times, until quite smooth.
2 Fill a deep heavy-based pan one third full of oil and heat to 180°C (350°F). Test the temperature by dropping a small ball of dough into the oil. The oil is ready if the dough rises immediately to the surface.
3 Using a piping bag with a 1 cm (½ inch) star nozzle, pipe short lengths of dough into the oil, cutting the dough off with a knife. Cook in manageable batches. They will rise to the surface and turn golden quickly. Remove with a slotted spoon and drain on crumpled paper towels. Serve the nibbles within 2 hours of cooking.

SMOKED SALMON AND ROCKET ROLLS

Preparation time: 20 minutes
Total cooking time: Nil
Makes 36

✷

200 g (6½ oz) ricotta cheese
¼ cup (60 g/2 oz) crème fraîche or
   sour cream
2 teaspoons wasabi paste
1 tablespoon lime juice
12 slices brown bread, crusts removed
300 g (10 oz) smoked salmon
100 g (3½ oz) baby rocket, trimmed
rocket leaves, extra, to garnish

1 Mix together the ricotta, crème fraîche, wasabi and lime juice.
2 Roll the bread out with a rolling pin to flatten.
3 Spread the ricotta over the bread, then top with the smoked salmon and rocket leaves, leaving a border. Roll up lengthways, wrap tightly in plastic wrap to hold the shape, then refrigerate for 30 minutes.
4 Unwrap, trim the ends and cut into 2 cm (¾ inch) slices. Garnish with rocket leaves.

POTATO NOODLE NIBBLES

Spoon the mixture into a piping bag with a star nozzle and pipe short lengths of dough into the oil, in small batches. Cut the dough off with a knife.

ABOVE: Potato noodle nibbles

BABY POTATOES

Preparation time: 10 minutes
Total cooking time: 40 minutes
Makes 30

★

30 baby new potatoes (see Note)
1 cup (250 g/8 oz) sour cream
2 tablespoons caviar

1 Preheat the oven to moderately hot 200°C (400°F/Gas 6). Prick the potatoes with a fork and place on a baking tray. Bake for 40 minutes, or until tender. Cool to room temperature.
2 Cut a large cross in the top of each potato, squeeze open, and top with a small dollop of sour cream and a little caviar.
IN ADVANCE: Cook the potatoes up to 4 hours ahead. Prepare up to 30 minutes before serving.
NOTE: Choose very small potatoes of the same size, so they take the same time to cook and are easy to eat. Use red or black caviar, or a combination. Caviar comes in different varieties and you may like to try various ones.

BEEF ROLLS

Preparation time: 30 minutes
Total cooking time: 30 minutes
Makes about 20

★

500 g (1 lb) beef fillet, 8 cm (3 inch) in diameter
3 tablespoons olive oil
1 1/2 tablespoons horseradish cream
1 1/2 tablespoons wholegrain mustard
1 zucchini (courgette), cut into fine strips
1 small carrot, cut into fine strips
1 small red pepper (capsicum), cut into fine strips
60 g (2 oz) snow peas (mangetout), cut into fine strips

1 Preheat the oven to moderately hot 200°C (400°F/Gas 6). Trim the beef of excess fat and sinew and brush with a little of the oil. Heat a heavy-based frying pan over high heat and brown each side of the beef fillet quickly, to seal in the juices. Transfer to a baking dish and bake for 20 minutes. Remove and set aside to cool.
2 Slice the cooled beef very thinly. Combine the horseradish cream and the mustard, then spread a little over each slice of beef.
3 Heat the remaining oil in a pan and cook the zucchini, carrot, pepper and snow peas quickly over high heat, and then allow to cool. Place a small bunch of the cooked vegetable strips on the end of each beef slice and roll up. Arrange on a platter and serve.
IN ADVANCE: The beef can be cooked and the vegetables prepared up to 2 hours in advance. Don't cook the vegetables or fill the rolls any earlier than 30 minutes before serving.

CORN MINI MUFFINS WITH PRAWNS AND DILL MAYONNAISE

Preparation time: 15 minutes
Total cooking time: 40 minutes
Makes about 50

★

2 cups (250 g/8 oz) plain flour, sifted
3/4 cup (110 g/3 1/2 oz) cornmeal
1 tablespoon baking powder
1/4 cup (60 g/2 oz) sugar
2 eggs, lightly beaten
125 g (4 oz) butter, melted
1 cup (250 ml/8 fl oz) milk
3 tablespoons finely chopped fresh dill
1 tablespoon lemon juice
1 teaspoon horseradish cream
1 1/2 cups (375 g /12 oz) whole egg mayonnaise
300 g (10 oz) small cooked prawns

1 Preheat the oven to moderately hot 200°C (400°F/Gas 6) and oil or spray two 12-hole mini muffin pans. Sift the flour into a large bowl and mix with the cornmeal, baking powder, sugar and 1/2 teaspoon salt. Add the eggs, butter and milk. Stir until just combined. Spoon small amounts into the muffin tins, filling the holes three-quarters full. Cook for 15–20 minutes, or until lightly browned. Turn onto a cake rack to cool. Repeat until you have used all the mixture.
2 Mix the dill, lemon juice and horseradish cream into the mayonnaise and add plenty of salt and black pepper.
3 When the muffins are cool, cut a circle from the top, as you would with a butterfly cake, and spoon a little dill mayonnaise into the cavity. Top with a prawn and some freshly ground black pepper.

DILL
This is a tall annual herb with delicate, long, thin leaves which have an intense aroma and distinctive taste. The leaves are chopped and served with fish, potatoes and other vegetables, or added to butters and sauces. The flavour also complements some soups and salads. The seeds are also used in cookery and are reminiscent of aniseed.

OPPOSITE PAGE: Baby potatoes (centre); Beef rolls

PARSLEY

Parsley is probably the most commonly used herb in the kitchen. Two different types are cultivated. This one, the curly-leafed variety, is commonly grown in the garden and is milder than the flat-leafed parsley. Parsley is used to flavour many sauces, vegetables, soups and casseroles and makes an attractive garnish. Parsley is a good source of some vitamins and minerals.

HERBED CHEESE CRACKERS

Preparation time: 40 minutes
Total cooking time: 8 minutes each tray
Makes 20

★

Biscuit pastry

1 cup (125 g/4 oz) plain flour

1/2 teaspoon baking powder

60 g (2 oz) butter

1 egg, lightly beaten

60 g (2 oz) Cheddar, grated

1 teaspoon chopped fresh chives

1 teaspoon chopped fresh parsley

Cheese filling

80 g (2 3/4 oz) cream cheese, softened

20 g (3/4 oz) butter

1 tablespoon chopped fresh chives

1 tablespoon chopped fresh parsley

1/4 teaspoon lemon pepper

90 g (3 oz) Cheddar, grated

1 Preheat the oven to moderately hot 190°C (375°F/Gas 5). Line two baking trays with baking paper.
2 To make the biscuit pastry, sift the flour and baking powder into a large bowl and add the chopped butter. Rub in with your fingertips, until the mixture resembles fine breadcrumbs.
3 Make a well in the centre and add the egg, cheese, herbs and 1 tablespoon iced water. Mix with a flat-bladed knife, using a cutting action until the mixture comes together in beads. Gently gather together and lift out onto a lightly floured surface. Press together into a ball.
4 Roll the pastry between sheets of baking paper to 3 mm (1/8 inch) thickness. Remove the top sheet of paper and cut the pastry into rounds, using a 5 cm (2 inch) cutter. Place the rounds onto the trays. Re-roll the remaining pastry and repeat cutting. Bake for about 8 minutes, or until lightly browned. Transfer to a wire rack to cool.
5 To make the filling, beat the cream cheese and butter in a small bowl with electric beaters until light and creamy. Add the herbs, pepper and cheese and beat until smooth. Spread half a teaspoon of filling on half of the biscuits and sandwich together with the remaining biscuits.
NOTE: You can use freshly chopped lemon thyme instead of parsley.

IN ADVANCE: The biscuits can be made 2 days ahead and stored in an airtight container, or frozen. The filling can be made a day ahead and stored, covered, in the refrigerator.

ABOVE: Herbed cheese crackers

Spread half the softened cream cheese over the egg layer with a spatula.

When set, gently ease the side of the tin away from the dip.

EGG AND CAVIAR MOULDED DIP

Preparation time: 1 hour + chilling
Total cooking time: 7 minutes
Serves 8–12

★ ★

7 eggs

3 tablespoons finely chopped fresh parsley

3 tablespoons whole egg mayonnaise

80 g (2¾ oz) chives, finely chopped

500 g (1 lb) cream cheese, softened to room temperature

90 g (3 oz) black caviar

300 g (10 oz) sour cream

extra chives, snipped, and black caviar, for serving

1 Fill a pan with cold water and gently add the eggs. Bring to the boil, then reduce the heat and simmer for 7 minutes. Drain and plunge the eggs in cold water to stop the cooking process. Cool thoroughly and drain.

2 Line a deep loose-based fluted flan tin (about 18 cm/7 inches in diameter) with plastic wrap, leaving a wide overhang to help you remove the moulded dip from the tin.

3 Peel and mash the eggs, add the parsley and mayonnaise, and season with salt and pepper.

4 Divide the egg mixture in half. Spoon one half into the lined tin. Firmly press down and smooth the surface with a spatula or the back of a spoon, pressing well into the side of the tin. Sprinkle with half the chives, pressing them down into the dip. Using a clean, warm spatula, spread with half the cream cheese to form another layer. Spoon half the caviar over the cream cheese and press down gently.

5 Repeat the layering with the remaining egg mixture, chives, cream cheese and caviar. Cover the moulded dip with plastic wrap, pressing down firmly so the layers stick together, and refrigerate for 2 hours.

6 Remove the top cover of plastic wrap and place a plate over the mould. Flip over onto the plate while holding the tin and gently ease the tin off. Carefully remove the plastic wrap, trying not to damage the fluted edges.

7 Spoon dollops of sour cream over the top of the mould and spread a little. Decorate with the extra snipped chives and a few spoonfuls of caviar. Serve with water crackers.

ABOVE: Egg and caviar moulded dip

PATES
Not strictly finger food—you will need a knife to spread them lusciously over crunchy toast—however, no occasion would be quite complete without a stylish pâté.

GRAND MARNIER PATE

Melt 90 g (3 oz) butter in a pan and cook 1 chopped onion and 1 crushed clove of garlic until the onion is tender. Add 250 g (4 oz) trimmed duck or chicken livers and cook for 5–10 minutes. Spoon into a food processor or blender with 2 tablespoons orange juice, 1 tablespoon Grand Marnier (or port or liqueur of your choice), 1 tablespoon sour cream and freshly ground pepper, to taste.

Process until smooth. To prepare the topping, arrange 2 orange slices (cut into quarters if you wish), and fresh chives or parsley in the base of a 2-cup (500 ml/ 16 fl oz) capacity serving dish. Sprinkle 1½ teaspoons gelatine over ½ cup (125 ml/4 fl oz) hot chicken stock and whisk vigorously with a fork to dissolve. Pour over the oranges to a depth of 1 cm (½ inch). Refrigerate until set. Spoon the pâté over the gelatine layer, tap gently

and smooth the top. Refrigerate until set. Unmould onto a serving plate. Serve with crackers or Melba toast. (Pâté can also be made without the gelatine topping, and served on cracker biscuits.) Serves 12–15.

SMOKED TROUT PATE

Mix 250 g (8 oz) skinned and boned smoked trout, 125 g (4 oz) softened butter and 125 g (4 oz) softened cream

cheese in a food processor for 20 seconds, or until smooth. Add 1 tablespoon lemon juice, 1 teaspoon horseradish cream, 15 g (1/2 oz) each of finely chopped fresh parsley and fresh chives and process for 10 seconds. Add salt and freshly ground black pepper, to taste, and more lemon juice, if liked. Transfer to a small serving dish. Serve with hot toasted brown bread. Serves 8–10.

LEMON PRAWN PATE

Melt 100 g (3 1/2 oz) butter in a frying pan. When it sizzles, add 3 crushed cloves garlic and 750 g (1 1/2 lb) peeled and deveined raw prawns and stir for 3–4 minutes, or until the prawns are pink and cooked through. Cool. Transfer to a food processor, add 1 teaspoon grated lemon rind, 3 tablespoons lemon juice and 1/4 teaspoon grated nutmeg and process for 20 seconds, or until roughly

puréed. Season and add 2 tablespoons each of mayonnaise and finely chopped fresh chives, then process for 20 seconds, or until combined. Spoon into a dish and chill for at least 1 hour, or until firm. Serves 6–8.

MUSHROOM PATE

Melt 40 g (1 1/4 oz) butter and 1 tablespoon oil in a large frying pan. Add 400 g (13 oz) chopped field mushrooms and 2 crushed cloves garlic. Cook until the mushrooms have softened and the mushroom liquid has evaporated. Stir in 3 chopped spring onions. Allow to cool, then process with 1 tablespoon lemon juice, 100 g (3 1/2 oz) ricotta cheese, 100 g (3 1/2 oz) soft cream cheese and 2 tablespoons chopped fresh coriander leaves. Process until smooth. Season, to taste, then spoon into a serving dish, cover and chill for 2 hours. Serves 8–10.

SOFT CHEESE PATE

Roughly chop 150 g (5 oz) toasted pine nuts in a food processor, add 500 g (1 lb) crumbled feta cheese, 3/4 cup (185 ml/6 fl oz) cream and 2 teaspoons coarsely ground pepper and mix until smooth. Add 30 g (1 oz) each of chopped fresh mint, dill and parsley and process until just combined. Line a 3-cup (750 ml/24 fl oz) capacity bowl with plastic wrap. Transfer the mixture to the bowl and press in firmly. Refrigerate, covered, for at least 1 hour, or until firm. Turn out onto a plate and smooth the surface with a knife. Serve with toast triangles. Serves 12–15.

PATES, CLOCKWISE, FROM LEFT: Grand Marnier; Smoked trout; Lemon prawn; Soft cheese; Mushroom

1 Combine the flour and seasoning in a plastic bag and toss with the chicken strips to coat; remove and shake off excess.

2 Beat the eggs lightly in a shallow bowl, and put the breadcrumbs in a plastic bag.

3 Working with a few chicken strips at a time, dip into the beaten egg, then toss in the breadcrumbs. Transfer to a baking tray covered with baking paper and refrigerate for about 30 minutes.

4 Heat 3 cm (1¼ inches) oil in a large frying pan to 180°C (350°F/Gas 4), or until a cube of bread dropped into the oil turns golden brown in 15 seconds. Fry the strips in batches for 3–5 minutes, or until golden brown. Drain on crumpled paper towels. Serve with the sauce.

5 For the sauce, combine the juice, vinegar, soy sauce, sugar and tomato sauce in a small pan. Stir over low heat until the sugar has dissolved. Blend the cornflour with 1 tablespoon water, add to the pan and stir constantly, until the mixture boils and thickens. Reduce the heat and simmer for 2 minutes.

CHICKEN STRIPS WITH SWEET AND SOUR SAUCE

Preparation time: 30 minutes + chilling
Total cooking time: 30 minutes
Makes 35–40

★ ★

½ cup (60 g/2 oz) plain flour
1 tablespoon chicken seasoning salt
4 chicken breast fillets, cut into 2 cm (¾ inch) wide strips
2 eggs
1½ cups (150 g/5 oz) dry breadcrumbs
oil, for shallow-frying

Sweet and sour sauce
1 cup (250 ml/8 fl oz) pineapple juice
3 tablespoons white wine vinegar
2 teaspoons soy sauce
2 tablespoons soft brown sugar
2 tablespoons tomato sauce
1 tablespoon cornflour

ABOVE: Chicken strips with sweet and sour sauce

BASIC SAUSAGE ROLLS

Preparation time: 30 minutes
Total cooking time: 15 minutes
Makes 36

★

3 sheets ready-rolled puff pastry
2 eggs, lightly beaten
750 g (1½ lb) sausage mince
1 onion, finely chopped
1 clove garlic, crushed
1 cup (80 g/2¾ oz) fresh breadcrumbs
3 tablespoons chopped fresh parsley
3 tablespoons chopped fresh thyme
½ teaspoon each ground sage, nutmeg, black pepper and cloves

1 Preheat the oven to 200°C (400°F/Gas 6). Cut the pastry sheets in half and lightly brush the edges with some of the beaten egg.

2 Mix half the remaining egg with the remaining ingredients in a large bowl, then divide into six even portions. Pipe or spoon the filling down the centre of each piece of pastry, then brush the edges with some of the egg. Fold the pastry over the filling, overlapping the edges and placing the join underneath. Brush the rolls with more egg, then cut each into 6 short pieces.

3 Cut two small slashes on top of each roll and place on lightly greased baking trays and bake for 15 minutes, then reduce the oven temperature to moderate 180°C (350°F/Gas 4) and bake for another 15 minutes, or until puffed and golden.

For a different flavour, select a filling from the recipes below and follow the method outlined for the basic sausage roll.

CURRIED PORK AND VEAL

Soak 3 dried Chinese mushrooms in hot water for 30 minutes, squeeze dry and chop finely. Cook 4 finely chopped spring onions, 1 crushed clove garlic, 1 finely chopped small red chilli and 2–3 teaspoons curry powder in 1 tablespoon oil. Transfer to a bowl and mix with 750 g (1½ lb) pork and veal mince, 1 cup (90 g/3 oz) fresh breadcrumbs, the dried mushrooms, 1 lightly beaten egg, 3 tablespoons chopped coriander and 1 tablespoon each soy and oyster sauce.

SPICY LAMB

Mix 750 g (1½ lb) lamb mince, 1 cup (90 g/ 3 oz) fresh breadcrumbs, 1 small grated onion, 1 tablespoon soy sauce, 2 teaspoons each of grated fresh ginger and soft brown sugar, 1 teaspoon ground coriander, ½ teaspoon each of ground cumin and sambal oelek. Lightly sprinkle the pastry rolls with poppy seeds after glazing and before baking.

SAUCY BEEF

Cook 1 finely chopped onion and 1–2 crushed cloves garlic in 20 g (⅔ oz) butter until the onion is softened. Mix 750 g (1½ lb) lean beef mince, the sautéed onion and garlic, 3 tablespoons finely chopped fresh parsley, 3 tablespoons plain flour, 3 tablespoons tomato sauce, 1 tablespoon each of Worcestershire and soy sauces and 2 teaspoons ground allspice until well combined.

CHUTNEY CHICKEN

Mix 750 g (1½ lb) chicken mince, 4 finely chopped spring onions, 1 cup (80 g/2¾ oz) fresh breadcrumbs, 1 finely grated carrot, 2 tablespoons fruit chutney and 1 tablespoon each of sweet chilli sauce and grated ginger. Sprinkle the pastry with sesame seeds after glazing, before baking.

BELOW: Basic sausage rolls (left); Sausage rolls with chutney chicken filling

SALMON SATAY WITH GINGER LIME MAYONNAISE

Preparation time: 30 minutes + chilling
Total cooking time: 4 minutes
Makes 24 skewers

★

500 g (1 lb) Atlantic salmon (or ocean trout) fillet
24 small wooden skewers
light olive oil

Ginger lime mayonnaise

1 cup (250 g/8 oz) whole egg mayonnaise
1/4 cup (60 g/2 oz) natural yoghurt
1 teaspoon finely grated fresh ginger
1 teaspoon finely grated lime rind
2 teaspoons lime juice

1 Remove the skin from the salmon. Use kitchen tweezers to remove any bones from the fish, then wrap the fish in plastic wrap and freeze for 1 hour. Soak small wooden satay sticks in cold water for 30 minutes (this will prevent them burning during cooking).
2 Cut the salmon fillets into 5 cm (2 inch) strips. Thread the strips loosely onto the satay sticks and place them on an oiled tray. Brush all over with oil and season, to taste, with salt and freshly ground pepper. Grill in two batches for 2 minutes, taking care not to overcook. Serve with the ginger lime mayonnaise.
3 To make ginger lime mayonnaise, place the mayonnaise in a small bowl and stir until smooth. Add the yoghurt, ginger and lime rind and juice. Add salt and pepper, to taste, and stir until blended thoroughly. Chill for at least 1 hour.
IN ADVANCE: The skewers can be assembled up to 1 hour in advance and refrigerated. Cook just prior to serving. Make the mayonnaise up to 2 days ahead and store, covered, in the refrigerator. The prepared skewers can be frozen in a single layer for up to 2 months.

MINI LENTIL BURGERS WITH TOMATO RELISH

Preparation time: 40 minutes
Total cooking time: 55 minutes
Makes 32

★

1 cup (185 g/6 oz) brown lentils
1 bay leaf
1 onion, roughly chopped
1 clove garlic, crushed
1 small leek, finely sliced
1 small carrot, finely grated
1 cup (80 g/2 3/4 oz) fresh breadcrumbs
2 egg yolks
2 tablespoons chopped fresh coriander
2 tablespoons oil
8 slices bread, cut into 4 cm (1 1/2 inch) squares
ready-made tomato relish, for serving

1 Place the lentils and bay leaf in a pan, cover with plenty of water, bring to the boil and simmer for 20–30 minutes, or until tender; drain well and discard the bay leaf.
2 Combine half the cooked lentils with the onion and garlic in a food processor until the mixture forms a smooth paste. Transfer to a bowl and mix with the remaining lentils, leek, carrot, breadcrumbs, egg yolks and coriander; season with salt and freshly ground black pepper. Form level tablespoons of the mixture into mini burgers.
3 Heat some of the oil in a non-stick frying pan and fry the mini burgers in batches until browned on both sides, adding more oil as necessary. Drain on paper towels and serve warm, on the bread squares (or toast), with a dollop of tomato relish on top. Garnish with fresh herbs.

OYSTERS WITH SALMON ROE

Spread rock salt all over a large plate to cover. Arrange 1 dozen freshly shucked oysters on the plate. Spoon 1 teaspoon of crème fraîche onto each oyster and top with 1/2 teaspoon salmon roe (you will need about 60 g/2 oz salmon roe). Season with black pepper. Garnish with fresh dill. Serve with lime wedges. (See cover illustration.)

BROWN LENTILS
Lentils come in various colours including brown, green and red. Some lentils are much bigger than others. Lentils have been used for thousands of years and are a good source of protein, fibre, potassium, magnesium and zinc, as well as some of the B vitamins. To prepare, lentils need to be picked over to remove any small stones, then, depending on the type, either soaked to soften before cooking, or simply cooked until soft. They are used in many recipes, including soups, casseroles, dhal and salads.

OPPOSITE PAGE: Salmon satay with ginger lime mayonnaise (top); Mini lentil burgers with tomato relish

CORNED BEEF, PARSNIP AND MINT PATTIES

Preparation time: 20 minutes
Total cooking time: 25 minutes
Makes 24

★★

ABOVE: Corned beef, parsnip and mint patties

2 parsnips, chopped

1 cup (100 g/3½ oz) dry breadcrumbs

200 g (6½ oz) piece cooked corned beef, finely chopped

1 egg yolk

¼ small onion, finely chopped

20 g (¾ oz) fresh mint leaves, finely chopped

1 tablespoon lemon juice

3 teaspoons wholegrain mustard

2 tablespoons plain flour

1 egg

1 tablespoon milk

¼ cup (60 ml/2 fl oz) olive oil

½ cup (140 g/4½ oz) spicy tomato chutney

24 small fresh mint leaves, to garnish

1 Cook the parsnip in a large pan of boiling water for 10 minutes, or until tender. Drain and mash until smooth. Set aside to cool.

2 Mix the parsnip with ⅓ cup 35 g (1¼ oz) of the breadcrumbs, the corned beef, egg yolk, onion, mint, lemon juice, mustard and salt and freshly ground black pepper.

3 Shape into 24 patties, pressing firmly together. Dust with flour and shake off any excess. Dip into the combined egg and milk, then coat in the remaining breadcrumbs.

4 Heat the oil in a large frying pan over medium-low heat and cook the patties in batches for 2–3 minutes each side, or until golden brown and heated through. Drain on crumpled paper towels. Spoon 1 teaspoon of tomato chutney onto each patty and top with a mint leaf. Serve immediately.

IN ADVANCE: The patties can be prepared a day ahead. Keep covered in the refrigerator until ready to cook.

MARINATED LAMB CUTLETS WITH SALSA VERDE

Preparation time: 30 minutes + marinating
Total cooking time: 20–25 minutes
Makes 24

✷ ✷

2 lemons
4 tablespoons virgin olive oil
1 tablespoon Dijon mustard
3 racks of 8 small lamb cutlets (about 1.1 kg), trimmed of fat
40 g (1¼ oz) flat-leaf parsley
3 drained anchovy fillets, finely chopped
1 clove garlic, crushed
1 tablespoon olive oil
1½ tablespoons baby capers, rinsed and drained

1 Finely grate the rind of the lemons and squeeze the juice from the fruit. Combine 1 teaspoon of the rind and 2 tablespoons of the juice with half the virgin olive oil and the mustard in a large bowl. Add the lamb racks and turn to coat thoroughly. Cover and refrigerate for at least 3 hours, or overnight.

2 To make the salsa verde, mix the parsley, anchovies, garlic, 1 tablespoon of the remaining lemon juice and 1 teaspoon of the rind in a food processor until finely chopped. With the motor running, add the remaining virgin olive oil and process until smooth and thickened. Transfer to a bowl, cover and refrigerate for at least 2½ hours.

3 Preheat the oven to moderately hot 200°C (400°F/Gas 6). Drain the lamb and discard the marinade. Heat the olive oil in a large baking dish over medium–high heat, add the lamb racks and cook, turning occasionally, for 5 minutes, or until the lamb is browned all over. Transfer the dish to the oven and bake for 15–20 minutes, or until the lamb is tender. Set aside for at least 10 minutes before slicing between the bones. Arrange in a single layer on a plate, top with salsa verde and sprinkle with capers.

NOTE: When you buy the racks of lamb, ask the butcher to cut through the bones at the base to make slicing into cutlets easier.

IN ADVANCE: Lamb can be prepared a day ahead, refrigerated, then brought to room temperature just before slicing and serving. Salsa verde can be made a day ahead and refrigerated until use.

OLIVE OIL
Olive oil is made by pressing olives from olive trees, native to the Mediterranean region. There are two methods of pressing olives. If cold-pressed, they are simply crushed, producing unrefined oil, whereas if pressed with the help of heat and treated in other ways, including the addition of preservatives, refined oil is the result. Olive oil is sold in different grades, which have different uses. Extra virgin olive oil, considered one of the best, is made from specially selected olives that are cold-pressed. It is used mainly for salad dressings or flavouring. Virgin olive oil is made with more mature olives and used in cooking and dressings. The cheaper all-purpose olive oil is made by the hot pressing method, sometimes with olives left after making extra virgin olive oil.

LEFT: Marinated lamb cutlets with salsa verde

FROM THE SHELL Some

foods need little dressing up—they seem to have been born to party. Shellfish are a

wonderful example—drizzle with sauce and serve in the shells nature gave them.

OYSTERS WITH PROSCIUTTO AND BALSAMIC VINEGAR

Place 24 fresh oysters on a baking tray and sprinkle with 2–3 tablespoons of balsamic vinegar. Chop 6 slices of prosciutto and sprinkle over the oysters. Sprinkle with cracked black pepper and place under a hot grill for 1 minute, or until the prosciutto is starting to crisp. Makes 24.

OYSTERS WITH TARRAGON

Remove 24 fresh oysters from their shells. Wash the shells and set aside. Combine the oysters with 1 tablespoon chopped fresh tarragon, 1 small finely chopped spring onion, 2 teaspoons white wine vinegar, 1 tablespoon lemon juice and 2 tablespoons extra virgin olive oil, cover and refrigerate for 30 minutes. Place the oyster shells on a serving plate

and spoon an oyster back into each shell. Drizzle with any remaining viniagrette. Makes 24.

SCALLOPS WITH LIME HOLLANDAISE SAUCE

Using a sharp knife, carefully cut 24 scallops from their shells, as cleanly as possible, and remove the veins. Wash the shells in warm water and warm

through on a baking tray in a moderate 180°C (350°F/Gas 4) oven for 5 minutes. Chargrill or fry the scallops for 2–4 minutes, then return to their shells. For the sauce, mix 1 egg yolk and 1 tablespoon lime juice in a food processor for 30 seconds. With the motor running, add 45 g (1½ oz) melted butter in a thin stream. (Beat in a bowl if you prefer.) Transfer to a bowl, add 1 tablespoon snipped chives and season with salt and pepper. Spoon 1 teaspoon over each scallop and serve. Makes 24.

CITRUS SAUCY SCALLOPS

Using a sharp knife, carefully cut 24 scallops from their shells, as cleanly as possible, and remove the veins. Wash the shells in warm water and warm through on a baking tray in a moderate 180°C (350°F/Gas 4) oven for 5 minutes.

Chargrill or fry the scallops for 2–4 minutes and return to their shells. For the sauce, combine 3 tablespoons lime juice, 1 tablespoon lemon juice, 1 finely chopped red chilli, 1 tablespoon fish sauce, 2 teaspoons sugar, 3 teaspoons chopped fresh coriander and 2 teaspoons chopped fresh mint. Spoon 1 teaspoon over each scallop and serve. Makes 24.

MUSSELS WITH BLOODY MARY SAUCE

Scrub 24 black mussels and remove the beards (discard any mussels which are open and don't close when tapped). Place in a large heavy-based pan with the juice of a lemon and 1 tablespoon water. Cover and steam over medium-low heat for 2–3 minutes, removing them as they open. (Discard any which haven't opened in that time.) Remove and discard the

top shell. Run a small knife along the shell under the mussel to detach it from the shell. Place the mussels in their shells on a baking tray which has been spread with a layer of salt (to keep them level and stop the filling falling out). For the sauce, combine 2 tablespoons vodka, 2 tablespoons tomato juice, 1 tablespoon lemon juice, 2 teaspoons Worcestershire sauce, a dash of Tabasco and ¼ teaspoon celery salt. Spoon 1 teaspoon into each shell and grill for a few seconds, or until the sauce is warm. Serve with a sprinkle of freshly ground black pepper. Makes 24.

FROM LEFT: Oysters with prosciutto and balsamic vinegar; Oysters with tarragon; Scallops with lime hollandaise sauce; Citrus saucy scallops; Mussels with bloody mary sauce

MINI EGGS FLORENTINE

Preparation time: 15 minutes + chilling
Total cooking time: 30 minutes
Makes 24

★ ★

Hollandaise sauce
3 egg yolks
2 tablespoons lime or lemon juice
125 g (4 oz) butter, melted

6–8 slices bread
oil spray
24 quail eggs
250 g (8 oz) English spinach, trimmed

1 Preheat the oven to moderate 180°C (350°F/ Gas 4). To make the hollandaise sauce, blend the yolks and juice in a food processor for 5 seconds, then gradually add the melted butter. Transfer to a bowl and refrigerate for about 30 minutes, until thickened.

2 Cut 24 rounds of bread with a 4 cm (1½ inch) cutter. Place on a baking tray, spray with oil and bake for 10 minutes. Turn over and bake for another 5 minutes, until dry and crisp.

3 Put about 2.5 cm (1 inch) water in a large non-stick frying pan and bring to simmering point. Reduce the heat so the water is not moving. Carefully crack the eggs into the water. Spoon a little water onto the top of the eggs as they cook, and when set, remove from the pan and drain on paper towels.

4 Steam or microwave the spinach for 2 minutes, or until wilted, then drain well. To assemble, put some spinach on the bread rounds, then top with egg and drizzle with hollandaise. Serve immediately.

NOTE: Quail eggs are available from speciality food stores or can be ordered from poultry shops. You can use bottled hollandaise. Any leftover hollandaise will keep in the refrigerator, covered, for up to five days.

HOLLANDAISE SAUCE
Although the origins of rich creamy hollandaise sauce are unknown, it translates from French into *Dutch sauce*. It was actually known by that name as long ago as the 16th century and until as recently as the early 20th century. Hollandaise sauce is used to embellish fish, eggs and vegetables, especially asparagus.

RIGHT: Mini eggs florentine

PAN-FRIED CHEESE SANDWICHES

Preparation time: 20 minutes
Total cooking time: 20 minutes
Makes about 40

★

20 thick slices white bread
2–3 tablespoons Dijon mustard
12 slices Cheddar
oil, for shallow-frying
plain flour, for dusting
3 eggs, lightly beaten
watercress, to garnish

1 Remove the crusts from the bread. Spread the bread with mustard, place a slice of cheese on top, then finish with another bread slice.
2 Heat a little oil in a frying pan. Dust the sandwiches lightly with flour and dip quickly into the beaten egg.
3 Cook the sandwiches on both sides until golden; drain on paper towels. Cut into quarters and garnish with watercress. Serve hot.
IN ADVANCE: Assemble the sandwiches up to 4 hours in advance, but don't dust with flour and dip in the egg until just before frying.

ALMOND-CRUSTED CHEESE BITES

Preparation time: 30 minutes + chilling
Total cooking time: 20 minutes
Makes 24

★ ★

500 g (1 lb) Cheddar, grated
250 g (8 oz) cold mashed pumpkin
1/3 cup (40 g/1 1/4 oz) plain flour
1 clove garlic, crushed
2 tablespoons chopped fresh chives or parsley
2 egg whites
250 g (8 oz) flaked almonds, roughly crushed
oil, for deep-frying

1 Combine the cheese, pumpkin, flour, garlic and chives in a large bowl. Beat the egg whites in a bowl until stiff, then stir into the pumpkin.
2 Mould small spoonfuls with your hands to form balls. Roll in the almonds, place on baking trays and refrigerate for 1 hour.
3 Fill a deep heavy-based pan one third full of oil and heat the oil to 180°C (350°F), or until a cube of bread dropped into the oil turns golden brown in 15 seconds. Deep-fry the balls in batches until golden brown; drain on crumpled paper towels.

PUMPKIN
This winter squash is sweet-tasting and very versatile. It can be baked, steamed, mashed or puréed, used in risotto and also made into a delicious soup. A whole pumpkin keeps in a cool, dark place for about six weeks. Once cut, however, it will tend to deteriorate quickly. Remove the seeds, wrap in plastic and refrigerate. Pumpkin is available in a variety of types and shapes, some of which are huge, others tiny, some round and fat, and others, such as the butternut, elongated. Make sure pumpkins are firm and heavy for their size when you buy them.

ABOVE: Pan-fried cheese sandwiches

OLIVE BASIL CHEESE SPREAD

Preparation time: 15 minutes
Total cooking time: Nil
Makes 2 cups

☆

250 g (8 oz) cream cheese, softened
200 g (6½ oz) feta cheese
20 g (¾ oz) basil leaves
3 tablespoons olive oil
15 Kalamata olives, pitted and roughly chopped

1 Combine the cream cheese, feta cheese, basil, 1 tablespoon of the oil and ¼ teaspoon cracked black pepper in a bowl and mix until smooth.
2 Fold in the olives and spoon into a serving bowl. Smooth the top with the back of the spoon. Pour the remaining oil over the top. Garnish with a little more cracked pepper and serve with warm bruschetta.

SMOKED SALMON PATE WITH CHIVE PIKELETS

Preparation time: 30 minutes + standing
Total cooking time: 40 minutes
Makes about 30

☆ ☆

125 g (4 oz) smoked salmon
2 teaspoons softened butter
1 small onion, chopped
1½ teaspoons horseradish cream
30 g (1 oz) soft butter, extra
3 teaspoons chopped tarragon
1 lime, cut into tiny wedges
red or black caviar, to garnish

Chive pikelets
½ cup (60 g/2 oz) self-raising flour
1 tablespoon coarsely chopped chives
1 egg yolk, lightly beaten
½ cup (125 ml/4 fl oz) milk

1 Roughly chop the salmon. Heat the butter in a small pan, add the onion and cook until soft. Put the smoked salmon, onion, horseradish cream and extra butter in a food processor. Season with salt and freshly ground black pepper and mix until smooth. Add the tarragon and process until the pâté is just combined.

2 For the pikelets, sift the flour and a pinch of salt into a bowl. Stir in the chives and make a well in the centre. Gradually whisk in the yolk and enough milk to form a smooth lump-free batter, the consistency of thick cream. Set aside for 15 minutes, then lightly grease a non-stick frying pan and drop teaspoons of the batter into the pan. When bubbles appear on the surface of the pikelets, turn them over and brown the other side. Transfer to a wire rack to cool. Repeat with the remaining batter.
3 Pipe or spread the pâté onto the pikelets, garnish with a slice of lime and some caviar.
IN ADVANCE: The pikelets may be assembled up to 3 hours ahead, covered and refrigerated.

OLIVE AND ALMOND PALMIERS

Preparation time: 30 minutes
Total cooking time: 20 minutes
Makes about 24

☆ ☆

75 g (2½ oz) black olives, pitted and chopped
95 g (3¼ oz) ground almonds
25 g (¾ oz) Parmesan, grated
2 tablespoons chopped fresh basil
3 tablespoons olive oil
2 teaspoons wholegrain mustard
2 sheets frozen puff pastry, thawed
¼ cup (60 ml/2 fl oz) milk

1 Preheat the oven to moderately hot 200°C (400°F/Gas 6). Line two baking trays with non-stick baking paper. In a food processor, process the olives, almonds, Parmesan, basil, oil, mustard, ¼ teaspoon salt and ½ teaspoon cracked black pepper until they form a paste.
2 Spread out one sheet of pastry and cover evenly with half the olive-almond paste. Fold two opposite ends into the centre to meet.
3 Fold the same way again. Brush the pastry with milk. Repeat the process with the remaining pastry and filling. Cut into 1.5 cm (⅝ inch) thick slices. Shape the slices into a V-shape, with the two sides curving out slightly. Bake on baking trays, leaving room for spreading, for 15–20 minutes, or until puffed and golden. Serve warm or at room temperature.
IN ADVANCE: Palmiers can be cooked up to 6 hours ahead and stored in an airtight container. Serve at room temperature, or warm.
NOTE: You can use ready-made olive paste.

PALMIERS
Traditional palmiers are small sweet puff pastry biscuits shaped a little like butterflies. Literally the word means 'palm tree' and it is believed their inventor thought the shape was reminiscent of the topknot of leaves on a palm. We have broken with tradition and given a savoury version.

OPPOSITE PAGE: Olive basil cheese spread (top); Smoked salmon pâté with chive pikelets

SWEET POTATO CREPES WITH DUCK FILLING

Bake the duck breasts on a wire rack in a baking dish until tender.

Measure the batter into a pan and quickly spread with the back of a spoon.

Fold the crepes in half to enclose the filling, then fold over into quarters.

ABOVE: Sweet potato crepes with duck filling

SWEET POTATO CREPES WITH DUCK FILLING

Preparation time: 25–30 minutes + chilling
Total cooking time: 55 minutes
Makes 24

★ ★ ★

1 cup (125 g/4 oz) plain flour

1/2 teaspoon bicarbonate of soda

3 eggs, lightly beaten

1 1/2 cups (375 ml/12 fl oz) milk

1 tablespoon light olive oil

2 teaspoons ground cumin

3 duck breast fillets (about 450 g/14 oz)

1/4 cup (60 ml/2 fl oz) olive oil

2 tablespoons orange juice

1 tablespoon lime juice

1 teaspoon pomegranate molasses

1/4 teaspoon finely grated orange rind

1/2 teaspoon sugar

pinch of ground cumin

60 g (2 oz) orange sweet potato, finely grated

2 tablespoons chopped fresh coriander

fresh coriander leaves, extra

1 Preheat the oven to moderately hot 200°C (400°F/Gas 6). Sift the flour and soda into a large bowl and make a well in the centre. Gradually add the combined eggs, milk, light olive oil and cumin, whisking to make a smooth, lump-free batter. Cover and refrigerate for 30 minutes.

2 Season the duck all over with salt and pepper. Heat a non-stick frying pan, brown the duck over medium-high heat, then bake, skin-side up, on a wire rack in a baking dish for 20 minutes, or until tender. Rest the duck in a warm place for at least 5 minutes.

3 Combine the olive oil, juices, molasses, orange rind, sugar and cumin in a screw-top jar and shake until well combined.

4 Discard the duck skin, then finely slice the duck across the grain or shred into thin pieces. Wrap in foil and keep warm in the oven.

5 Press the sweet potato between sheets of paper towel to extract as much moisture as possible. Stir into the batter with the coriander leaves. Spoon 1 tablespoon of batter into a non-stick or greased crepe pan. Quickly spread with the back of a spoon so the crepe measures about 12 cm (5 inches) across. Cook for 1 minute, or until lightly browned underneath. Turn and brown on the other side. Repeat to make 24 crepes. The crepes can be stacked, wrapped loosely in foil and kept warm in the oven.

6 To assemble, lay the crepes flat, and pile even amounts of duck in one quarter of each. Drizzle with pomegranate dressing and top with the extra coriander leaves. Fold the crepes in half to enclose the filling, then into quarters. Serve.
NOTE: Pomegranate molasses is available from gourmet speciality stores.
IN ADVANCE: The crepes and duck can both be prepared a day ahead, covered separately in the refrigerator, then reheated in foil. The dressing can be made a day ahead, refrigerated and brought to room temperature before serving.

CHIPOLATA SAUSAGES WITH HORSERADISH CREAM

Preparation time: 15 minutes
Total cooking time: 25 minutes
Makes 12

✹

2 tablespoons virgin olive oil
2 red onions, cut into thin wedges
2 tablespoons dark brown sugar
3 teaspoons balsamic vinegar
100 g (3 1/2 oz) spreadable cream cheese
1 tablespoon horseradish cream
12 chipolata sausages
12 par-baked mini bread rolls
100 g (3 1/2 oz) rocket leaves, stalks removed

1 Preheat the oven to hot 220°C (425°F/Gas 7). Heat 1 1/2 tablespoons olive oil in a small pan. Add the onion and 1 1/2 tablespoons water, cover, and cook over medium heat for about 10 minutes, stirring occasionally, until the onion is soft and starting to brown. Stir in the sugar and vinegar and cook, uncovered, for 3 minutes, or until thick. Season and keep warm.
2 Meanwhile, in a small bowl, mix the cream cheese and horseradish cream until smooth.
3 Heat the remaining oil in a large frying pan and cook the sausages in batches over medium-low heat for 6–8 minutes, or until brown and cooked. Remove; drain on crumpled paper towels.
4 Meanwhile, heat the bread rolls according to the manufacturer's instructions. When hot, slice vertically, three-quarters of the way through, and spread with the horseradish mixture. Fill the rolls with rocket and a sausage, then onion. Serve.
NOTE: If you can't get chipolatas, you can use thin sausages and twist them through the centre.

BALSAMIC VINEGAR
Good-quality balsamic vinegar is quite expensive because of the length of time involved in processing the Trebbiano grapes from which it is made. Genuine balsamic vinegar, which is aged for 30–50 years, is made by about 40 families in Italy, so only a small quantity is produced. You can usually tell the quality by the price. However, some of the cheaper vinegars, although not aged for as long, are still quite good. Avoid especially cheap ones as they are poor imitations. Balsamic vinegar is used in many salad dressings, marinades and sauces, and is also brushed directly onto food before grilling.

ABOVE: Chipolata sausages with horseradish cream

259

CHICKPEAS

The chickpea is the seed of a leguminous plant, native to Asia. Chickpeas are an excellent source of protein as well as dietary fibre, iron, B vitamins and potassium and so are an excellent staple in a vegetarian diet. As dried chickpeas need overnight soaking before being cooked, sometimes it is easier to use canned chickpeas, which are readily available.

ABOVE: Chicken felafel with tabbouli cones

CHICKEN FELAFEL WITH TABBOULI CONES

Preparation time: 30 minutes + standing
Total cooking time: 20 minutes
Makes 24

★ ★ ★

¹/4 cup (45 g/1¹/2 oz) cracked wheat (burghul)
4 pieces Lavash bread 30 x 23 cm (12 x 9 inch)
2 spring onions, thinly sliced
1 large tomato, seeded, finely chopped
1 small Lebanese cucumber, finely chopped
15 g (¹/2 oz) fresh flat-leaf parsley, chopped
1 tablespoon lemon juice
1 tablespoon virgin olive oil
1 tablespoon olive oil
1 onion, finely chopped
1 clove garlic, crushed
2 teaspoons ground coriander
1 teaspoon cumin seeds
¹/2 teaspoon ground cinnamon
250 g (8 oz) chicken mince
300 g (10 oz) can chickpeas, rinsed, drained and mashed
10 g (¹/4 oz) fresh flat-leaf parsley, extra, chopped
10 g (¹/4 oz) fresh mint leaves, chopped
2 tablespoons plain flour
vegetable oil, for shallow-frying
¹/4 cup (60 g/2 oz) Greek-style natural yoghurt

1 Soak the cracked wheat in hot water for 20 minutes. Slice the bread into thirds widthways, then cut in half. Keep the bread covered with a damp cloth to prevent it drying out. Cut some baking paper the same size as the bread. Roll the paper up around the bottom half of the bread to form a cone and secure. Twist at the bottom. You will need 24 bread cones.
2 Drain the wheat in a fine mesh sieve, pressing out as much water as possible. Transfer to a bowl and mix with the onion, tomato, cucumber, parsley, lemon juice and virgin olive oil. Season.
3 Heat the olive oil in a pan, add the onion and garlic and cook, stirring over medium-low heat, for 5 minutes, or until the onion is soft. Add the spices and cook for another minute, or until the spices are aromatic.
4 Place the onion mixture, chicken mince, chickpeas, parsley and mint in a bowl, season with salt and pepper and mix until combined.

Shape into 24 patties, pressing firmly together. Toss in the flour and shake off the excess.

5 Fill a deep, heavy-based pan one third full of oil and heat to 180°C (350°F), or until a cube of bread dropped into the oil turns golden brown in 15 seconds. Cook the felafels in batches for 3–4 minutes each side, or until golden and heated through. Drain on crumpled paper towels.

6 To assemble, place a felafel in each bread cone, top with tabbouli, then 1/2 teaspoon yoghurt.

IN ADVANCE: The salad is best made on the day of serving. The felafel can be prepared up to a day ahead and cooked just before serving.

FRIED CALAMARI WITH TARTARE SAUCE

Preparation time: 30 minutes
Total cooking time: 10 minutes
Serves 8

★★

1 kg (2 lb) small, cleaned calamari tubes
4 tablespoons cornflour
4 eggs, lightly beaten
2 cloves garlic, crushed

1 tablespoon grated lemon rind
2 cups (200 g/6 1/2 oz) dry breadcrumbs
oil, for deep-frying

Tartare sauce
1 cup (250 g/8 oz) mayonnaise
2 tablespoons chopped chives
2 small pickled onions, finely chopped
1 tablespoon seeded mustard

1 Thinly slice the calamari, toss in cornflour and shake off the excess. Dip into the combined egg, garlic and lemon rind. Coat with breadcrumbs and shake off the excess.

2 Fill a deep heavy-based pan one third full of oil and heat the oil to 180°C (350°F). The oil is ready when a cube of bread dropped into the oil turns golden brown in 15 seconds. Gently lower small batches of calamari into the oil and cook for 1 minute, or until just heated through and lightly browned. Remove with a slotted spoon. Drain on crumpled paper towels and keep warm while cooking the remainder.

3 To make tartare sauce, combine the mayonnaise, chives, pickled onions and mustard. Mix well and serve with the calamari.

ABOVE: Fried calamari with tartare sauce

LEEKS

This vegetable has a long history, dating back at least as far as Ancient Egypt when leeks were part of the rations given to the builders of the pyramids. The leek is the national emblem of Wales and, in a battle in the seventh century, the Welsh wore leeks in their caps as identification so they wouldn't kill the wrong fighters. On St David's Day, Welsh men wear pieces of leek in their buttonholes in memory of this victory. Leeks can be steamed, braised, used in soups, pies and stir-fries, or added to dressed salads.

OPPOSITE PAGE: Parsnip and chicken patties with crispy leek (left); Honey veal tagine on pappadums

PARSNIP AND CHICKEN PATTIES WITH CRISPY LEEK

Preparation time: 15 minutes
Total cooking time: 25 minutes
Makes 24

★ ☆

1 large parsnip, chopped
500 g (1 lb) English spinach leaves
250 g (8 oz) chicken mince
4 spring onions, thinly sliced
1 egg yolk
1/2 cup (50 g/1 3/4 oz) dry breadcrumbs
1 tablespoon lemon juice
2 teaspoons chopped fresh thyme
2 tablespoons polenta
1 leek
1/4 cup (60 ml/2 fl oz) light olive oil
1/2 cup (125 g/4 oz) light sour cream
50 g (1 3/4 oz) creamy blue cheese

1 Cook the parsnip in a large pan of boiling water for 10 minutes, or until tender. Drain and mash until smooth. Set aside to cool.
2 Trim the spinach, rinse and add to a pan of boiling water. Boil for 1 minute, drain and rinse under cold water; drain thoroughly. Squeeze the spinach with your hands to remove as much liquid as possible; chop finely.
3 In a bowl, mix the parsnip, spinach, chicken, spring onion, egg yolk, breadcrumbs, lemon juice, thyme and salt and pepper. Shape into 24 patties, pressing firmly together. Dust with polenta and shake off any excess.
4 Remove the tough green portion of the leek and trim the base. Cut the leek widthways into 6 cm (2 1/2 inch) lengths, then cut lengthways into thin strips. Heat the oil in a large frying pan over medium–high heat and cook the leek until golden brown; drain on crumpled paper towels. Add the patties to the pan and cook, in batches, for 3–4 minutes each side, or until golden and heated through. Drain on crumpled paper towels.
5 Meanwhile, combine the sour cream and blue cheese in a small bowl and season with salt and pepper. To assemble, spoon 1 teaspoon of blue cheese mixture on top of each patty and top with crispy leek. Serve immediately.
IN ADVANCE: The patties can be made a day ahead and covered in the refrigerator until ready to cook, or frozen for up to 2 months. Crispy leek is best made close to serving.

HONEY VEAL TAGINE ON PAPPADUMS

Preparation time: 20 minutes
Total cooking time: 1 hour 10 minutes
Makes 24

★ ☆

2 tablespoons olive oil
650 g (1 lb 5 oz) whole piece leg veal, cut into small cubes
1 onion, chopped
2 cloves garlic, crushed
1 cinnamon stick
2 teaspoons ground cumin
1 teaspoon coriander seeds, crushed
1/4 teaspoon ground cardamom
1 1/4 cups (315 ml/10 fl oz) chicken stock
24 small pappadums
3 pitted dates, thinly sliced
4 pitted prunes, finely chopped
3 teaspoons honey
1/2 cup (125 g/4 oz) Greek-style natural yoghurt
fresh coriander leaves, to garnish

1 Heat 1 tablespoon of the olive oil and brown the veal in batches over high heat. Transfer the veal and any juices to a bowl.
2 Heat the remaining oil in the same pan, add the onion and garlic and stir over medium heat for 5 minutes, or until the onion is slightly softened. Add the spices and cook for another minute, or until the spices are aromatic. Return the veal to the pan, pour in the stock and bring to the boil. Reduce the heat and simmer, covered, over low heat for 30 minutes.
3 Uncover and simmer for 30 minutes, or until the mixture is thickened and the veal is tender. Meanwhile, cook the pappadums according to the manufacturer's instructions.
4 Stir the dates, prunes and honey into the veal mixture. To assemble, spoon the veal tagine in the centre of the pappadums, top each with 1 teaspoon of yoghurt and sprinkle with coriander leaves. Serve immediately.
IN ADVANCE: Veal tagine can be prepared a day ahead, refrigerated and reheated just before serving. Pappadums can be cooked a day ahead and stored in an airtight container.

VEGETABLE FRITTATA WITH HUMMUS AND BLACK OLIVES

Preparation time: 30 minutes
Total cooking time: 35 minutes
Makes 30

★ ★

Hummus

425 g (14 oz) can chickpeas, drained
2 cloves garlic, crushed
1/3 cup (80 ml/2¾ fl oz) lemon juice
2 tablespoons natural yoghurt

2 large red peppers (capsicums)
600 g (1¼ lb) orange sweet potato
500 g (1 lb) eggplant (aubergine)
3 tablespoons olive oil
2 leeks, finely sliced
2 cloves garlic, crushed
250 g (8 oz) zucchini (courgettes), thinly sliced
8 eggs, lightly beaten
2 tablespoons finely chopped fresh basil
125 g (4 oz) Parmesan, grated
60 g (2 oz) black olives, pitted and halved,
   to garnish

1 In a food processor, purée the chickpeas, garlic, lemon juice, yoghurt and black pepper.
2 Quarter the peppers, remove the seeds and membrane and cook, skin-side-up, under a hot grill until the skin is black and blistered. Cool in a plastic bag, then peel.
3 Cut the sweet potato into 1 cm (½ inch) thick slices and cook until just tender; drain.
4 Cut the eggplant into 1 cm (½ inch) slices. Heat 1 tablespoon oil in a 23 cm (9 inch) round, high-sided frying pan and stir the leek and garlic over medium heat for 1 minute, or until soft. Add the zucchini and cook for another 2 minutes. Remove from the pan and set aside.
5 Heat the remaining oil in the same frying pan and cook the eggplant slices, in batches, for 1 minute each side, or until golden. Line the base of the pan with half the eggplant and spread the leek over the top. Cover with the roasted peppers, remaining eggplant and sweet potato.
6 Combine the eggs, basil, Parmesan and some black pepper in a jug, pour over the vegetables and cook over low heat for 15 minutes, or until almost cooked. Place the frying pan under a preheated grill for 2–3 minutes, until the frittata is golden and cooked. Cool for 10 minutes before inverting onto a cutting board. Trim the edges and cut into 30 squares. Top with hummus and olives. Serve cold or at room temperature.

FRITTATA

This is an Italian version of an omelette but differs in the way it is cooked. The filling ingredients are mixed with the egg instead of being folded inside, and the egg is cooked slowly until set, not served soft and creamy. Frittata is cooked on both sides, not folded over. It can be flipped, but most people cook the underside, then put the pan under a grill to cook the top.

RIGHT: Vegetable frittata with hummus and black olives

BAGUETTE WITH EGG, DILL PESTO AND PROSCIUTTO

Preparation time: 20 minutes
Total cooking time: 25 minutes
Makes 30

★★

8 thin slices prosciutto
45 g (1 1/2 oz) fresh dill sprigs
75 g (2 1/2 oz) pine nuts, toasted
60 g (2 oz) Parmesan, finely grated
2 cloves garlic, crushed
1/3 cup (80 ml/2 3/4 fl oz) virgin olive oil
1 French bread stick, sliced diagonally
2 teaspoons butter
7 eggs, lightly beaten
1/3 cup (80 ml/2 3/4 fl oz) milk
1 tablespoon light sour cream

1 Preheat the oven to moderately hot 200°C (400°F/Gas 6). Spread the prosciutto on a baking tray lined with baking paper. Bake for 5 minutes, or until sizzling and lightly crisp. Set aside.
2 Finely chop the dill, pine nuts, Parmesan and garlic together in a food processor. With the motor running, add the oil in a thin stream and process until smooth. Season.
3 Arrange the bread on baking trays and grill until golden on both sides. Spread with dill pesto.
4 Heat the butter in a large non-stick frying pan over low heat. Add the combined eggs and milk. As the egg begins to set, use a wooden spoon to scrape along the base with long strokes to bring the cooked egg to the surface in large lumps. Repeat several times over 10 minutes, or until the mixture is cooked but still creamy-looking. Remove from the heat and stir in the sour cream. Season with salt and pepper.
5 Divide the egg among the toasts and top with torn prosciutto. Serve immediately.
IN ADVANCE: Pesto can be made 3 days ahead and refrigerated. Use at room temperature.

SOUR CREAM
Sour cream, used in many recipes, was originally made by leaving cream at room temperature to sour. Today, commercial sour cream is made by adding a lactic acid culture to cream, thus providing the characteristic slightly acidic tang. Keep sour cream refrigerated and discard if any mould forms.

ABOVE: Baguette with egg, dill pesto and prosciutto

SOMETHING SWEET

Where on earth did the phrase 'sweet nothings' arise from? What a dreadful contradiction in terms. For most of us, sweet food is definitely not 'nothing'; it is one of life's greatest pleasures. The sensation of chocolate melting on the lips, cream oozing from a tiny pastry, or the tang of fresh berries catching on the tastebuds, is not something to be taken lightly. So round off your evening with a platter of sweet treats and watch your guests' eyes light up. Or, for those with a really sweet tooth, do away with the savoury food altogether and have a 'sweets only' party.

TEARDROP
CHOCOLATE CHERRY
MOUSSE CUPS

Just before the chocolate sets, bring the short edges together to form a teardrop shape. Hold together with your fingers.

Use a small sharp knife to trim around the outer edge of each teardrop, then leave until set completely.

TEARDROP CHOCOLATE CHERRY MOUSSE CUPS

Preparation time: 1 hour
Total cooking time: Nil
Makes about 24

★ ★ ★

glossy contact paper
200 g (6½ oz) dark chocolate melts or buttons
¾ cup (150 g/5 oz) stoneless black cherries, well drained

Chocolate mousse
60 g (2 oz) dark cooking chocolate, melted
1 tablespoon cream
1 egg yolk
½ teaspoon gelatine
⅓ cup (80 ml/2¾ fl oz) cream, extra
1 egg white

1 Cut glossy contact into 24 rectangles 4 x 11 cm (1½ x 4½ inches). Line a tray with baking paper.
2 Place the chocolate melts in a small heatproof bowl. Bring a small pan of water to the boil and remove from the heat. Sit the bowl over the pan, making sure the bowl does not touch the water. Stir occasionally until the chocolate has melted and the mixture is smooth. Using a palette or flat-bladed knife, spread a little of the chocolate over one of the contact rectangles. Just before the chocolate starts to set, bring the short edges together to form a teardrop shape. (Leave the contact attached.) Hold together with your fingers until the shape holds by itself and will stand up. Repeat with some of the remaining chocolate and rectangles. (The chocolate will need to be re-melted several times. To do this, place the bowl over steaming water again.)
3 Spoon about 1½ teaspoons of the remaining chocolate on the tray and spread into an oval about 5 cm (2 inches) long. Sit a teardrop in the centre of it and press down gently. Repeat with the remaining teardrops. Allow to almost set.
4 Using a sharp small knife or scalpel, cut around the outer edge of each teardrop. Allow the cups to set completely before lifting away from the baking paper. Carefully break away the excess chocolate from the bases to form a neat edge on the base. Carefully peel away the contact. Set the cups aside. Cut the cherries into quarters and drain on crumpled paper towels.
5 For the mousse, mix the chocolate, cream and yolk in a bowl until smooth. Sprinkle the gelatine in an even layer over 2 teaspoons water in a small heatproof bowl and leave until spongy. Bring a small pan of water to the boil, remove from the

ABOVE: Teardrop
chocolate cherry
mousse cups

heat and place the bowl over the pan. The water should come halfway up the side of the bowl. Stir the gelatine until clear and dissolved. Stir into the chocolate mixture.

6 Working quickly, so the gelatine does not set, beat the extra cream with electric beaters until soft peaks form; fold into the chocolate. Using electric beaters, beat the egg white in a clean dry bowl until soft peaks form. Fold into the chocolate.

7 Place a few pieces of cherry inside each teardrop cup. Spoon the chocolate mousse over the cherries. (Fill to slightly over the brim as the mousse will drop during setting.) Chill until set.

CHOCOLATE CUPS WITH CARAMEL

Preparation time: 40 minutes
Total cooking time: 5–10 minutes
Makes 24

★★★

150 g (5 oz) dark chocolate melts
24 small foil confectionery cups
80 g (2³/₄ oz) Mars® bar, chopped
¹/₄ cup (60 ml/2 fl oz) cream
50 g (1³/₄ oz) white chocolate melts

1 Place the dark chocolate in a small heatproof bowl. Bring a small pan of water to the boil and remove from the heat. Sit the bowl over the pan, making sure the bowl does not touch the water. Stir occasionally until the chocolate has melted and the mixture is smooth.

2 Using a small new paintbrush, brush a thin layer of chocolate inside the foil cases. Stand the cases upside-down on a wire rack to set. (Return the remaining chocolate to the pan of steaming water for later use.)

3 Combine the Mars® bar and cream in a small pan and stir over low heat until the chocolate has melted and the mixture is smooth. Transfer to a bowl and leave until just starting to set, then spoon into each cup leaving about 3 mm (about ¹/₄ inch) of space at the top.

4 Spoon the reserved melted chocolate into the caramel cases and allow the chocolate to set. Melt the white chocolate in the same way as the dark chocolate. Place in a small paper piping bag and drizzle patterns over the cups. Carefully peel away the foil when the chocolate has set.

NOTE: Ensure the chocolate is set before piping the white chocolate on the top.

IN ADVANCE: Caramel cups can be made up to 3 days ahead.

ABOVE: Chocolate cups with caramel

thickness of 3 mm (¼ inch). Cut out rounds with a 5 cm (2 inch) fluted cutter. Lift gently with a flat-bladed knife and line each muffin hole with pastry. Spread the pine nuts onto a flat baking tray and bake for 2–3 minutes, or until just golden. Remove from the tray and cool; divide the nuts among the pastry cases.

4 Combine the melted butter, syrup and sugar in a jug and whisk with a fork, then pour over the pine nuts. Bake for 15 minutes, or until golden. Cool in the trays for 5 minutes before lifting out onto a wire rack to cool completely. Dust with icing sugar before serving, if desired.

NOTE: You can use chopped walnuts or pecans instead of the pine nuts.

IN ADVANCE: The tarts can be made up to 8 hours ahead. Store in an airtight container.

GULAB JAMUN

Preparation time: 20 minutes
Total cooking time: 25 minutes
Makes 35

✷ ✷

1 cup (100 g/3½ oz) milk powder
50 g (1¾ oz) blanched almonds, ground
150 g (5 oz) plain flour
1 teaspoon baking powder
½ teaspoon ground cardamom
30 g (1 oz) butter, chopped
¼ cup (60 g/2 oz) natural yoghurt
oil, for deep-frying
1 cup (250 g/4 oz) sugar
a few drops of rose water

1 Sift the dry ingredients into a large bowl and add the butter. Rub the butter into the flour with your fingertips until the mixture resembles fine breadcrumbs. Make a well, then add the yoghurt and 2–3 tablespoons of water. Mix with a flat-bladed knife to form a soft dough (alternatively, use a food processor). Shape the dough into small balls about the size of quail eggs, cover with a damp cloth and set aside.

2 Fill a heavy-based pan one third full of oil and heat to 180°C (350°F). The oil is ready when a cube of bread dropped into the oil turns golden brown in 15 seconds. Deep-fry the jamuns in several batches until deep brown. Do not cook them too quickly or the middle won't cook through. They should puff up a little. Drain in a sieve set over a bowl.

PINE NUT TARTS

Preparation time: 25 minutes
Total cooking time: 15 minutes
Makes 24

✷ ✷

½ cup (60 g/2 oz) plain flour
60 g (2 oz) butter, chopped
40 g (1¼ oz) pine nuts
20 g (¾ oz) butter, melted
½ cup (175 g/6 oz) golden syrup
2 tablespoons soft brown sugar

1 Preheat the oven to moderate 180°C (350°F/ Gas 4). Grease two 12-hole mini muffin tins.
2 Sift the flour into a bowl and add the chopped butter. Rub into the flour with your fingertips until the mixture comes together. Turn onto a lightly floured surface and gather together.

ABOVE: Pine nut tarts

3 Roll out on a lightly floured surface to a

3 Place the sugar and 1½ cups (375 ml/12 fl oz) water in a heavy-based pan and stir until the sugar has dissolved. Bring to the boil, reduce the heat and simmer for 5 minutes. Stir in the rose water. Place the warm jamuns in a deep bowl and pour the syrup over. Leave to soak and cool until still slightly warm. Drain and serve piled in a small bowl.

BAKLAVA FINGERS

Preparation time: 30 minutes
Total cooking time: 20 minutes
Makes 24

✳ ✳

Filling
90 g (3 oz) walnuts, finely chopped
1 tablespoon soft brown sugar
1 teaspoon ground cinnamon
20 g (¾ oz) butter, melted

8 sheets filo pastry
50 g (1¾ oz) butter, melted

Syrup
1 cup (250 g/8 oz) sugar
2 tablespoons honey
2 teaspoons orange flower water, optional

1 Preheat the oven to hot 210°C (415°F/ Gas 6–7). Brush a baking tray with oil or melted butter.
2 To make the filling, place the walnuts, sugar, cinnamon and butter in a small bowl and stir until combined.
3 Remove one sheet of filo and cover the rest to prevent drying out. Place the sheet of filo pastry on a work bench, brush with melted butter and fold in half. Cut the sheet into three strips and place a heaped teaspoon of filling close to the front edge of the pastry. Roll up, tucking in the edges. Place on the prepared tray and brush with melted butter.
4 Repeat with the remaining pastry sheets. Bake for 15 minutes, or until golden brown.
5 To make the syrup, combine the sugar, honey and ½ cup (125 ml/4 fl oz) water in a small pan. Stir over low heat, without boiling, until the sugar has completely dissolved. Bring to the boil, reduce the heat and simmer for 5 minutes. Remove from the heat and add the orange flower water.

6 Transfer to a wire rack over a tray and spoon the syrup over the pastries while both the pastries and syrup are still warm.
IN ADVANCE: Store in an airtight container for up to 2 days.

CHOCOLATE STRAWBERRIES

Brush 250 g (8 oz) strawberries with a dry pastry brush to remove any dirt. Melt 150 g (5 oz) dark chocolate in a small heatproof bowl over a pan of steaming water and dip the bottom half of each strawberry in the chocolate. Place on a baking paper-covered baking tray and leave to set. When set, melt 100 g (3½ oz) white chocolate in a small bowl, dip the tips of the strawberries in the chocolate and allow to set.

ABOVE: Baklava fingers

RICH CHOCOLATE TRUFFLES

Preparation time: 40 minutes + chilling
Total cooking time: 5 minutes
Makes about 30

✷ ✷

3/4 cup (185 ml/6 fl oz) thick (double) cream
400 g (13 oz) dark chocolate, grated
70 g (2¼ oz) butter, chopped
2 tablespoons Cointreau
dark cocoa powder, for rolling

1 Place the cream in a small pan and bring to the boil. Remove from the heat and stir in the chocolate until it is completely melted. Add the butter and stir until melted. Stir in the Cointreau. Transfer to a large bowl, cover and refrigerate for several hours or overnight, or until firm enough to roll.
2 Quickly roll tablespoons of the mixture into balls, and refrigerate until firm. Roll the balls in the cocoa, shake off any excess and return to the refrigerator. Serve at room temperature.
IN ADVANCE: Truffle mixture can be made and rolled up to 2 weeks ahead. You will need to roll the balls in cocoa again close to serving time.

RUM-AND-RAISIN TRUFFLES

Preparation time: 30 minutes + soaking
  and chilling
Total cooking time: 5 minutes
Makes about 40

✷ ✷

60 g (2 oz) raisins, finely chopped
1/4 cup (60 ml/2 fl oz) dark rum
200 g (6½ oz) chocolate-coated wheatmeal
  biscuits, crushed
1/3 cup (60 g/2 oz) soft brown sugar
1 teaspoon ground cinnamon
50 g (1¾ oz) pecans, finely chopped
1/4 cup (60 ml/2 fl oz) cream
250 g (8 oz) dark chocolate, chopped
1/4 cup (90 g/3 oz) golden syrup
125 g (4 oz) pecans, finely ground

1 Marinate the raisins in the rum in a small bowl for 1 hour. Put the biscuits, sugar, cinnamon and pecans in a large bowl and mix until combined.

2 Stir the cream, chocolate and golden syrup in a pan over low heat until melted. Pour onto the biscuit mixture, add the raisins and rum mixture and stir until well combined. Refrigerate until just firm enough to roll into balls.
3 Roll tablespoons of the mixture into balls, then roll the balls in the ground pecans. Refrigerate until firm.
IN ADVANCE: Truffles can be made up to 2 weeks ahead.

WHITE CAKE TRUFFLES

Preparation time: 25 minutes
Total cooking time: Nil
Makes about 25

✷

2 cups (250 g/8 oz) Madeira cake crumbs
2 tablespoons chopped glacé orange peel or
  glacé apricots
1 tablespoon apricot jam
2 tablespoons cream
100 g (3½ oz) white chocolate, melted

Chocolate coating

150 g (5 oz) white chocolate, chopped
20 g (¾ oz) white vegetable shortening
  (Copha), chopped

1 Line a baking tray with foil. Combine the cake crumbs in a bowl with the chopped peel or apricots, jam, cream and melted chocolate. Mix until smooth, then roll into balls using 2 teaspoons of mixture for each.
2 To make the chocolate coating, combine the chocolate and shortening in a heatproof bowl. Bring a pan of water to the boil, remove from the heat and sit the bowl over the pan, making sure the bowl does not touch the water. Stir occasionally until the chocolate and shortening have melted. Dip the balls in chocolate, wipe the excess off on the edge of the bowl and leave them to set on the tray. Decorate with gold leaf, if desired.
NOTE: For decorating, you can buy 24 carat edible gold leaf from speciality art shops or cake decorating suppliers.
IN ADVANCE: These truffles can be made up to 2 weeks ahead.

WHITE CHOCOLATE
White chocolate is not strictly a chocolate as it contains no cocoa liquor. It is a blend of cocoa butter, sugar, vanilla flavouring, milk solids and a stabilizer. It is softer than real chocolate and is not as easy to handle. Because of its different chemistry, it cannot be easily substituted for other chocolates in recipes.

OPPOSITE PAGE: Rich chocolate truffles (top); Rum-and-raisin truffles

CASTER SUGAR

Often used on baking day in cakes, meringues and biscuits, caster sugar is simply finely ground white sugar. It is used because it dissolves more easily and is also good to use when making custards or sauces. In America, it is called superfine sugar.

ABOVE: Amaretti

AMARETTI

Preparation time: 15 minutes + standing
Total cooking time: 20 minutes
Makes 40

★

1 tablespoon plain flour
1 tablespoon cornflour
1 teaspoon ground cinnamon
2/3 cup (160 g/5 1/2 oz) caster sugar
1 teaspoon grated lemon rind
1 cup (185 g/6 oz) ground almonds
2 egg whites
1/4 cup (30 g/1 oz) icing sugar

1 Line two baking trays with baking paper. Sift the plain flour, cornflour, cinnamon and half the caster sugar into a large bowl; add the lemon rind and ground almonds.
2 Place the egg whites in a small, dry bowl. With electric beaters, beat the egg whites until soft peaks form. Add the remaining caster sugar gradually, beating constantly until the mixture is thick and glossy, stiff peaks form and all the sugar has dissolved. Using a metal spoon, fold the egg white into the dry ingredients. Stir until the ingredients are just combined and the mixture forms a soft dough.
3 With oiled or wetted hands, roll 2 level teaspoons of mixture at a time into a ball. Arrange on the prepared tray, allowing room for spreading. Set the tray aside, uncovered, for 1 hour before baking.
4 Heat the oven to moderate 180°C (350°F/ Gas 4). Sift the icing sugar liberally over the biscuits. Bake for 15–20 minutes, or until crisp and lightly browned. Transfer to a wire rack to cool.

IN ADVANCE: The biscuits can be stored in an airtight container for up to 2 days.
NOTE: You can use orange rind instead of lemon rind. These biscuits have a chewy texture and are perfect served with coffee.

STUFFED FIGS

Preparation time: 20 minutes
Total cooking time: 5 minutes
Makes 30

★

100 g (3¹/₂ oz) blanched almonds
30 soft dried figs
²/₃ cup (125 g/4 oz) mixed peel
200 g (6¹/₂ oz) marzipan, chopped

1 Preheat the oven to moderate 180°C (350°F/
Gas 4). Place the almonds on a baking tray and
bake for 5 minutes, or until lightly golden. Leave
to cool.
2 Remove the hard stem ends from the figs. Cut
a cross in the top of each fig halfway through to
the base and open out like petals.
3 Chop the mixed peel and almonds in a food
processor until fine. Add the marzipan and
process in short bursts until fine and crumbly.
4 With your hands, press 2 teaspoons of
marzipan filling together to make a ball. Place
a ball inside each fig and press back into shape
around it. Serve at room temperature.
IN ADVANCE: Store the stuffed figs in a single
layer in a covered container in the refrigerator
for up to 2 days. Return to room temperature
before serving.
NOTE: As a variation, you can dip the bases of
the figs into melted chocolate.

PANFORTE

Preparation time: 15 minutes
Total cooking time: 40 minutes
Makes about 32 pieces

★ ★

115 g (4 oz) blanched almonds, toasted
70 g (2¹/₄ oz) hazelnuts, toasted
60 g (2 oz) walnuts
90 g (3 oz) raisins
180 g (6 oz) glacé apricots, cut into 8 pieces
45 g (1¹/₂ oz) mixed peel
²/₃ cup (85 g/3 oz) plain flour
2 tablespoons cocoa powder
1 teaspoon ground cinnamon
50 g (1³/₄ oz) dark chocolate, chopped
¹/₃ cup (90 g/3 oz) caster sugar
¹/₃ cup (115 g/4 oz) honey

1 Preheat the oven to warm 160°C (315°F/
Gas 2–3). Lightly grease a shallow 20 cm (8 inch)
round cake tin and cover the base with non-stick
baking paper. Combine the almonds, hazelnuts,
walnuts, raisins, apricots and peel in a large bowl.
Add the sifted flour and cocoa and cinnamon to
the fruit mixture and stir to combine.
2 Combine the chocolate, sugar and honey in a
small pan and stir over low heat until melted.
Make a well in the centre of the dry ingredients
and add the melted mixture. Mix until all the
ingredients are just combined. You will need to
use your hand after the initial mixing with a
spoon, as the mixture will be very stiff.
3 Press the mixture evenly into the prepared tin.
Wet your hand slightly to prevent the mixture
sticking. Smooth the top with the back of a
spoon. Bake for about 35 minutes, or until the
panforte is just firm to touch in the centre.
Allow to cool completely in the tin.
4 When cold, remove from the tin, dust
generously with icing sugar and cut into thin
wedges for serving.

ABOVE: Stuffed figs

MINI PARIS-BREST

Preparation time: 30 minutes
Total cooking time: 35 minutes
Makes 15

★ ★ ★

1/2 cup (60 g/2 oz) plain flour
60 g (2 oz) butter, chopped
2 eggs, lightly beaten

Custard filling

1 1/4 cups (315 ml/10 fl oz) milk
3 egg yolks
2 tablespoons caster sugar
1 tablespoon plain flour
1 tablespoon custard powder
few drops almond essence, to taste

Toffee

1 cup (250 g/8 oz) caster sugar
2/3 cup (60 g/2 oz) flaked almonds,
   lightly toasted

1 To make choux pastry, sift the flour onto a sheet of baking paper. Put the butter in a pan with 1/2 cup (125 ml/4 fl oz) water, stir over low heat until melted, then bring to the boil. Remove from the heat, add the flour in one go and quickly beat it into the water with a wooden spoon. Return to the heat and continue beating until the mixture forms a ball and leaves the side of the pan. Transfer to a large clean bowl and cool slightly. Beat with electric beaters to release any more heat. Gradually add the beaten egg, about 3 teaspoons at a time. Beat well after each addition until all the egg has been added and the mixture is smooth and glossy.
2 Preheat the oven to moderately hot 190°C (375°F/Gas 5). Line 3 baking trays with baking paper. Place the choux pastry into a piping bag with a 5 mm (1/4 inch) star nozzle. Pipe 3 cm (1 1/4 inch) circles of choux onto the paper. Bake for 10 minutes then reduce the heat to moderate 180°C (350°F/Gas 4). Bake for 15–20 minutes more, or until well browned and puffed. Pierce the sides to allow the steam to escape and cool on a wire rack.
3 For the filling, heat 1 cup (250 ml/8 fl oz) milk to simmering point in a pan. In a bowl, whisk together the remaining milk, egg yolks, sugar, flour and custard powder and slowly pour on the hot milk, whisking vigorously until well combined. Pour back into the clean pan and stir over medium heat until the mixture boils and thickens. Stir in the essence. Transfer to a bowl, cover and cool.
3 To make the toffee, combine the sugar and 1/2 cup (125 ml/4 fl oz) water in a small pan, stirring constantly over low heat until the sugar has dissolved. Bring to the boil and boil rapidly without stirring for about 10 minutes, or until just golden. Place the pan immediately over another pan of hot water to stop the toffee setting.
4 Immediately dip the choux tops into the toffee, decorate with a few toasted flaked almonds and place on a wire rack to set. Split the choux rings in half, pipe or spoon the filling in and top with the toffee lids.

PETITS PITHIVIERS

Preparation time: 40 minutes + chilling
Total cooking time: 15 minutes
Makes 26

★ ★ ★

Almond filling

45 g (1 1/2 oz) butter
1/3 cup (40 g/1 1/4 oz) icing sugar
1 egg yolk
70 g (2 1/4 oz) ground almonds
1 teaspoon finely grated orange rind
few drops almond essence

3 sheets puff pastry
1 egg, lightly beaten

1 To make the filling, beat the butter and icing sugar with electric beaters until light and creamy. Add the egg yolk and beat well. Stir in the ground almonds, rind and essence.
2 Preheat the oven to hot 210°C (415°F/ Gas 6–7) and lightly grease 2 baking trays. Lay the puff pastry on a work surface and cut into 5 cm (2 inch) circles with a cutter. Divide the almond filling among half the circles, using about 1 1/2 teaspoons filling for each. Leave a 5 mm (1/4 inch) border. Brush the border with egg.
3 Place the remaining pastry circles over the filling and press the edges firmly to seal. Transfer to the baking trays and chill for 30 minutes. With a blunt-edged knife, press up the edges gently at intervals. Carefully score the tops of the pastries into wedges, then brush with beaten egg. Bake on the greased trays for 10 minutes, or until lightly golden.

PARIS-BREST
This classic French pastry is meant to resemble the wheel of a bicycle and the name is taken from a bicycle race that was run in the late 19th century between the two cities Paris and Brest.

OPPOSITE PAGE: Mini Paris-Brest (top); Petits pithiviers

TINY TREATS There is only one thing

better than a huge cheesecake, and that's a plateful of miniature cheesecakes... so

you can sneak back and eat as many as you want without anyone noticing.

CHOCOLATE LIQUEUR CHEESECAKES

Grease four deep 12-hole patty tins and place a thin strip of baking paper in the bases, extending up the sides. Finely crush 250 g (8 oz) sweet biscuits, stir in 125 g (4 oz) melted butter, then firmly press 1 heaped teaspoon into each base. Refrigerate. Dissolve 3 teaspoons gelatine in ¼ cup (60 ml/2 fl oz) boiling water. Beat 250 g (8 oz) soft cream cheese with ⅓ cup (90 g/3 oz) caster sugar, then add 150 g (5 oz) melted chocolate, 2 teaspoons

grated orange rind and 3 tablespoons Tia Maria and beat until smooth. Stir in the gelatine, spoon onto the bases and refrigerate for 2 hours, or until firm. Whip 300 ml (10 fl oz) cream, spoon over the cheesecakes and garnish with chocolate curls. Makes 48.

BAKED CHEESECAKES

Preheat the oven to warm 160°C (315°F/ Gas 2–3). Grease three deep 12-hole patty tins and place a thin strip of baking paper in the bases, extending up the sides.

Finely crush 250 g (8 oz) sweet biscuits, stir in 125 g (4 oz) melted butter, then firmly press 1 heaped teaspoon into each base. Refrigerate. Beat 250 g (8 oz) soft cream cheese, ½ cup (125 g/4 oz) sour cream and ½ cup (125 g/4 oz) caster sugar, until smooth. Mix in 2 egg yolks, 1 tablespoon lemon juice and 2 teaspoons plain flour. Beat 2 egg whites until stiff peaks form, then fold through the cream cheese mixture. Spoon 1 tablespoon filling into each base and bake for 15–20 minutes, until set. Cool. Makes 36.

CUSTARD AND FRUIT TARTS

Preheat the oven to moderate 180°C (350°F/Gas 4). Grease three shallow 12-hole patty tins. Using a 7 cm (2¾ inch) round cutter, cut rounds from 4 sheets of ready-rolled sweet shortcrust pastry. Place in the tins and prick the bases several times with a fork. Bake for 12–15 minutes, or until golden brown. Remove and cool. Cut a vanilla pod in half and place in a saucepan with 1¼ cups (315 ml/10 fl oz) milk. Slowly bring to the boil, remove from the heat and cool slightly. In a large heatproof bowl whisk 2 egg yolks and 2 tablespoons sugar until thick and pale. Add 3 tablespoons plain flour, then gradually whisk in the vanilla milk. Return to a clean pan and heat slowly, stirring constantly for 5–10 minutes, or until it boils and thickens. Allow to cool, then spoon evenly into each pastry case and top with some sliced fruit. Glaze with warmed sieved apricot jam. Makes 36.

MINI LIME MERINGUE PIES

Preheat the oven to moderate 180°C (350°F/Gas 4). Grease three shallow 12-hole patty tins. Cut rounds with a 7 cm (2¾ inch) cutter from 4 sheets of ready-rolled sweet shortcrust pastry. Place in the tins and prick the bases well with a fork. Bake for 12–15 minutes, or until golden brown, then cool. Put ½ cup (125 g/4 oz) caster sugar, ¼ cup (30 g/1 oz) cornflour, 2 teaspoons lime rind, ⅓ cup (80 ml/2¾ fl oz) lime juice and ¾ cup (185 ml/6 fl oz) water in a large pan. Stir over medium heat until the mixture boils and thickens. Remove from the heat and add 30 g (1 oz) butter, then mix. Gradually mix in 2 egg yolks. Spoon heaped teaspoons into each pastry case. Beat 3 egg whites into stiff peaks, gradually add ½ cup (125 g/4 oz) sugar and beat until the sugar dissolves and is glossy. Spoon 1 tablespoon over each tart. Bake for 4–5 minutes, or until lightly golden. Makes 36.

PEACH AND ALMOND STRUDELS

Preheat the oven to moderate 180°C (350°F/Gas 4). Grease two deep patty tins. Mix a 425 g (14 oz) can pie peaches, 60 g (2 oz) slivered almonds, 60 g (2 oz) sultanas and 1 tablespoon soft brown sugar. Brush a sheet of filo pastry with melted butter, then top with another sheet. Cut into 4 and cut each piece into 4 again. Repeat with another 4 sheets of filo. Place 4 squares in each base and bake for 10 minutes. Place 1 tablespoon of filling in each pastry case, sprinkle with cinnamon and bake for 5–10 minutes, until the pastry is golden. Makes 24.

FROM LEFT: Chocolate liqueur cheesecakes; Baked cheesecakes; Custard and fruit tarts; Mini lime meringue pies; Peach and almond strudels

SACHER CAKE

The original Sacher Torte was a two-layered dense chocolate cake separated by apricot jam and covered with smooth chocolate. Created by Franz Sacher, chief pastrycook to the Austrian statesman Metternich during the Congress of Vienna (1814–15), the cake was later the subject of a protracted argument between some of Sacher's descendants and Vienna's famous Demel pâtisserie as to whether in its true form it had two layers or was just a cake spread with jam and iced.

BELOW: Sacher squares

SACHER SQUARES

Preparation time: I hour
Total cooking time: 40 minutes
Makes 24

★ ★ ★

Base
I cup (125 g/4 oz) plain flour
60 g (2 oz) butter, chopped
1/4 cup (60 g/2 oz) sugar
2 egg yolks, lightly beaten

Cake
I cup (125 g/4 oz) plain flour
1/3 cup (40 g/1 1/4 oz) cocoa powder
I cup (250 g/4 oz) caster sugar
100 g (3 1/2 oz) butter
2 tablespoons apricot jam
4 eggs, separated
I cup (315 g/10 oz) apricot jam, extra

Topping
250 g (4 oz) dark chocolate
3/4 cup (185 ml/6 fl oz) cream

1 Preheat the oven to moderate 180°C (350°F/ Gas 4). To make the base, sift the flour into a large bowl and add the butter. Rub in until the mixture resembles fine breadcrumbs. Stir in the sugar and make a well in the centre. Add the egg yolks and 1 1/2 teaspoons iced water and mix with a flat-bladed knife, using a cutting action, to a firm dough, adding more water if necessary. Gently gather the dough together and lift onto a lightly floured surface. Roll out the pastry to an 18 x 28 cm (7 x 11 inch) rectangle. Bake on a tray covered with baking paper for 10 minutes, or until just golden. Cool completely.

2 To make the cake, keep the oven at moderate 180°C (350°F/Gas 4). Lightly grease a shallow 18 x 28 cm (7 x 11 inch) tin and line the base and side with baking paper, extending over two sides. Sift the flour and cocoa into a large bowl. Make a well in the centre. Combine the sugar, butter and jam in a small pan and stir over low heat until the butter has melted and the sugar has dissolved. Remove from the heat. Add the butter mixture to the dry ingredients and stir until just combined. Mix in the egg yolks.

3 Place the egg whites in a small clean dry bowl and beat with electric beaters until soft peaks form. Using a metal spoon, fold the egg whites into the cake mixture. Pour into the prepared tin

and bake for 30 minutes or until a skewer comes out clean when inserted into the centre of cake. Leave in the tin for 15 minutes before turning out onto a wire rack to cool.

4 Warm the extra jam in a microwave or in a small pan, then push through a fine sieve. Brush the pastry base with 3 tablespoons of the jam. Place the cake on the base. Trim the sides evenly, cutting the hard edges from the cake and base. Using a serrated knife, cut into 24 squares.

5 Brush the top and sides of each square with apricot jam. Place the squares on a large wire rack, over a piece of baking paper, leaving at least 4 cm (1¹/₂ inches) between each.

6 To make the topping, break the chocolate into small pieces and place in a small bowl. Place the cream in a small pan and bring to the boil. Remove from the heat, pour over the chocolate and leave for 5 minutes, then stir until the mixture is smooth. Cool slightly. Working with one at a time, spoon the topping over each square and use a flat-bladed knife to cover completely. Scrape the excess topping from the paper, with any left over, and spoon into a small paper piping bag. Seal the open end, snip off the tip and pipe an 'S' onto each square.

IN ADVANCE: Store for up to 5 days in an airtight container.

WALNUT CHOCOLATES

Preparation time: 30 minutes + chilling
Total cooking time: 2–3 minutes
Makes 30

★

100 g (3¹/₂ oz) walnut pieces
¹/₂ cup (60 g/2 oz) icing sugar
2 teaspoons egg white
200 g (6¹/₂ oz) dark chocolate
30 walnut halves

1 Chop the walnut pieces in a food processor. Sift the icing sugar and process with the walnuts and egg white until a moist paste forms. Cover and refrigerate for 20 minutes.

2 Roll teaspoons of walnut paste into balls and flatten slightly. Place the chocolate in a heatproof bowl. Bring a pan of water to the boil and remove from the heat. Sit the bowl over the pan, making sure the base of the bowl does not sit in the water. Stir occasionally until the chocolate has melted.

3 Dip the walnut rounds in the chocolate and transfer to a piece of greaseproof paper or foil. Press the walnut halves gently into the top of each round and leave to set.

IN ADVANCE: Can be made 4 days ahead.

WALNUTS
Various types of walnut have been used in cookery for thousands of years. The most commonly available is believed to have originated in Persia and been transported to Europe. Other types are native to Asia, America and Europe. Many other countries now grow walnuts. Store the peeled walnuts in the refrigerator or freezer.

ABOVE: Walnut chocolates

oil and heat the oil to 180°C (350°F). The oil is ready when a cube of bread dropped into the oil turns golden brown in 15 seconds. Fry 3 or 4 khvorst at a time, until golden brown on both sides. Drain on crumpled paper towel. Sift icing sugar over the pastry after it is fried but before it gets cold.

IN ADVANCE: These will keep for up to 2 weeks in a dry airtight container.

BABY FLORENTINES

Preparation time: 20 minutes
Total cooking time: about 50 minutes
Makes about 50

✷ ✷

90 g (3 oz) butter
1/2 cup (125 g/4 oz) caster sugar
1 tablespoon honey
45 g (1 1/2 oz) slivered almonds, chopped
55 g (2 oz) dried apricots, finely chopped
2 tablespoons chopped glacé cherries
45 g (1 1/2 oz) mixed peel
1/2 cup (60 g/2 oz) plain flour
150 g (5 oz) dark chocolate

1 Preheat the oven to 180°C (350°F/Gas 4). Cover two baking trays with non-stick baking paper. Melt the butter, sugar and honey in a saucepan. Remove from the heat and stir in the almonds, apricots, glacé cherries, mixed peel and the flour. Mix well to combine (the mixture may feel oily).
2 Roll teaspoonfuls into balls and place on the prepared trays, allowing plenty of room for spreading. Press lightly with your fingertips into 3 cm (1 1/4 inch) rounds.
3 Bake for 8–10 minutes, or until golden brown. Cool on the trays until slightly firm, then using a spatula, carefully remove and cool completely on wire racks. Repeat with the remaining mixture.
4 Bring a pan of water to the boil and remove from the heat. Put the chocolate in a heatproof bowl and sit the bowl over the pan, making sure the base of the bowl does not sit in the water. Stir occasionally until the chocolate has melted. Spread a thin layer of chocolate quickly over the backs of the florentines. A little of the chocolate will come through the florentine. Leave to set chocolate-side-up. When set, store in an airtight container in a cool place or keep refrigerated for up to 2 weeks .

SWEET TWISTS

Preparation time: 40 minutes
Total cooking time: 10 minutes
Makes 45

✷ ✷

1 egg
1 1/2 tablespoons sugar
1/2 cup (125 ml/4 fl oz) milk
2 cups (250 g/8 oz) plain flour
oil, for deep-frying
1 3/4 cups (215 g/7 oz) icing sugar

1 Beat the egg with the sugar in a bowl, then stir in the milk. Sift the flour with 1/2 teaspoon salt and mix in to form a stiff dough, adding more milk if necessary. Roll out on a lightly floured work surface. Cut into strips about 10 cm (4 inches) long and 3 cm (1 1/4 inches) wide. Make a slit along the length, like a buttonhole. Tuck one end through the slit and pull through to make a twist.
2 Fill a deep heavy-based pan one third full of

ABOVE: Sweet twists

PETITS FOURS

Preparation time: 45 minutes
Total cooking time: 20 minutes
Makes 32

☆☆

2 eggs
¹/₄ cup (60 g/2 oz) caster sugar
²/₃ cup (85 g/3 oz) plain flour
30 g (1 oz) butter, melted

Topping
1 cup (315 g/10 oz) apricot jam, warmed
   and strained
2 teaspoons liqueur
200 g (6¹/₂ oz) marzipan
400 g (13 oz) ready-made soft icing, chopped

1 Preheat the oven to moderate 180°C (350°F/Gas 4). Brush two 26 x 8 x 4.5 cm (10¹/₂ x 3 x 1³/₄ inch) bar tins with melted butter or oil. Line the bases and sides with baking paper.
2 Using electric beaters, beat the eggs and sugar in a bowl for 5 minutes, until very thick and pale. Fold in the sifted flour and melted butter quickly and lightly, using a metal spoon. Divide between the tins and bake for 15 minutes, until lightly golden and springy to the touch. Leave in the tins for 3 minutes before turning out onto a wire rack to cool.
3 Using a 3 cm (1¹/₄ inch) round cutter, cut shapes from the cakes. Brush the top and sides of each with the combined jam and liqueur. Roll the marzipan out to a thickness of 2 mm (¹/₈ inch) and cut out rounds and strips to cover the top and sides of the cakes.
4 Place the icing and 2 tablespoons water in a heatproof bowl and stand the bowl over a pan of simmering water. Stir until the icing has melted and the mixture is smooth; cool slightly.
5 Place the marzipan-covered cakes on a wire rack over a tray. Spoon the icing over each cake and use a flat-bladed knife to spread evenly over the base and sides. Reheat the icing over the pan if it begins to thicken. Leave the cakes to set. Carefully lift from the rack and place each in a paper petit four case. Decorate with small coloured fondant flowers if desired.
NOTE: Fondant flowers for decorating are found in some supermarkets and in speciality shops.
IN ADVANCE: Petits fours will keep for up to 2 days in an airtight container in a cool, dark place. Store in a single layer.

MINI TOFFEE APPLES

Peel 2 large apples and use a melon baller to cut out balls, or cut the apples into cubes. Push a cocktail stick into each ball or cube. Sprinkle 200 g (6¹/₂ oz) sugar in an even layer over the base of a pan and melt over low heat, slowly tipping the pan from side to side to make sure the sugar melts evenly. Keep the sugar moving so it does not start to colour on one side before the other side has melted. When the caramel starts to colour, keep swirling until you have an even colour, then remove the pan from the heat and stop the cooking by plunging the base into cold water. Reheat the caramel gently until runny. Dip each piece of apple in the caramel, coating completely. Leave to dry, standing upright on a piece of baking paper. Reheat the caramel when necessary.

PETITS FOURS
A petit four is a small dainty biscuit, cake or sweet, often decorated or iced. It is usually served at the end of a meal. The French term *petit four* literally means 'small oven' and probably refers to the fact that the little cakes or biscuits were baked at a low temperature.

ABOVE: Petits fours

EGG TARTS

Place the inner dough on the centre of the outer dough and fold over the edges to enclose.

When cooled slightly, slip a knife down the side of each tart and transfer the tarts to a wire rack.

EGG TARTS

Preparation time: 10 minutes + standing
Total cooking time: 20 minutes
Makes 18

★ ★ ★

Outer dough

1¹/₃ cups (165 g/5¹/₂ oz) plain flour
2 tablespoons icing sugar
2 tablespoons oil

Inner dough

1 cup (125 g/4 oz) plain flour
100 g (3¹/₂ oz) lard, chopped

Custard

¹/₄ cup (60 g/2 oz) caster sugar
2 eggs, lightly beaten

1 Preheat the oven to hot 210°C (415°F/Gas 6–7). Lightly grease 18 holes in shallow 12-hole patty tins.
2 For the outer dough, sift the flour and sugar into a bowl. Make a well and pour in the oil and ¹/₃ cup (80 ml/2³/₄ fl oz) water. Stir quickly, then knead to form a soft dough. (If the dough is very dry, you may need a little extra water.) Cover and set aside for 15 minutes.
3 For the inner dough, sift the flour into a bowl. Add the lard and rub in with your fingertips until the mixture resembles coarse breadcrumbs, then press together to form a very short-textured pastry. Cover and set aside for 15 minutes.
4 On a lightly floured surface, roll the outer dough into a rectangle 20 x 10 cm (8 x 4 inch). Roll the inner dough on a lightly floured surface into a rectangle one-third the size of the other. Place the inner dough on the centre of the outer dough. Fold over the edges to thoroughly enclose, then pinch the ends together to seal.
5 Roll the dough out on a lightly floured surface into a long rectangle, about half as thick as it was previously. Take the left-hand edge and bring it towards the centre. Repeat with the right-hand edge. Wrap the dough in plastic wrap and leave in a cool place for 30 minutes.
6 For the custard, place the sugar and ¹/₃ cup (80 ml/2³/₄ fl oz) water in a pan and bring to the boil. Reduce the heat and simmer, uncovered, until the sugar has dissolved. Cool for 5 minutes, then whisk into the eggs until just combined. Strain into a jug.
7 Turn the pastry so that the fold is on the left-hand side. Working on a lightly floured surface, roll the pastry out to a rectangle about 3 mm

RIGHT: Egg tarts

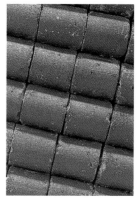

(1/8 inch) thickness. Cut out rounds with a 7 cm (2³/4 inch) fluted cutter and put in the tins.

8 Fill each pastry case two thirds full of egg custard, then cook for 15–18 minutes. Do not overcook; the filling should be just set. Leave for 3 minutes, then slip a flat-bladed knife down the sides to lift out onto a rack. Serve warm or cold.

NOTE: If you prefer, use 3 sheets of ready-rolled shortcrust pastry.

IN ADVANCE: Can be cooked 2 days ahead and stored in an airtight container.

THAI STICKY RICE

Preparation time: 15 minutes + overnight soaking
Total cooking time: 1 hour
Makes 25–30

★★

2¹/2 cups (500 g/1 lb) glutinous rice
2¹/2 cups (600 ml/20 fl oz) coconut milk
¹/2 cup (125 g/4 oz) caster sugar

Topping

1 cup (90 g/3 oz) desiccated coconut
¹/4 cup (60 ml/2 fl oz) coconut milk, heated
90 g (3 oz) palm sugar, grated

1 Put the rice in a large glass bowl and cover with water. Soak for 8 hours or overnight; drain. Line a 30 x 20 cm (12 x 8 inch) shallow tin with baking paper, overlapping the two long sides. Line a large bamboo steamer with baking paper.

2 Spread the steamer base with rice, cover and place over a wok. Half-fill the wok with boiling water. Steam for 45–50 minutes, or until the grains are softened. Top up the wok with water when necessary.

3 Put the rice, coconut milk and sugar in a large heavy-based pan. Stir over low heat for 10 minutes, or until all the coconut milk is absorbed. Spoon into the tin and flatten the surface. Set aside to cool and firm.

4 For the topping, put the coconut in a small bowl and mix in the coconut milk. Put the palm sugar and 3 tablespoons water in a small pan and stir over low heat for 3 minutes, or until the sugar has dissolved and the syrup has thickened slightly. Stir in the coconut and continue to stir until the mixture holds together. Cover and set aside to cool. Spread the topping over the rice base. Cut into diamonds for serving. Serve at room temperature.

NOTE: These are best eaten on the same day. Chilling firms the mixture and it loses its flavour. Glutinous rice and palm sugar are available from Asian speciality stores. Palm sugar can be crushed with a rolling pin.

GLUTINOUS RICE
As no rice contains any gluten, this name is a bit of a misnomer. Sometimes it is called *sticky rice*. The stickiness comes from a particular type of starch highly prevalent in sticky rice. This type of rice is most commonly used for making sweets, but in parts of Laos, Cambodia and Vietnam it is the main crop and the preferred rice for all dishes. Most sticky rices are short-grained.

ABOVE: Thai sticky rice

285

SORBET BALLS

Scoop out balls of sorbet, put on a tray and push a cocktail stick into each ball.

Thoroughly coat each frozen sorbet ball with melted chocolate.

SORBET BALLS

Preparation time: 15 minutes + overnight freezing
Total cooking time: 35 minutes
Makes 24

★★★

400 g (13 oz) sorbet
250 g (8 oz) dark chocolate melts or buttons

1 Soften the sorbet slightly (if you do this step as soon as you get home it will probably be the right consistency and will save having to refreeze it) and spread it out in a shallow container to a depth of about 2.5 cm (1 inch). Put in the freezer until solid.
2 Cover a baking tray with baking paper and place in the freezer. Using a melon baller, scoop out tiny balls of sorbet and place them on the prepared tray. Put a cocktail stick in each sorbet ball. Cover the tray tightly with plastic wrap, ensuring it is completely covered (see Note), then refreeze overnight so the balls are solid.
3 Place the chocolate in a heatproof bowl. Bring a pan of water to the boil, then remove the pan from the heat. Sit the bowl over the pan, making sure the base of the bowl does not touch the water. Stir occasionally until the chocolate has melted. Remove the bowl and set aside to cool a little.
4 The next part is quite tricky so you need to be careful. Ladle some of the chocolate into a separate bowl so that if anything goes wrong you won't ruin the whole batch. Work with just a few balls at a time so they do not melt. Dip each sorbet ball in the chocolate, making sure it is thoroughly coated and place it back on the tray. Return to the freezer. Reheat the chocolate if necessary. It must be liquid enough not to coat too thickly. Add more melted chocolate to the bowl when necessary, but if it seizes, start with a new bowl and a new batch. Freeze until you are ready to serve.
NOTE: In a frost-free freezer, the sorbet will dry out if not properly covered.

Serve these on a bed of dry ice or pile them into a bowl set inside an ice bowl. To make an ice bowl, fill a bowl half full of water and float some flower petals and herb leaves in it, place another bowl inside and weight it down so it sits down in the water but does not sink to the bottom. The water should form a bowl-shaped layer between the two bowls. Freeze overnight. Separate the bowls by rubbing a cloth dipped in hot water over them and twisting them apart.

MINI PAVLOVAS

Preparation time: 50 minutes
Total cooking time: 50 minutes
Makes 35–40

★

3 egg whites
1 cup (125 g/4 oz) icing sugar
150 g (5 oz) dark chocolate, melted
1 cup (250 ml/8 fl oz) thick (double) cream
1 tablespoon icing sugar, extra
1 teaspoon finely grated orange rind
assorted fresh fruit for garnish, such as strawberries, cut into thin wedges, sliced pawpaw and kiwi fruit, and passionfruit pulp

1 Preheat the oven to slow 150°C (300°F/ Gas 2). Place the egg whites in a large bowl and beat until stiff peaks form. Set the bowl over a large pan of simmering water and add the icing sugar to the egg whites while continuing to beat. Add it carefully or it will fly all over the place. At this stage it is best to use electric beaters as you must now beat the meringue until thick and very solid.
2 Using a cutter as a guide, draw 4 cm (1½ inch) circles onto two sheets of baking paper, then invert these sheets onto baking trays (so the pencil won't come off on the base of the pavlovas). Spread a little of the meringue mixture over each round—this will be the base of the pavlova. Spoon the remaining meringue into a piping bag fitted with an 5 mm (¼ inch) plain piping nozzle.
3 Pipe three small circles on top of each other on the outer edge of each base, leaving a small hole in the centre. Bake for 30 minutes, or until firm to touch. Leave to cool in the oven with the door slightly ajar.
4 When cold, dip the bases of the meringues into the melted chocolate to come about 2 mm (⅛ inch) up the sides of the meringues, then place on trays covered with baking paper and allow to set.
5 Combine the cream, extra icing sugar and rind, stirring until just thick. If necessary, beat slightly. Spoon into a piping bag fitted with a small plain nozzle and pipe into the meringues. Top with fruit and passionfruit pulp.
IN ADVANCE: Chocolate-dipped meringues without the filling can be made up to a week ahead and stored in an airtight container. Fill them close to serving time, otherwise they will soften.

OPPOSITE PAGE: Sorbet balls (top); Mini pavlovas

CHOCOLATE PRALINE TRIANGLES

When the praline mix is cold and set, break it up roughly, put it in a plastic bag, then crush with a rolling pin.

Spread the chocolate praline over the prepared loaf tin and smooth the surface. Tap gently on the bench to level.

Press a whole toasted almond onto each triangle. Lift each triangle with two forks and dip into the melted chocolate to coat.

ABOVE: Chocolate praline triangles

CHOCOLATE PRALINE TRIANGLES

Preparation time: 40 minutes + chilling
Total cooking time: 3 minutes
Makes 36

✶ ✶

60 g (2 oz) slivered almonds

1/2 cup (125 g/4 oz) caster sugar

150 g (5 oz) dark chocolate, chopped

40 g (1 1/4 oz) butter

1/4 cup (60 ml/2 fl oz) cream

80 g (2 3/4 oz) blanched almonds, toasted

200 g (6 1/2 oz) dark compound chocolate, melted

50 g (1 3/4 oz) white compound chocolate, optional

1 Line a baking tray with foil and brush lightly with oil. Line a 20 x 10 cm (8 x 4 inch) loaf tin with foil.
2 Combine the almonds and sugar in a small pan and place over low heat. Watch carefully, without stirring, for 3–5 minutes, until the sugar is melted and golden. (Swirl the pan slightly to dissolve the sugar.) Pour onto the tray and leave until set and completely cold. Break into chunks, place in a plastic bag and crush with a rolling pin, or chop in a food processor until crumbly.
3 Put the chopped chocolate in a heatproof bowl. Combine the butter and cream in a small pan and stir over low heat until the butter melts. Bring to the boil, then remove from the heat. Pour the hot cream mixture over the chocolate. Leave for 2 minutes, then stir until the chocolate is smooth. Cool slightly, then stir in the crushed praline.
4 Spread the mixture into the loaf tin and smooth the surface. Tap gently on the bench to level. Cover with plastic wrap, then refrigerate for 1 hour, or until set. Lift from the tin, peel away the foil and cut into 36 small triangles.
5 Line a tray with foil. Press a whole toasted almond onto each triangle. Using two forks, dip the triangles one at a time into the chocolate to coat. Lift out, drain off the excess chocolate and place on the tray to set. Pipe with white chocolate to decorate, if desired.
NOTE: Refrigerate in warm weather.

EGGS
Many recipes call for just egg yolks but you don't have to waste the white as it is easily transformed into tempting little sweet meringues. To make them successfully, make sure you bring the egg whites to room temperature, that the bowl and utensils are clean, and be careful when separating the eggs that no yolk slips into the white.

CHOCOLATE MERINGUE KISSES

Preparation time: 20 minutes
Total cooking time: 40 minutes
Makes 25

★★

2 egg whites, at room temperature
1/2 cup (125 g/4 oz) caster sugar
1/4 teaspoon ground cinnamon

Filling
125 g (4 oz) dark chocolate melts or buttons
1/3 cup (90 g/3 oz) sour cream

1 Preheat the oven to slow 150°C (300°F/ Gas 2). Line two oven trays with baking paper.
2 Using electric beaters, beat the egg whites in a small clean dry bowl until soft peaks form. Gradually add the sugar, beating well after each addition until stiffened and glossy peaks form. Add the cinnamon and beat until just combined.
3 Transfer the mixture to a piping bag fitted with a 1 cm (1/2 inch) fluted nozzle. Pipe small stars of 1.5 cm (5/8 inch) diameter onto the trays, 3 cm (11/4 inches) apart. Bake for 30 minutes, or until pale and crisp. Turn off the oven and leave the meringues to cool in the oven with the door ajar.
4 To make the filling, place the chocolate and sour cream in a small heatproof bowl. Bring a pan of water to the boil, remove from the heat and sit the bowl over the pan, making sure the bottom of the bowl does not sit in the water. Stir occasionally until the chocolate has melted. Remove from the heat and cool slightly. Sandwich the meringues together with the chocolate filling.
NOTE: You can use white chocolate instead of dark and other ground spices such as ground cloves, allspice or nutmeg. Meringues should be cooked slowly. The ideal texture is crunchy on the outside and soft inside.
IN ADVANCE: Unfilled meringues can be made several days ahead. Store in an airtight container, between sheets of greaseproof paper.

ABOVE: Chocolate meringue kisses

1 teaspoon of chocolate in each. Use a small new paintbrush to coat the inside with chocolate, making sure it is thick and there are no gaps. Turn the cups upside down on a wire rack and leave until firm. Set the remaining chocolate aside.

3 Combine the cream, white chocolate and Tia Maria in a heatproof bowl. Stir over a pan of simmering water until smooth. Cool slightly, then spoon into the chocolate cups. Press half a coffee bean into each cup. Allow to set.

4 Remelt the reserved chocolate. Spoon it over the filling and tap to level, then leave to set.

CHOCOLATE CLUSTERS

Preparation time: 35 minutes
Total cooking time: Nil
Makes about 40

☆

125 g (4 oz) dark chocolate melts
125 g (4 oz) white chocolate melts
2/3 cup (125 g/4 oz) dried mixed fruit
125 g (4 oz) glacé ginger, chopped
30 g (1 oz) each dark chocolate and white
    chocolate melts or buttons, extra, melted

1 Put the dark chocolate in a heatproof bowl. Bring a pan of water to the boil, remove from the heat. Sit the bowl over the pan, making sure the base of the bowl is not touching the water. Stir occasionally until the chocolate has melted. Cool slightly. Repeat with the white chocolate.

2 Stir the mixed fruit into the dark chocolate. Combine the ginger with the white chocolate.

3 Drop spoonfuls of the mixtures onto foil-lined trays, and leave to set at room temperature. Drizzle with the extra melted chocolate.

CHOCOLATE-COFFEE CUPS

Preparation time: 40 minutes
Total cooking time: 10 minutes
Makes 20

☆ ☆

200 g (6 1/2 oz) dark chocolate melts
20 foil cups
1 tablespoon cream
50 g (1 3/4 oz) white chocolate, chopped
1 tablespoon Tia Maria
10 coffee beans, halved

1 Put the dark chocolate in a heatproof bowl. Bring a pan of water to the boil, remove from the heat and sit the bowl over the pan, making sure the base of the bowl does not sit in the water. Stir occasionally until the chocolate has melted. Cool slightly.

2 Working with one foil cup at a time, put

ABOVE: Chocolate clusters (top); Chocolate-coffee cups

FRUIT BITES WITH WARM CHOCOLATE SAUCE

Thread two or three chopped pieces of fresh fruit onto small skewers and serve with warm chocolate sauce. In a small pan, combine 250 g (8 oz) good quality dark chocolate, 3/4 cup (185 ml/6 fl oz) cream, 50 g (1 3/4 oz) butter, 1 tablespoon golden syrup and 2 tablespoons coffee-flavoured liqueur. Stir over low heat until melted and serve in a bowl beside the fruit.

CHOCOLATE TARTS

Preparation time: 40 minutes + chilling
Total cooking time: 30 minutes
Makes about 45

☆ ☆

1¼ cups (155 g/5 oz) plain flour
75 g (2½ oz) butter, chopped
¼ cup (60 g/2 oz) caster sugar
2 egg yolks
250 g (4 oz) dark chocolate, finely chopped
1 cup (250 ml/4 fl oz) cream
1 tablespoon orange-flavoured liqueur
1 orange
½ cup (125 g/4 oz) caster sugar, extra

1 Lightly grease two 12-hole tartlet tins. Sift the flour into a large bowl and add the butter. Rub in with your fingertips until the mixture resembles fine breadcrumbs. Stir in the sugar. Make a well and add the egg yolks and up to 2 tablespoons water. Mix with a flat-bladed knife using a cutting action, until the mixture comes together in beads. Gather together and lift out onto a lightly floured work surface. Press into a ball and flatten slightly into a disc. Wrap in plastic and refrigerate for 20 minutes.

2 Preheat the oven to moderate 180°C (350°F/ Gas 4). Roll the dough between two sheets of baking paper and cut rounds with a 5 cm (2 inch) cutter. Press into the tins.

3 Bake for about 10 minutes, or until lightly browned. Remove from the tins and cool. Repeat to use all the pastry. Allow to cool.

4 Put the chocolate in a heatproof bowl. Bring the cream to the boil in a small pan and pour over the chocolate. Leave for 1 minute, then stir until the chocolate has melted. Stir in the liqueur. Allow to set, stirring occasionally until thick.

5 Meanwhile, thinly peel the orange, avoiding the bitter white pith, and cut into short thin strips. Combine the extra sugar, rind and ½ cup (125 ml/4 fl oz) water in a small pan, stir over heat until the sugar has dissolved, then simmer for about 5–10 minutes, or until thick and syrupy. Remove the rind with tongs and drain on baking paper; allow to cool.

6 Spoon the chocolate mixture into a piping bag fitted with a 1 cm (½ inch) plain piping nozzle. Pipe three small blobs of ganache into the pastry case, pulling up as you pipe so the ganache forms a point. Dust with cocoa, decorate with the orange rind and refrigerate until ready to serve.

ORANGES
Oranges are in plentiful supply all year round with different varieties available in opposite seasons. Summer and spring are *Valencia* time, whereas autumn through to spring are the times for the seedless *Navel* orange. Blood oranges, with red flesh, and the *Seville*, a bitter orange used for marmalade, are available in winter. Navel oranges have thick, easy to peel skin, whereas the Valencia skin is smooth and thin. Valencias are ideal for making juice, with a high yield. Store oranges in the refrigerator or in a dry, cool area.

LEFT: Chocolate tarts

BRANDY SNAPS
WITH COFFEE
LIQUEUR CREAM

Drop level teaspoons of
mixture onto the covered
tray and spread into rounds
using the broad side of
a knife.

While the biscuits are still
hot, wrap them around the
handle of a wooden spoon.

Spoon the cream mix into
a piping bag and fill the
cooled biscuits.

BRANDY SNAPS WITH COFFEE LIQUEUR CREAM

Preparation time: 12 minutes + chilling
Total cooking time: 20 minutes
Makes 25

★ ★ ★

60 g (2 oz) butter
2 tablespoons golden syrup
1/3 cup (60 g/2 oz) soft brown sugar
1/4 cup (30 g/1 oz) plain flour
1 1/2 teaspoons ground ginger
80 g (2 3/4 oz) dark chocolate, melted

Coffee liqueur cream
2/3 cup (170 ml/5 1/2 fl oz) cream
1 tablespoon icing sugar, sifted
1 teaspoon instant coffee powder
1 tablespoon coffee liqueur

1 Preheat the oven to moderate 180°C (350°F/
Gas 4). Line two baking trays with baking paper.
Combine the butter, syrup and sugar in a small
pan. Stir over low heat until the butter has
melted and the sugar has dissolved; remove from
the heat. Add the sifted flour and ginger and,
using a wooden spoon, stir until well combined;
do not overbeat.
2 Drop 1 level teaspoon of mixture at a time
onto the trays, about 12 cm (5 inches) apart.
(Prepare only three or four biscuits at a time.)
Use a palette knife to spread the mixture into
8 cm (3 inch) rounds. Bake for 6 minutes, or
until lightly browned. Leave on the trays for
30 seconds, then lift off the tray and wrap
around the handle of a wooden spoon while still
hot. If the biscuits harden on the trays, return to
the oven to soften again, then roll. Set aside to
cool. Repeat with the remaining mixture.
3 To make the coffee liqueur cream, combine
all the ingredients in a small bowl and stir until
just combined. Cover with plastic wrap and
refrigerate for 1 hour. Using electric beaters, beat
until the mixture is thick and forms stiff peaks.
Fill the biscuits. (You can spoon the cream into a
small paper icing bag, seal the open end and snip
off the tip, then pipe into the snaps.) Pipe or
drizzle with melted chocolate before serving.
IN ADVANCE: Store in an airtight container for
up to 2 days, or freeze snaps for up to 1 month
without filling.

*ABOVE: Brandy snaps
with coffee liqueur cream*

CHINESE FORTUNE COOKIES

Preparation time: 15 minutes
Total cooking time: 5 minutes each tray
Makes about 30

★★

3 egg whites
1/2 cup (60 g/2 oz) icing sugar, sifted
45 g (1 1/2 oz) butter, melted
1/2 cup (60 g/2 oz) plain flour

1 Preheat the oven to moderate 180°C (350°F/
Gas 4). Line a baking tray with baking paper.
Draw three 8 cm (3 inch) circles on the paper.
Turn the paper over.
2 Place the egg whites in a bowl and whisk until
just frothy. Add the icing sugar and butter and
stir until smooth. Add the flour and mix until
smooth. Set aside for 15 minutes. Using a flat-
bladed knife, spread 1 1/2 level teaspoons of
mixture over each circle. Bake for 5 minutes,
or until slightly brown around the edges.

3 Working quickly, remove from the trays by
sliding a flat-bladed knife under each round.
Place a folded written fortune message inside
each cookie.
4 Fold in half, then in half again over a blunt-
edged object. Allow to cool on a wire rack.
Cook the remaining mixture the same way.
NOTE: Make only two or three fortune cookies
at a time, otherwise they will harden too quickly
and break when folding. If this happens, return
the tray to the oven and warm through.

IN ADVANCE: The fortune cookies can be
cooked up to 2 days ahead and stored in an
airtight container.

**CHINESE
FORTUNE COOKIE**
This is a small biscuit or
cake containing a slip of
paper with a horoscope,
joke or proverb printed
on it. Chinese Americans
invented the idea early in
the 20th century.

*ABOVE: Chinese
fortune cookies*

293

INDEX

Page numbers in *italics* refer to photographs. Page numbers in **bold** type refer to margin notes.

Cover illustration (from top): Asparagus Boats (p.72); Beef en Croute with Béarnaise (p.79); Cucumber Bites (p.235); Caviar Eggs (p.230); Smoked Salmon Pikelets (p.47); Marinated Trout and Cucumber Tarts (p.80)

ACKNOWLEDGEMENTS

HOME ECONOMISTS: Miles Beaufort, Anna Beaumont, Anna Boyd, Wendy Brodhurst, Kerrie Carr, Rebecca Clancy, Bronwyn Clark, Michelle Earl, Maria Gargas, Wendy Goggin, Kathy Knudsen, Michelle Lawton, Melanie McDermott, Beth Mitchell, Kerrie Mullins, Justine Poole, Tracey Port, Kerrie Ray, Jo Richardson, Maria Sampsonis, Christine Sheppard, Dimitra Stais, Alison Turner, Jody Vassallo

RECIPE DEVELOPMENT: Roslyn Anderson, Anna Beaumont, Wendy Berecry, Janelle Bloom, Wendy Brodhurst, Janene Brooks, Rosey Bryan, Rebecca Clancy, Amanda Cooper, Anne Creber, Michelle Earl, Jenny Grainger, Lulu Grimes, Eva Katz, Coral Kingston, Kathy Knudsen, Barbara Lowery, Rachel Mackey, Voula Mantzouridis, Rosemary Mellish, Kerrie Mullins, Sally Parker, Jacki Passmore, Rosemary Penman, Tracey Port, Jennene Plummer, Justine Poole, Kerrie Ray, Jo Richardson, Tracy Rutherford, Stephanie Souvilis, Dimitra Stais, Beverly Sutherland Smith, Alison Turner, Jody Vassallo

PHOTOGRAPHY: Jon Bader, Paul Clarke, Joe Filshie, Andrew Furlong, Chris Jones, Andre Martin, Luis Martin, Andy Payne, Hans Sclupp, Peter Scott

STYLISTS: Marie-Helene Clauzon, Georgina Dolling, Kay Francis, Mary Harris, Donna Hay, Vicki Liley, Rosemary Mellish, Lucy Mortensen, Sylvia Seiff, Suzi Smith

The publisher wishes to thank the following for their assistance in the photography for this book:

The Bay Tree Kitchen Shop, NSW;
Made in Japan, NSW;
MEC-Kambrook Pty Ltd, NSW;
Orson & Blake Collectables, NSW;
Royal Doulton Australia Pty Ltd, NSW;
Ruby Star Traders Pty Ltd, NSW;
Sunbeam Corporation Ltd, NSW;
Villery & Boch Australia Pty Ltd, NSW;
Waterford Wedgwood Australia Ltd, NSW.